AF709288

Paradox 4 Programming Guide

The Lance A. Leventhal Microtrend Series

Paradox 4 Programming Guide

Valerie Schmieder

Copyright © 1993 Valerie M. Schmieder

All rights reserved. No part of this book may be reproduced or transmitted in any form or by any means, electronic or mechanical, including photocopying, recording or by any information storage and retrieval system without written permission from the copyright holder, except for the inclusion of brief quotations in a review.

Library of Congress Card Catalog Number: 92-32255

Library of Congress Cataloging-in-Publication Data
Schmieder, Valerie M.
Paradox 4 Programming Guide
Valerie M. Schmieder
p. cm. — (Lance A. Leventhal Microtrend series)
Includes index.
ISBN 0-915391-62-7 (pbk.)
1. Data base management 2. Paradox (Computer program)
I. Title II. Series
QA76.9.D3S295 1993
005.75'65—dc20
CIP

Microtrend™ Books
Slawson Communications, Inc.
2075 Corte Del Nogal, Suite E
Carlsbad, CA 92009-1414

Edited by Lance A. Leventhal, Ph.D., San Marcos, CA
Front cover design by John Odam Design Associates
Produced by Joanne Roth, Slawson Communications, Inc.

Printed in the United States
10 9 8 7 6 5 4 3 2 1

Table of Contents

List of Tables

List of Programs

List of Figures

About the Author

Valerie M. Schmieder is the principal of V.S. Systems, a consulting and training company established in 1979 specializing in Paradox applications. She works with a variety of businesses, including banks, insurance companies, hospitals, and manufacturers.

Mrs. Schmieder teaches seminars in Paradox and PAL programming throughout New England. She has also been an adjunct faculty member at Western Connecticut State University lecturing on database design, software engineering, and Pascal programming. She has given presentations to many groups, including Borland's International Paradox Conference. V.S. Systems publishes a quarterly newsletter, CheckPlus, with Paradox and PAL tips, product reviews, and industry news.

Mrs. Schmieder holds a B.A. in mathematics from Western Connecticut State University and an M.A. in computer science from the University of New Haven. She is a member of ACM, Connecticut Computer Society, and the Independent Computer Consultants Association.

About the Series Editor

Lance A. Leventhal is the author of 25 books, including *80386 Programming Guide*, *68000 Assembly Language Programming*, *Turbo C Quickstart*, and *Microcomputer Experimentation with the IBM PC*. His books have sold over 1,000,000 copies and have been translated into many foreign languages. He has also helped develop microprocessor-based systems and has been a consultant for Disney, Intel, NASA, NCR, and Rockwell.

Dr. Leventhal served as Series Editor on Personal Computing for Prentice-Hall and as Technical Editor for the Society for Computer Simulation. He has lectured on microprocessors, C programming, and operating systems throughout the United States for IEEE, IEEE Computer Society, and other groups.

Dr. Leventhal's background includes affiliations with Linkabit Corporation, Intelcom Rad Tech, Naval Electronics Laboratory Center, and Harry Diamond Laboratories. He received a B.A. degree from Washington University (St. Louis, Missouri) and M.S. and Ph.D. degrees from the University of California, San Diego. He is a member of ACM, IEEE, and IEEE Computer Society.

Acknowledgments

I started this book on a dare from my husband who got tired of my complaining about how there are never any good books available. I would like to thank him for his support and encouragement (even though Paradox is a conundrum to him).

I have used much of this material in my Paradox and PAL seminars. My thanks to the many students who found errors, suggested changes, and gave encouragement, especially Cindy Arndt, Darrah Ballou, Ray Cassidy, Dick Marshall, and Scott Sante.

Thanks to my editor, Lance Leventhal, who believed in a first time author and nursed me through the process. As James L. Brooks once said, "The thing that usually gets me through the writing is that my feelings of wretched inadequacy are irregularly punctuated by brief flashes of omnipotence."

Thanks also to Joanne Roth who did the production.

Dedication

To my daughter, Erin, who had endless patience when told not to bother mommy while she's writing.

Preface

Why Program in Paradox?

This book is about programming in PAL, the Paradox Application Language. J.D. Powers and Associates has consistently rated Paradox among the leading PC database products in recent years. Its reputation is well deserved.

I have been a database consultant for over ten years (although I am getting younger all the time) using products such as dBASE, Clipper, and FoxPro. I was always looking for the magic formula that would eliminate the drudgery (programming yet another data entry routine or menu) inherent in every application so I could focus on the enjoyable part—solving the problem. Actually, getting paid is the best part, but it usually requires that I solve the problem anyway.

Several years ago, I participated in a database analysis for a major helicopter manufacturer. Paradox emerged the clear winner because of its network support and rapid prototyping with an excellent screen editor. The company used it for several projects, including an on-line reference of historical aircraft attributes and a cost estimating package for a new model. Although (being a mercenary) I still support clients with older systems written in other languages, Paradox is my choice for all new development.

One reason for PAL's versatility is that it can integrate Paradox facilities directly into applications with little difficulty. I can easily give users Query by Example and access to the report or graphics editor under program control. Using these proven facilities speeds development and thus saves money (who has enough of that?) and reduces the number of system errors.

What Is in This Book?

I am basically an engineer at heart, so this book is a highly practical guide to getting the most from PAL. It does not spend time discussing the history of Paradox or the philosophy behind its design. Those topics may be interesting, but most of us are too busy working to wade through them!

The book contains many practical examples derived from actual systems developed for typical clients who wanted the impossible, delivered early, at little or no cost. The amount of work in any organization always overwhelms available resources (namely you!); productivity increases are essential just to stay even.

I have also tried to keep my sense of humor as I wrote, remembering that if you are not laughing, you are probably crying.

Each chapter includes a general discussion of the topic, tips and warnings, and PAL code to illustrate important points. Chapters also have CheckPoints where you can test your Paradox and PAL knowledge by writing PAL programs. Appendix E contains the answers. Most chapters include a How to DO_IT! section with major examples including fully documented and tested source code.

Chapter 1 introduces Paradox and PAL programming. Besides presenting a list of Paradox's features, it describes three typical applications and discusses trends in Paradox and PAL.

Chapter 2 discusses PAL's basic building blocks. It explains how to move easily from Paradox to PAL by recording keystrokes and saving queries. It presents PAL commands and functions and introduces arrays. The How to DO_IT! section covers loading menu selections from tables into arrays, trapping possibly destructive keystrokes such as Del during data entry, and doing a wildcard search on a Paradox field.

Chapter 3 shows how to convert PAL programs (called scripts) into procedures and libraries so they execute faster and can use Paradox's memory management facilities. It also explains how to package an application for distribution. The How to DO_IT! section presents a recursive procedure that can save programming time by allowing you to reuse the same code to display different menus. By changing the table name passed to the procedure, you change the menu it displays.

Chapter 4 describes PAL arrays and presents major routines for copying them, deleting and finding elements, and storing table structure information. PAL supports only one-dimensional arrays, but the chapter shows how to simulate multi-dimensional ones. The How to DO_IT! section features a technique for displaying records in a multi-record form with a scrolling highlight bar.

Chapter 5 presents techniques to control the user interface. It discusses PAL commands specific to workspace and canvas windows and presents a table maintenance procedure you can modify for applications. The chapter shows you how to build dialog boxes with pick lists, text areas, and control buttons. It shows an example of event-driven programming and discusses how to add events to data entry applications. It also describes how to give users access to Paradox facilities such as Query by Example and the report editor under program control. The How to DO_IT! section shows how to add popup help to dialog boxes.

Chapter 6 discusses error proofing applications and describes the limitations of Paradox ValChecks. It also covers how to handle key violations, and how to maintain master and detail table relationships. It points out potential trouble spots in PAL applications and presents solutions. The How to DO_IT! section includes a data dictionary procedure to preserve referential integrity without employing Paradox forms.

Chapter 7 focuses on multiuser applications and explains how to control concurrent access to Paradox objects such as tables and reports using explicit locks. It describes Paradox network control files and discusses typical network problems and solutions. The How to DO_IT! section presents an extensive example of a multiuser system using group locks to assure maximum concurrent table use.

Chapter 8 shows how to integrate Paradox with WordPerfect and Quattro Pro. The techniques are extensible to other word processors and spreadsheets. WordPerfect techniques include mail merging, logically attaching documents to Paradox records, and transferring a name and address from Paradox to type a letter or memo. The final section covers the use of Paradox Access to take advantage of Quattro's superior mathematical and desktop publishing capabilities.

Chapter 9 describes how table driven programs can save you time by processing system information stored in tables with general purpose procedures. Changing the table changes the application. You need not modify the code at all. The result can be programs that are like a magician's magic hat. You can be constantly getting new things out of them without ever appearing to put anything in. The chapter concludes with an extensive sample application that implements an inventory system.

Chapter 10 discusses improving performance. If your programs already run as fast as users want, you are a lucky programmer (send me your favorite lottery numbers). If not, look in this chapter for programming techniques, memory management tips, indexing options, and hardware improvements that will help you make an application run as fast as possible.

Appendix A contains a table of Paradox keycodes. Appendix B has an ASCII character set table. Appendixes C and D contain brief descriptions of all Paradox commands and functions. Appendix E has answers to the CheckPoint questions. The book also has an acronym list and a glossary.

Who Needs This Book?

This book will be especially useful for developers of Paradox applications. It is also suitable for advanced users, systems analysts, teachers, trainers, programmers, VARs, consultants, support personnel, and students. It assumes an understanding of and experience with Paradox, but it does not presume any programming background. It is thus well-suited to Paradox programming classes given as short courses or in adult or continuing education.

How Should You Use This Book?

PAL beginners should scan Chapter 1, then start with Chapter 2 to gain a good understanding of the language. Experienced PAL programmers or the legion of curious can focus on individual areas of interest. Each chapter is as self-contained as possible. There are occasional references to procedures in previous chapters, but this is unavoidable because of our emphasis on reusing code!

I have tested and documented program examples carefully, trying to follow my own stated rules for proper structure and form. Hypocrisy often saves time and effort, but I always seem to get caught at it. (My editor was relentless!) The code is all available on the included disk.

How Will You Benefit from This Book?

Like Lewis Carroll's White Rabbit in Alice in Wonderland, I am often "Late for a very important date". This book will help you write better PAL programs in less time. It will also help you create the interfaces that today's users expect, including pulldown menus and popup boxes. Besides offering an attractive appearance, an application must protect data integrity, simplify data entry, and provide appropriate help. This book addresses these issues and many more. It also describes how to design and program multiuser applications. It shows how to handle runtime errors ("What, me worry?") and recover gracefully, if possible. This book will help you gain the skills required to deliver an attractive, fast, and error-free system in time for you to attend the tea party. Bring your own clean cup!

Valerie M. Schmieder
Danbury, CT
July 1992

1

Meet Your PAL

A man may love a paradox without either losing his wit or his honesty.

—Emerson

Introduction

A worried radiologist crouches nervously beside a hospital administrator. Finally, the computer they are watching blinks, beeps, emits a small belch, and reports, "No such number on file." What has happened to a perfectly good paying patient? How can we assess our standard outrageous charges if we cannot even find the person's record?

If only we could ask for information by patient name, doctor, or date of visit! Unfortunately, cries of anguish, tough sounding threats of pulling the plug or making a trip to the junkyard, and even the most beautifully arranged plates of burnt offerings have no effect on a heartless machine.

But, fortunately, help is available. The receptionist sees the unavailing struggle and says confidently, "Let me handle this." She locates the patient's records using a database query with a partial last name. She also sends an electronic request to the film room where a clerk obtains the patient's previous x-rays. The clerk uses a bar code reader to check the films out. After the new procedures are completed, a transcriptionist listens to the radiologist's diagnosis on a headset and types the report into a word processor. She also files the procedure history in the database. All this easily accessible information comes from a system developed with Paradox and PAL (Paradox Application Language).

What Is Paradox?

Paradox is an easy to use yet powerful relational database from Borland. It is relational because it allows users to obtain information from many files simultaneously based on relationships among them. Table 1-1 summarizes its major features.

Table 1-1. Paradox's Major Features

Feature	Description
Table Oriented	Operations such as maintenance and queries apply both to data tables and to their associated families of forms, reports, and indexes. **Advantage:** No need to handle related entities separately, thus simplifying design, coding, and maintenance. You cannot forget a family member, as Paradox binds them all together!
Relational Forms and Reports	Can build forms and reports using fields from many related tables. **Advantage:** Easy to create forms and reports based on related files such as customers and orders, or patients and procedures.
Query-By-Example	Lets the user specify the desired information on a form rather than by creating a complex expression. **Advantage:** User can formulate queries easily by selecting fields and entering search criteria. The results are available in a new file for further analysis.
Multiuser	Built-in multiuser support for efficient data sharing. **Advantage:** User need not worry about data integrity when sharing information on a network.
Modes	Paradox keeps detailed track of what it is doing (its *mode*), thus allowing it to recognize invalid or improper actions. **Advantage:** Paradox can determine automatically whether an action such as deleting a record is valid in the current context. This simplifies the monitoring of network users and allows immediate recognition of errors.

Windows	Actions occur in windows that users can move, resize, close, and stack. **Advantage:** Users can see several views of a single table or can perform unrelated actions in different windows. They can switch between windows as required.

Tables and Their Families

Tables are Paradox's basic elements. They consist of rows or records, each representing an entity such as a customer or patient. Each record consists of columns or fields containing information such as company name or patient telephone number.

A table can have a group of associated objects called its *family*. Its members include forms, reports, and indexes (but no in-laws, thank goodness!). Paradox manages the relationship between a table and its family automatically. For example, if you restructure a table, Paradox checks each form and report in its family and removes fields you deleted. Families always travel together (and without quarreling!). When you use Paradox to copy a table, for example, it also copies the family. Paradox thus lets you build systems with many forms and reports, yet simplifies maintenance through the family approach. You need not remember which files are related logically, as Paradox keeps track for you. Your own handy genealogist and promoter of family values!

Designing Forms and Reports

Paradox has built-in form and report generators for working with related objects. You can design a table form with up to nine detail tables and reports with up to five tables. That is, each form or report belongs to a single master table such as customers, and may include links to related detail tables such as orders, invoices, and payments. A link contains shared data such as a customer number.

Thus, for example, you can include the customer's name and address at the top of an order report by linking to the customer table. This saves disk space and simplifies maintenance. If a customer moves, for example, you need only change the address in one place. It is not stored with each order; Paradox looks it up when necessary.

Asking Questions

The query facility also uses the relational approach to access data. To ask a question, you fill out a form, placing check marks in the fields you want, enter search criteria such as customer name, and press the Do_It! key. Paradox creates a new table with records that match your request. In the hospital application, for example, you can get a list of a doctor's patients (in case he or she is ill or called out of town for an urgent golf match), a history of a patient's procedures, or a summary of how many people are scheduled for a particular procedure. No matter what information local administrators, insurance companies, or government agencies suddenly decide they want, you can probably get it quickly without writing any programs.

Sharing Data

All Paradox actions including maintenance, form and report design, and asking questions will work on a network. Paradox is network ready right out of the box. That is, it handles contention automatically. For example, if a user is editing an invoice record, Paradox will not let anyone else change it until he or she finishes.

It also controls data integrity during queries. If you ask a question and someone changes a table before Paradox finishes responding, it can restart the query automatically to assure a correct answer. You also can continue the query regardless of table changes if a rough estimate is sufficient. Now everyone in the hospital can know whether Mrs. Smith has a broken left arm or a bruised right leg. "Don't worry, madam, fortunately we have our two casts for the price of one special this week only."

Modes Control the Action

A mode is a Paradox state that determines if a request such as a query is valid, based on the current context. Paradox always starts in Main mode and switches to one of 14 others automatically, depending on the user's menu selections. The current mode is indicated on the screen. It limits what a user can do. For example, if someone on a network selects the menu path Modify/Edit, Paradox changes to Edit, a single user mode. No one else can view or change the table or modify its forms or reports until the first user finishes. This is essential for activities such as month end closing where you do not want people changing data while the system is trying to post totals to a history file.

On the other hand, if someone chooses the path Modify/Coedit, Paradox switches to Coedit, a multiuser mode. It then lets people change other records in the same table simultaneously.

Paradox checks the mode before executing a request and notifies the user if it is invalid. Users can thus perform different jobs without interfering with each other.

Windows on the World

A window is a rectangular screen area that may contain a Paradox object. There can be a different mode in each window. For example, you can edit a table in one window (Edit mode) and open a text file in another (File Editor mode). When you switch between them, Paradox changes modes automatically. The topmost window is always the active (current) one, and its mode determines what you can do.

When you select something from a menu, Paradox automatically opens a new window at the very top, puts the object in it, and switches to the corresponding mode. You switch to another window by pointing the mouse at its border and clicking. Paradox moves it to the top of the stack and transfers control to it. You may also close a window by clicking on its close button, or move and resize windows by dragging them.

What Is PAL?

As powerful as Paradox is, you will surely want to do things that are impossible interactively. For example, you may want to make a report run automatically or develop an entire application for inventory, billing, or payroll.

PAL, the Paradox Application Language, is procedure-oriented. With it, you write instructions that tell Paradox what to do. For example, you can write a program to select a table, pick a form, and let a user enter data. The user plays the program and thus need not select from Paradox menus and lists; the form pops up on the screen ready to accept information. PAL can automate repetitive actions and thus simplify the user's job. Table 1-2 summarizes its major features.

Table 1-2. PAL's Major Features

Feature	Description
Relationship to Paradox	Includes all features of Paradox in its commands and functions. **Advantage:** Simplifies moving from Paradox.
Modern Interface	Includes commands to create attractive user interfaces with popups, pulldowns, and dialog boxes. **Advantage:** Reduces programming time. Makes it easier to develop sophisticated looking applications.
Data Entry Control	Can limit valid keys and define program actions for them. Also can trap mouse events such as click, and table movement such as leaving a record. **Advantage:** Easy to control data entry because you can trap actions and execute a corresponding series of instructions. For example, you can close a table when a user presses F2.
Multiuser	Includes commands for explicit record and table locking. **Advantage:** Program can control transactions within a single table or ones involving many tables.
Paradox Facilities	Programs can include built-in facilities such as Query-by-Example and the sort editor. **Advantage:** Reduces programming time, presents a familiar interface, and reduces the number of application errors.

Moving from Paradox to PAL

It is easy to move from interactive Paradox to PAL because of their close relationship. Any job you can do interactively you can also do using PAL commands and functions that represent actions such as pressing a key or selecting from a menu. For example, you use the following menu path in Paradox to edit a Customer table.

```
Modify/Edit/Customer
```

The PAL equivalent is

```
EDIT "Customer"
```

The menu path and the equivalent PAL command generally use the same terminology. PAL also has many features not available interactively. It can manage windows, control data entry, direct printer output, and lock records and files in multiuser applications to assure maximum concurrent use. For example, there is no way to check printer status in Paradox. If you send a report to a printer that is disconnected, out of paper, or off-line, Paradox keeps trying to print it forever. However, the following function can check printer status easily in a PAL program.

```
Ok = PRINTERSTATUS()
```

PRINTERSTATUS returns True if the printer is on-line and False otherwise.

The Very Model of a Modern User Interface

Paradox has a modern interface with pulldown menus and dialog boxes; you can incorporate it into your own applications using PAL commands. Menus may have submenus and dividers, and options may be disabled if they are currently inappropriate. For example, you can disallow queries until the user selects a table.

You can store menu choices in a table for easy system maintenance. If you add to or revise them, you need change only the table, not the PAL code. When the application next reads the table, it will pick up the changes automatically.

PAL also has commands that use dialog boxes in a variety of ways to pose questions, display lists, and accept text. The user may respond or make selections using the cursor or the mouse.

Data Entry Control

You may also include pulldown menus in a data entry procedure. You first design a master form that may contain data from detail tables. You control data entry by trapping actions such as clicking the mouse on a menu choice, pressing a function key, or using cursor control keys. You tell Paradox what event to watch for, and what to do when it occurs. The following example opens the Customer table for editing (Edit mode) and lets the user insert, delete, and edit records until he or she presses F2 to finish the session. It then terminates data entry and returns to Main mode.

```
EDIT "Customer"
WAIT TABLE
   PROMPT "Press F2 to finish editing"
UNTIL "F2"
DO_IT!
```

The application can respond differently to each event. For example, it could open a dialog box to request search criteria when a user clicks on a menu choice, terminate data entry when he or she presses F2, or update a record when he or she moves to a new one using an arrow key.

Controlling Multiuser Systems

You can easily program data entry on a network. PAL has commands to lock records and tables to assure that an operator can complete a job such as adding an item to a customer order.

For example, the program could accept an item number, move to the inventory table, locate and lock the item record for exclusive use (or deny access if another user has already locked it), update the quantity ordered, and finally unlock it so it is available to other users.

I have used PAL to develop a multiuser application for a hospital radiology department with a 100,000 record history file. Access time for a complete patient history (with four concurrent users) is about 5 seconds. Amazingly enough, users grumble about response time even though the old manual procedures often took hours! As Groucho Marx once wrote, "I only cite the annoyances to show you that it isn't necessary to have relatives in Kansas City to be unhappy."

Using Paradox Facilities

Regardless of whether I am creating small applications or large multiuser ones with thousands of lines of PAL code, I always look for shortcuts to speed development time and save clients money. After all, I want them to invite me back for the next project! PAL lets me include Paradox facilities such as Query-By-Example in applications and control active keys. The results are less coding, fewer bugs, and applications that are delivered early (or at least on time!).

For example, you can turn control over to Paradox temporarily to monitor actions during a query. It provides special features such as letting the user press F6 to check fields. It also catches syntax errors such as >6 and < 10 instead of >6,<10 and asks the user to correct them. When he or she presses F2, Paradox optimizes the query automatically and executes it. It is as if your application steps out of the way temporarily to let Paradox control the action.

You can also let users specify sort fields, design reports and forms, create graphs, and index tables. Besides speeding application development, this technique provides a familiar interface and thus reduces training time.

When to Use Paradox

Like Sherlock Holmes, I recognize the solution to a problem by investigating the clues and making educated guesses. You should use Paradox when you must develop applications quickly, relate separate files such as inventory and orders, and give users flexibility so they can ask ad-hoc questions. It is also an excellent tool for building network applications because of its data integrity safeguards. Thus, it is well-suited to small single-user applications such as expense tracking and survey tabulation as well as to large multiuser order entry and inventory systems.

Users often wait until the last minute to decide they need a computer system and generally underestimate the required work. You can develop applications quickly in Paradox by designing forms and reports interactively, recording keystrokes to run them, and using PAL to create attractive popup or pulldown menus. This approach also makes your applications simple to change as users refine (or completely revamp!) their requirements.

Paradox makes it easy to include data from many files on forms and reports. Thus, it is a good solution when an application stores related information such as customers and orders separately, but includes fields from each on data entry forms and reports.

You can save many programming hours by using Paradox facilities such as Query-by-Example. It is often hard for you to predict what questions a user will ask; he or she frequently does not even know ahead of time! The advantages of including QBE in an application are that it is flexible, presents a familiar interface, and is bug free.

Developing a network application is much more difficult than writing a stand-alone one. Besides making sure it works correctly, you must let multiple users enter data simultaneously without interfering with each other. Interactive Paradox enforces data integrity automatically on forms, and PAL has commands to provide even more control. Paradox is thus suitable for multiuser applications such as order entry, inventory control, and accounts receivable.

Case Studies

The following case studies illustrate the use of Paradox and PAL to solve varied information management problems.

Case 1-1. Warehouse Fulfillment

Problem

A warehouse fulfillment company must control a diverse inventory for multiple clients. Each has unique order processing and reporting needs.

Parameters

- 30 clients
- 100 - 200 different items per client
- 1,000 - 50,000 items in stock
- 100 - 200 orders per week

Issues

- Multiple clients, each with its own inventory.
- Each item stored in several locations.
- Items received and shipped in different quantities.
- Order processing differs for each client.
- Reporting requirements constantly changing.
- Must be multiuser.

Solution

- Multiuser Paradox and PAL system.
- One inventory table with products stored by client and item.

- Receipts standardized for all clients.
- Items stored at multiple locations by date of receipt for first in, first out shipping.
- Inventory maintained on piece rather than package basis.
- Order processing differs for each client, but printing is standardized.
- Users can add or change reports.

A warehouse fulfillment company stores products for 30 clients. Items range from museum posters (stunningly sophisticated!) packaged in dozens to electric beer signs (how plebeian!) packaged singly. Clients often have hundreds of items and send hundreds of orders per week. The company stores items in multiple warehouses and ships the oldest products first.

Items may be received individually or in packages, but can be repackaged and shipped in different quantities. Due to the shifting nature of receiving and shipment lots, the company maintains inventory on a piece rather than a package basis.

The company maintained its inventory manually until doing so became impossible. Problems included lost orders, wrong items or quantities, and inability to handle back orders. Clients also wanted reports sorted by sales territory and largest volume items; the company either could not provide them at all, or they required huge amounts of manual labor.

Standard inventory systems do not fit the way the company does business. It uses a standard receiving procedure, but inventory and order processing differs for each client. We wrote a multiuser Paradox and PAL application to do the job.

Operators enter received items by number of packages, but the system stores inventory as pieces. A clerk can split the incoming shipment and place different amounts in several locations. The system maintains each client's inventory separately and uses different order entry procedures. The company standardized on a single order form, thus allowing shared printing procedures.

The system stores menu options and the corresponding program names in Paradox tables, so adding or revising reports is easy. When a client asks for something new, a user designs it and records the keystrokes required to run it. He or she then adds the text and program name to the table of menu options. As if by magic, the new report appears on a menu the next time someone runs the application.

The approach gives company personnel some independence from the developer, lets them respond quickly to client requests, and saves them money. They need not call the developer every time a client asks for new or different reports.

Conclusion:

The multiuser Paradox and PAL inventory system lets warehouse company personnel operate the way they want without restricting them to a standard package designed for a different type of business. Customer service is fast and flexible. And the company feels free to charge clients accordingly!

Case 1-2. Royalty Calculations

Problem

Publisher must print semiannual royalty statements based on past six months net sales volume.

Parameters

- 300 new books per 6 month season
- 200 authors

Issues

- Only three days to develop system. Talk about a last minute call!
- Some information stored only in paper files.
- Books may have coauthors. Royalties must be split.
- No identification number for a particular title, as hardback and paperback versions have separate numbers.
- System used just twice a year. Must be simple enough so user can run it without retraining each time.

Solution

- Single user Paradox and PAL system.
- Simple data entry for advances, payments, and net sales.
- Books stored by title rather than by number.
- Royalty calculations allow coauthors with uneven split.
- Royalty statements printed on letterhead using a Hewlett-Packard LaserJet.

A small publisher produces about 300 childrens' books per year. It pays royalties to authors and illustrators semiannually based on the number of copies sold less returns and advances. The company first did the calculations using a spreadsheet because it was a familiar tool and the number of books was small.

The company moved the files to Paradox when the calculations became more complicated. New factors included having coauthors and illustrators for some titles, selling foreign publication rights, and disposing of leftover lots at varied prices.

The system references books by title rather than by number. The hardback and paperback editions have different numbers, so title is the only way to relate sales to authors and print a single statement.

The data entry forms let users assign multiple advances to authors based on titles. The system also records royalty payments and net sales for each edition. It calculates royalties for the current period, splitting the amount for coauthored books. It prints the statements on company letterhead to save the time and cost of creating a custom form. The system also prints mailing labels.

At the end of each royalty period, the publisher posts sales and royalty information to a history file.

Conclusion:

We developed the single user Paradox and PAL system in three days to meet an urgent need to print royalty statements. Even with such short notice, we were able to include popup menus, multi-table data entry screens, and printer utilities. PAL is powerful enough to let developers respond quickly to customer requests.

Case 1-3. On-Line Bank Transaction Tracking

Problem

Bond transactions handled by an old mainframe system that did not provide timely feedback for customer service personnel. For example, there was no way to answer queries about current account status.

Parameters

- 1,000 - 2,000 transactions per year
- 1 part-time data entry clerk

Issues

- Mainframe system could not be changed.
- Turnaround time from submittal to returned report was several weeks.
- No history available.
- No audit trail of submitted transaction requests.

Solution

- Single user Paradox and PAL system.
- Enter transactions on local PC and create file to upload to mainframe in card format.
- Design screens and reports to show total customer history.

A large bank processes thousands of bond transactions annually. They can be as simple as a name change or as complex as a sell order. It used a mainframe punched card system developed millions of years ago by extinct dinosaurs (well almost). The deposit maintenance department wrote transaction data on transmittal sheets, combined them into batches, and sent them to be keypunched daily. They did not receive a report until weeks later. If there was a mistake, the department had to submit another request and wait weeks more to verify the correction. Meanwhile, customers wanted their balances (unavailable), complained about statement discrepancies (almost uncorrectable), and asked for account history (unbelievable). The only good point was the continuing employment of several hopelessly obsolete keypunchers.

There was absolutely no way to get corporate information center personnel to rewrite the system, but they did agree to accept transactions in a computer file rather than on transmittal sheets. We designed a Paradox system to enter customer changes, print transaction logs, and create files to upload to the mainframe.

The deposit maintenance group runs the application on a single machine (no new hardware!). A single clerk enters daily transactions, creates the upload file, and transmits it. Data is available immediately, rather than waiting weeks for the mainframe report. The group can now build account histories and use the Paradox Query-by-Example facility to answer customer questions.

Conclusion:

Customers are happy, the department is relieved, and corporate data processing need not cope with punched cards. (Besides the ultimate disgrace of people snickering at you when you carry your card box around!) In these days of recycling, there are only so many Christmas wreaths, bookmarks, door stops, and paper dolls you can make out of old cards.

Future Trends

Given this wide variety of applications, what is Paradox's future? Previous upgrades have emphasized the user interface, network performance, memory management, client server technology, and interfaces to other Borland products.

Although I am no soothsayer (Madam Valerie, Palm Reading and Paradox Consulting), and cannot commit Borland to future improvements, I can look into my crystal ball and predict the future based on history.

Improving the User Interface

Borland has recognized the trend toward graphical user interfaces, in particular Microsoft Windows. The DOS version is not a true Windows product, but it does include many text-based windowing features. You work with Paradox objects such as tables and forms in windows you can move, resize, and close with a mouse. Windows have attributes such as color and title that you can control with PAL commands. The interface also includes popup and pulldown menus along with dialog boxes for pick lists and text.

The form and report generators do not yet implement the mouse fully. Future versions will surely extend its use in both design and data entry.

Paradox now includes event handling, so PAL programs can trap mouse events such as clicking on a menu item, keypresses such as F2 to close a session, and triggers such as the PgUp key to move to another record. Paradox transfers control to a PAL procedure when an event occurs. This is Borland's first try at providing event support and, although it works, programming would be easier if you could specify different procedures for different types of events. Borland will surely expand event support to respond to constant user requests for a more intuitive interface.

Borland has also added a new field type, the BLOB (Binary Large Object), to Paradox. No, it is not a creature from the black lagoon or even your mother-in-law during a bad week. A BLOB can be a picture in a format such as PCX, a WordPerfect document, a spreadsheet, or almost any other type of non-Paradox data. You could use a BLOB to store a picture of a house with its real estate listing, a spreadsheet of repair expenses with a leased car record, or a WordPerfect contract with a client record.

Currently, you can specify just one BLOB editor such as PC Paintbrush or WordPerfect. So your Paradox tables can contain just one type of BLOB. Borland will certainly extend the feature to allow multiple types of foreign objects. Watch for BLOB2 or 'Return of the Killer BLOB'.

Networking Improvements

Paradox has always had flexible record and file locking abilities to simplify interactive table sharing. Programming a multiuser system, on the other hand, was a feat worthy of Houdini.

Borland recognized the recent trend toward *downsizing*, moving large applications off mainframes and distributing data on local area networks. They improved network data management by introducing group locks. Now a programmer need only lock the group of records required to complete a job.

They have also improved the way Paradox tracks locks to reduce the number of disk accesses. I expect the trend toward simpler network programming and higher speed will continue.

Memory Management

Paradox has provided improved memory management with Microsoft Windows compatibility. Applications can now run under Windows in protected mode, using as much RAM as is available. Unfortunately, the changes also mean you can no longer run Paradox in 640K; it requires at least 2 MB of extended memory, and the more the better. In practice, you will not be able to run applications on most 286 machines. But what poor soul would have such an obsolete computer these days anyway? You might as well be living in the Dark Ages without a fax machine, voice mail, or an electric pencil sharpener!

Client Server Technology

With increased network use comes increased traffic to slow applications to a crawl. The local PC is still making the decisions, and the network server is merely a big filing cabinet. For example, if you query a 5000 record table, all 5000 records travel across the network to your PC. It decides whether they fit your search criteria. If your private directory is located on the network and 3000 records match your request, they also travel across the network. Even with network police, there are sure to be rush hour traffic jams.

Client server technology changes the scenario by moving the decision making ability to the network level. So when you ask Paradox a question, it sends only the request across the network. All processing occurs on the server, and the Answer table stays there too. This reduces traffic, improving performance dramatically.

Borland provides SQL (Structured Query Language) Link, an add-on product to interface Paradox with database servers such as Microsoft's SQL Server. It adds commands to PAL to access data stored on SQL servers, thus reducing LAN traffic. Unfortunately, the current product cannot perform on-line updates. This limits its use to systems with heavy query requirements and low data entry needs. Future releases will improve data entry abilities and increase network performance even more.

Other Product Interfaces

Borland is committed to interfacing its products with each other. Quattro Pro, the Borland spreadsheet, includes Paradox Access. It lets a user query Paradox tables from Quattro and copy Answer tables automatically. There is a PAL command to transfer control to Quattro.

Borland also provides the Paradox Engine that lets C and Pascal programmers access Paradox tables for jobs such as interpreting bar codes, producing graphics and animation, and implementing communications with remote computers that PAL cannot handle. Rather than try and make PAL do tasks for which it is ill-suited, Borland constantly improves its links to other products.

Summary

Paradox and PAL provide the tools to implement both large and small database applications. Paradox uses an object-oriented technique of storing data in tables and lets you design related family objects such as forms and reports. The family approach simplifies application development and system maintenance. Paradox also includes a powerful query facility that you can include in applications with little programming.

You can use PAL to solve problems that would be impossible in interactive Paradox, such as developing a full featured order entry system. You may use all the Paradox interface elements in PAL programs, including popups, pulldowns, and dialog boxes. Data entry is based on the event model. You can trap mouse operations such as clicking on a menu option or field, keystrokes such as F2 to end a session, and triggers such as pressing the down arrow to leave a record. PAL transfers control to a procedure you write to handle events.

We presented three cases of using Paradox to solve varied business problems. The inventory application was multiuser and handled hundreds of items and orders. The publisher needed an elegant but fast way to print royalty statements. The bank had to work around an ancient mainframe system that was unresponsive to customer inquiries.

Finally we looked at the future of Paradox. Although my ouija board is barely functional, I think Borland is on the PC database stage to stay. The same cannot be said for other actors in this arena. Besides, I like a company that can produce great software and a good jazz band at the same time!

2

PAL Basics

In language, clarity is everything.

—Confucius

Introduction

This chapter describes the building blocks of PAL, the Paradox Application Language. It contains background information required to understand the rest of the book. Beginners should read all of it, and experienced PAL programmers should browse it for a quick review.

Paradox programming is built around a stage metaphor. "All the world's a stage," as Bacon (or whoever pretended to be Shakespeare) once wrote. We refer to PAL programs as **scripts** and to direct action in Paradox as occurring in **workspace** and **canvas windows**. There is obviously a mixed metaphor here; I don't think Michelangelo used scripts or Shakespeare wrote on canvas windows.

Workspace windows are the areas where you control tables, forms, and reports in interactive Paradox. In applications, you can hide the action by lowering canvas windows like theater curtains. Or raise them to show the audience what is happening. People seldom need to see (or hear) black-garbed stagehands struggling with heavy props in the dark.

If you use Paradox, you already know more PAL than you might think. Without programming, you can record keystrokes to automate common jobs, save queries, and use the Value and Miniscript commands to get system information. When you are ready for more, you can use the

Paradox editor to create programs. We discuss how to write custom scripts with it and play them.

Paradox and PAL are closely related. Any key you can press interactively you can put in scripts as a keypress or abbreviated menu command. But PAL has additional programming commands and functions. They manage fields and tables in workspace windows, direct screen and printer output, control program flow, lock records and tables for multiuser applications, and manipulate variables and arrays.

PAL has commands to control text-based windows. They can contain Paradox objects, such as tables in form or table view, query forms, report and form designs, and PAL canvases. Windows have attributes such as size, screen position, and color that you can control. Objects in them exhibit standard Paradox behavior. For example, you can insert and delete records from a table displayed in a window as long as it is in Coedit, Edit, or DataEntry mode.

PAL also provides commands to handle application events. They include keystrokes such as F2, mouse actions such as click or double click (but not running up or down clocks), and triggers (no relation to Roy Rogers' horse) such as entering or leaving fields, records, or tables. You can direct Paradox to watch for selected events and execute procedures based on them.

How to DO_IT!

This section describes the following useful techniques:

- Loading menu selections from tables into arrays for maximum flexibility
- Trapping keystrokes with destructive or surprising effects to avoid problems during data entry
- Locating records with similar field values (such as the last names Smith, Smyth, and Smythe) using a secondary index.

Recording Keystrokes

A simple way to create programs is by recording keystrokes. Paradox's multilevel menus make it easy to use, but most jobs require you to press many keys. If you perform a task repeatedly, you may want to record the keystrokes and play them back when needed. Think of it as like preparing a roll for a player piano (surely easier and more dependable than repeating the piece and requires far less boring practice besides!)

Paradox provides the **Instant** script as a quick way to record menu choices. Good name, as instant gratification is the goal of our era! Alt-F3 is the toggle that begins and ends recording. Program 2-1 shows an Instant script to display a customer report. Note that Paradox places each keystroke inside curly braces.

You can duplicate the sequence with the Paradox editor by typing the braces yourself. When you play the script, Paradox does not know (or care) whether the keys were recorded or typed. It responds to them the same either way.

```
;Instant.sc
;Recorded keystrokes to display a customer report
{Report} {Output} {Customer} {1} {Screen}
```

Program 2-1. *Instant Script to Display a Report*

Press Alt-F4 to play the Instant script or choose the menu path Scripts/Play/Instant.

You can record a script under any name by entering it after selecting Scripts/BeginRecord. Recording continues until you select Scripts/EndRecord.

CheckPoint 2-1. Recording Scripts

Objective: Record an Instant script to sort a table by any field and store the result in a new table Sorttbl.

Saving Queries

Saving queries is another quick PAL technique. You build a query on the workspace in interactive Paradox and save it with Scripts/QuerySave under a name you choose. This saves time if you must repeat it or if you want users to play it on their own. You can also test the query by itself and then include it in a script as part of a larger job.

Paradox cannot save the graphic check marks and reverse video of your example elements, so it substitutes words and text symbols. Program 2-2 shows a saved query for a customer table. You would select Ask/Customer to put the form on the workspace. Press F6 to check the fields and F2 to test whether the query works. Then use Scripts/QuerySave to save it. Note that the word "check" replaces the check mark. Paradox saves example elements with a leading underscore. When you play the script query, Paradox rebuilds the workspace accordingly, but does not actually run anything. You must either press the Do_It! key or add the PAL command DO_IT! at the end.

```
;QrySave.sc
;Save a customer query with Cust Id, Name, and Address

Query
 Customer  | Cust Id | Name    | Address  |
           | Check   | Check   | Check    |

Endquery
```

Program 2-2. *Saving a Customer Query*

Value and Miniscript

The Value and Miniscript choices on the PAL menu are two other useful ways to avoid programming. Paradox presents the menu when you press Alt-F10. I use **Value** to perform numeric calculations such as TODAY() + 30 to display the date thirty days from now. TODAY is a PAL function that returns the system date. Results appear immediately in the lower right corner when I press the Enter key. I also use Value to get system information. For example, entering MEMLEFT() makes Paradox report how much memory is available.

I use **Miniscript** to perform a quick sequence of PAL commands without using the editor. You can enter as many instructions (separated by spaces) as will fit in 175 characters. For example, the following Miniscript displays five menu choices from an array and waits for the user to press a key after Paradox displays each element:

```
FOR Choice FROM 1 TO 5 ? MyMenu[Choice] Ans=GETCHAR() ENDFOR
```

Paradox plays it when you press the Enter key. Unfortunately, you cannot save the script in a file, so you must write it down as you go! As George Eliot wrote, "Early youth . . . has no long memories." You can edit the current Value or Miniscript by selecting the option again and pressing Ctrl-E. The same key combination lets you add an expression to the beginning by entering commands.

Writing Scripts

You can write your own scripts if the quick methods of keystroke recording, saving queries, and using Miniscripts are inadequate. PAL commands can do much more than play keystrokes and queries. However, you cannot record them; instead, you must use an editor to add them to scripts.

The script editor is the same program you use to edit memos. You can start it from Paradox by pressing Alt-E or from the main menu by selecting Script/Editor, followed by New to create a new file or Open to open an existing one. You can edit any ASCII file with the Paradox editor, not just scripts.

Table 2-1 summarizes the editor's control keys. Its menu selections are File, Edit, Search, Options, Go, Do_It!, and Cancel.

File creates a new file, opens an existing one, and saves or prints the current file. You can also use it to insert a file at the current cursor position.

Edit cuts, copies, and pastes text blocks to and from the clipboard. You can toggle to the clipboard and edit text there as well as in the main file. You can also erase blocks and move around the file.

Search finds and replaces text.

Options toggles autoindenting, word wrap, and case sensitivity on or off.

Go leaves the editor, saving the script, and plays it.

Do_It! saves the current script and returns control to Paradox. It is quite harmless despite its free-spirited and suggestive name!

Cancel ends the editing session without saving anything.

Table 2-1. Paradox Editor Keys

Keys	Action
Alt-A	Replace next value
Alt-Z	Find next value (ZoomNext)
Ctrl-A	Replace a value
Ctrl-Ins	Copy highlighted area to clipboard
Ctrl-Left Arrow	Move left one word
Ctrl-PgDn	Move to last character in file
Ctrl-PgUp	Move to first character in file
Ctrl-Right Arrow	Move right one word
Ctrl-T	Delete from cursor to end of word
Ctrl-V	Show cursor position
Ctrl-Y	Delete line cursor is in
Ctrl-Z	Find a value (Zoom)
Del	Delete character at cursor or block
Down Arrow	Move down one line
End	Move to last character in current line
Enter	Move to beginning of next line or insert a line
F10	Display editor menu
Home	Move to first character in current line
Ins	Toggle between insert and overwrite modes
Left Arrow	Move left one character
PgDn	Move down one window screen
PgUp	Move up one window screen
Right Arrow	Move right one character
Shift-Ctrl Left	Highlight one word left
Shift-Ctrl PgDn	Highlight from cursor to end of file
Shift-Ctrl PgUp	Highlight from beginning of file to cursor

Shift-Ctrl Right	Highlight one word right
Shift-Del	Cut highlighted area to clipboard
Shift-Down Arrow	Highlight one line down
Shift-End	Highlight from cursor to end of line
Shift-Home	Highlight from beginning of line to cursor
Shift-Ins	Insert clipboard text at cursor
Shift-Left Arrow	Highlight one character left
Shift-PgDn	Highlight from cursor down one window
Shift-PgUp	Highlight from cursor up one window
Shift-Right Arrow	Highlight one character right
Shift-Up Arrow	Highlight one line up
Up Arrow	Move up one line

You can use the mouse to move the cursor and highlight text. To select it, point to the starting position and click. Hold the button down and move the mouse to highlight the area, then release it.

Formatting Scripts

Scripts are freeform. You can put as many commands on a line as you want—just separate them with spaces. You can continue on the next line as long as you do not split keywords, names, or values. The following examples are fine:

```
IF Lname = "Smith" THEN Ok = True ENDIF

IF Lname = "Smith" THEN
  Ok = True
ENDIF

IF Lname = "Smith"
  THEN Ok = True
ENDIF
```

Although PAL does not require them, blank lines and indentation make scripts easier to read. A leading semicolon indicates a comment. It can either be on a line by itself or at the end of a command line.

> **Tip**
>
> Limit scripts to one keyword per line to make errors easier to locate. The debugger indicates the problem line when a runtime error occurs.

Paradox ignores case in variables and keywords. For example, it treats the variables Lname, LNAME, and lname as the same. It also treats RUN, Run, and run identically.

> **Tip**
>
> Use an initial capital letter in variable names and all capitals in reserved words such as RUN. This convention makes scripts easier to read and interpret.

Playing Scripts

Scripts do not need special line delimiters. When one plays, execution starts with the first instruction and proceeds sequentially. Structures such as WHILE and IF change the flow of control. The commands EXIT and QUIT end play immediately. You might say they bring down the curtain! EXIT returns control to DOS, whereas QUIT returns to Paradox. The workspace still shows the active tables and forms unless you clear it.

If one script calls another, the RETURN command returns control to the caller. It may return a value. At the top level, RETURN stops play and returns control to Paradox.

You can play scripts with the path Scripts/Play or from the DOS command line. The following command loads Paradox and plays the Startup script.

```
C:> Paradox Startup
```

Paradox pre-parses a script and creates a new file with the extension SC2 the first time you play it. It then plays the SC2 version, not the original. This speeds execution (after the first time), because Paradox need not recheck the program for syntax errors such as misspelled words and missing punctuation. It recreates the SC2 version if you change the original script and play it. A bit less romantic than "Play it again, Sam!" but more efficient.

Watching Script Action

The screen goes blank when you play a script. It's like waiting for your computer to do its self-test when you turn it on. PAL lowers the full screen canvas to hide table manipulation on the workspace. In the following example, the screen stays blank until Paradox loads the Items table. All three tables then appear simultaneously.

```
CLEAR
VIEW "Customer"
VIEW "Orders"
VIEW "Items"
```

You can see what is happening on the workspace by using Scripts/ShowPlay instead of Scripts/Play. Now, like a playwright who is also the director, you can watch as PAL runs your script. You see the results as each command executes. As you might expect, this is especially useful for debugging. I personally never make a mistake, but I do make a lot of on-stage improvements! You may compare the process to revising a play during rehearsals or out-of-town tryouts. "Give my regards to Broadway!"

PAL Commands

You use the editor to build scripts containing PAL commands. We mentioned one type called a keypress action; it is an interactive key name inside curly braces. PAL also includes commands unavailable in interactive Paradox, such as LOCATE to find records with particular values in fields.

Abbreviated menu commands are a third type. They replace a series of menu choices. For example, COEDIT "Customer" replaces the path Modify/Coedit/Customer.

Keypress Actions

Keypress actions have the same effect as pressing keys in interactive Paradox. You can select from menus and use special keys and strings.

You make menu selections by placing them inside curly braces. For example, the menu path View/Customer becomes {View} {Customer}.

You cannot put a variable inside braces. Instead, you must use the SELECT command to store menu choices in variables or calculate them at runtime. The following example prints customer report 1.

```
Rptnumber = 1
{Report} {Output} {Customer} SELECT Rptnumber {Printer}
```

You can use a key's name to produce the effect of pressing it. If you are Coediting a table in a script, for example, the DEL command works the same as pressing the Del key. Table 2-2 lists Paradox's special script keys.

Table 2-2. Special Script Keys

Key	Script Name	Key	Script Name
Special Keys		**Function Keys**	
Backspace	Backspace	F1	Help
Del	Del	F2	Do_It!
End	End	F3	Upimage
Esc	Esc	F4	Downimage
Home	Home	F5	Example
Ins	Ins	F6	Checkmark
PgUp	PgUp	F7	Formkey
PgDn	PgDn	F8	Clearimage
Shift-Tab	Reversetab	F9	Editkey
Tab	Tab	F10	Menu
Up Arrow	Up		
Down Arrow	Down	**Ctrl Function Keys**	
Right Arrow	Right		
Left Arrow	Left	Ctrl-F6	Check Descending
		Ctrl-F7	Graphkey
Control Keys			
		Alt Function Keys	
Ctrl-Backspace	Ctrlbackspace		
Ctrl-Break	Ctrlbreak	Alt-F3	Instantrecord

Ctrl-End	Ctrlend
Ctrl-Home	Ctrlhome
Ctrl-PgDn	Ctrlpgdn
Ctrl-PgUp	Ctrlpgup
Ctrl-Right	Ctrlright
Ctrl-Left	Ctrlleft
Ctrl-D	Ditto
Ctrl-F	Fieldview
Ctrl-L	Resynchronize
Ctrl-O	Dos
Ctrl-R	Rotate
Ctrl-U	Undo
Ctrl-V	Vertruler
Ctrl-Y	Delete Line
Ctrl-Z	Zoom

Alt Keys

Alt-E	Editor
Alt-K	Keylookup
Alt-L	Lockkey
Alt-O	Dosbig
Alt-R	Refresh
Alt-X	Crosstab
Alt-Z	Zoomnext
Alt-F4	Instantplay
Alt-F5	Fieldview
Alt-F6	Checkplus
Alt-F7	Instantreport
Alt-F8	Clearall
Alt-F9	Coeditkey

Shift Function Keys

Shift-F6	Groupby

Programming Commands

Scripts can do much more than just automate the pressing of keys. PAL commands can show menus, specify loops, display messages, and do almost anything else you can imagine! But not what you're thinking of just now. The nine command categories with examples are:

- Table control

```
COEDIT "Customer"
WAIT TABLE
  PROMPT "Press F2 to finish"
UNTIL "F2"
DO_IT!
```

Lets the user Coedit the Customer table in table view until he or she presses F2.

- Screen and printer input/output commands

```
@ 1,0 ?? "Enter Customer Id==>"
ACCEPT "S" TO Custid
```

Prompts the user to enter a Customer Id value (a small integer).

- Program control structures

```
IF NOT Retval THEN
  MESSAGE "Customer not on file"
ENDIF
```

Displays a message after failing to locate a customer record.

- Multiuser commands

```
LOCKRECORD
```

Tries to lock the current record. If successful, the record is reserved for exclusive use until it is unlocked.

- Variable and array manipulation

```
SHOWMENU
  "Add"  : "Add a record",
  "Edit" : "Edit a record",
  "Quit" : "Return"
TO Moption
```

Displays a popup menu and assigns the user's choice to variable Moption.

- Canvas and workspace control

```
PAINTCANVAS ATTRIBUTE 31 0,0,24,79
```

Paints the screen with a white foreground and blue background, coloring text already displayed.

- Dialog commands

```
SHOWDIALOG "State Selection"
  @ 5,5 HEIGHT 10 WIDTH 50
  @ 2,15 ?? "Enter State"

  ACCEPT @ 2,27
    WIDTH 5 "A2"
    TAG " "
    TO State

  PUSHBUTTON @ 4,18 WIDTH 10
    "Accept"
    OK
    DEFAULT
    VALUE "OK"
    TAG "Yes"
    TO Button

ENDDIALOG
```

Creates a dialog box to accept a state abbreviation. It contains an "Accept" pushbutton.

- Procedure and library commands

```
INFOLIB("Ordlib")
```

Creates a temporary List table with a record for each procedure in the library Ordlib containing its name and size in bytes. You can print a report based on List to document application procedures.

- Window commands

```
WINDOW CREATE @ 10,15
  HEIGHT 10
  WIDTH 50
  TO AdviceWindow

  @ 3,6 ?? "Never eat more than you can lift"
  @ 3,7 ?? "          Miss Piggy"
```

Creates a canvas window at row 10 column 15 ten lines high by fifty characters wide and displays two text strings in it.

We describe programming commands in later chapters as we need them. For example, we discuss record and file locking when developing multiuser applications.

Program 2-3 is an example of combining commands to do a specific job. It uses a WHILE loop, an IF statement, several PAL functions, and keypress actions. It checks whether the printer is ready, and allows the user three tries to correct a problem. If the printer is ready, it prints a report.

```
;Chkprt.sc
;Check if printer is ready to print report. Users have
; three tries to fix a problem. They must press a key
; after each one.

Ctr = 1
WHILE Ctr < 4
  ;Test ready status
  IF NOT PRINTERSTATUS() THEN
    MESSAGE "Check printer - press any key to continue"
    ;Wait for keypress
    Ans = GETCHAR()
    MESSAGE "Checking..."
    Ctr = Ctr + 1
  ELSE
    ;Print report
    MESSAGE "Printing report..."
    {Report} {Output} {Customer} {1} {Printer}
    QUITLOOP
  ENDIF
ENDWHILE
```

Program 2-3. *Check Printer Status*

CheckPoint 2-2. PAL Commands

Objective: Change the Chkprt script (Program 2-3) to display a message if the printer is not ready after the third try.

Hint: What is the value of Ctr after the third try?

Abbreviated Menu Commands

Besides specifying keypress actions in curly braces and using PAL programming commands, you can use abbreviated menu commands as shortcuts for a series of Paradox menu choices. They mean less typing when writing PAL programs and, for me, that means fewer mistakes!

The following sequences produce the same result. The first simulates pressing keys to copy report 1 from the Customer table to the Newcust table. The second uses the equivalent abbreviated menu command.

```
Menu {Tools} {Copy} {Report} {DifferentTable} {Customer} {1}
{Newcust} {1}
```

```
COPYREPORT "Customer" "1"  "Newcust" "1"
```

Table 2-3 lists the abbreviated menu commands.

> **Warning**
>
> Abbreviated commands provide automatic confirmation instead of displaying the Paradox Cancel/Replace menu. If Newcust already had a report 1, COPYREPORT would simply overwrite it.

Table 2-3. Abbreviated Menu Commands

Menu Command	System Mode	Menu Path
Add	Main	Tools/More/Add
Canceledit	Edit,Form,Report	Cancel/Yes
Coedit	Main	Modify/Coedit
Copy	Main	Tools/Copy/Table/Replace
Copyform	Main	Tools/Copy/Form/Replace
Copyreport	Main	Tools/Copy/Report/Replace
Create	Main	Create
Delete	Main	Tools/Delete/Table/Ok
Dos	Main	Tools/More/ToDos
Edit	Main	Modify/Edit
Empty	Main	Tools/More/Empty/Ok
Exit	Main	Exit/Yes
Index	Main	Tools/QuerySpeedup
Lock	Main	Tools/Net/Lock Tools/Net/ PreventLock
Moveto	Main	Image/Zoom/Record, Field, or Value
Pickform	Main,Edit,Coedit	Image/Pickform
Play	All	Scripts/Play
Protect	Main	Tools/More/Protect/Password /Table
Rename	Main	Tools/Rename/Table/Replace
Report	Main	Report/Output/Printer
Setdir	Main	Tools/More/Directory/Ok
Setprivatedir	Main	Tools/Net/SetPrivate
Setusername	Main	Tools/Net/UserName
Sort	Main	Modify/Sort
Subtract	Main	Tools/More/Subtract
Undo	Edit,Coedit	Undo/Yes
Unlock	Main	Tools/Net/Lock Tools/Net/ PreventLock
Unpassword	Main	Tools/More/Protect/ ClearPassword
View	Main	View

Building Expressions

You often need more flexibility than a simple PAL command provides. If your program has a runtime error, for example, you might want to display the Paradox error message. Really, you would like to slink away behind the canvas, but the users always find you! You can employ PAL expressions to extend commands and make them more useful. The PAL command to display the current error message in the bottom right screen corner is:

```
MESSAGE "Error is: " + ERRORMESSAGE()
```

The expression consists of the PAL MESSAGE command, a string constant ("Error is: "), and the Paradox ERRORMESSAGE function. The plus sign combines the constant and error message into a string for MESSAGE to display.

PAL expressions can include constants, variables, arrays, operators, field specifiers, and functions. They produce a value that is a PAL data type: alphanumeric, memo, numeric, short number, currency, or date. They can also produce a logical result of True or False. Expressions may be up to 132 characters long.

You can mix some data types in expressions. PAL assigns a default type to the result (see Table 2-4). For example, if Days is a numeric variable and Invoice_Date is a date, the following expression produces a date.

```
New_Date = Invoice_Date + Days
```

Table 2-4. Data Types Produced by Mixed Expressions

	A	D	L	N	S	$
A	A	*	*	*	*	*
D	*	N	*	D	D	*
L	*	*	L	*	*	*
N	*	*	*	N	N	$
S	*	*	*	N	S	$
$	*	*	*	$	$	$

Data types are: A (Alphanumeric)
D (Date)
L (Logical, True/False)
M (Memo)
N (Number)
S (Short Number)
$ (Currency)
* Invalid combination

Note: A string of 1 to 255 characters evaluates to an alphanumeric type. Paradox converts longer strings to the memo type.

Using Constants

PAL has four types of constants: alphanumeric, date, logical, and numeric. Alphanumeric constants are strings such as "Hello". Numeric ones consist of digits with an optional decimal point and minus sign. Date constants can have any of the following formats: mm/dd/yy, dd-Mon,yyy, or dd.mm.yyyy. Logical constants, also called Boolean values, are either True or False.

Using Variables

Variables can hold any PAL data type. Their names must start with a letter and can be up to 132 characters long. They cannot contain spaces, but you can use underscores instead as in Next_Payment_Due.

You need not declare variables before using them. They get their types when assigned values. The most common way to do this is with an equal sign. For example,

```
Lname = "Smith"
```

assigns the string *Smith* to the variable Lname. The TYPE function returns a variable's data type. In this example, it would return A for alphanumeric.

PAL commands such as SHOWMENU assign values to variables as a side effect. The following example displays a popup menu with three choices. It assigns the user's selection to the string variable Moption.

```
SHOWMENU
  "Maint"    :  "Customer Maintenance",
  "Reports"  :  "Customer Reports",
  "Return"   :  "Return to Operating System"
TO Moption
```

PAL provides a special type of variable called a tilde (~) variable. You use it in queries when you want Paradox to substitute its value rather than take it literally. For example, suppose you want a list of all customers in a particular state. You simply use its abbreviation (for example, "NY") as the selection criterion. Paradox looks for exact matches and places their records in the Answer table. But what if you want the user to select a state at runtime? Put a tilde variable in the criterion!

Program 2-4 asks the user to enter a state abbreviation and stores it in the variable State. PAL replaces State with its value before executing the query.

```
;Tildeqry.sc
;User enters a state abbreviation and Paradox substitutes
; it for the tilde variable before executing the
; query.

@ 10,15 ?? "Enter State ==>"
ACCEPT "A2" TO State
Query

Customer | Cust Id | State  |
         | Check   | ~State |

Endquery
DO_IT!
```

Program 2-4. *Using Tilde Variables in a Query*

Paradox also has a special variable called Retval. It is a system variable that PAL sets after certain operations such as trying to lock a record. In this case, PAL returns True if the lock succeeds and False if it fails. Table 2-5 lists commands that set Retval.

Table 2-5. Commands That Set Retval

Command	Sets Retval to
ACCEPT	True if user entered a value, False if user pressed Esc
FORMTABLES	True if there are embedded tables on the form, False if not
LOCATE	True if record found, False if no match
LOCK	True if locked all tables in list, False if could not lock all tables
LOCKRECORD	True if record locked, False if could not lock record

REPORTTABLES	True if there are linked tables on the report, False if not
SHOW COMMANDS	True if user made a selection, False if user pressed Esc
UNLOCK	True if unlocked a locked table, False if tried to unlock an unlocked table
UNLOCKRECORD	True if unlocked a locked record, False if tried to unlock an unlocked record
WAIT	Key used to end WAIT. Can be a string such as "F2" or the ASCII value of a key.

Arrays

A PAL array is a collection of related information such as 12 months of sales data. You could use 12 separate variables (Jan...Dec), but that complicates programming. To compute total annual sales, you would need an expression such as:

```
Yrsales = Jan + Feb + ... + Dec
```

If you must handle sales for 1000 salespeople, this approach is impractical! An array lets you assign a name to the entire set and specify how many elements it has. PAL has two types of arrays, fixed and dynamic. For the monthly sales example, the fixed PAL array is:

```
ARRAY Sales[12]
```

This allocates memory space for an array Sales with 12 elements.

PAL arrays are one-dimensional, and their elements may be of different types. You can declare as many arrays as you want, and each fixed one may have up to 15,000 elements. Dynamic arrays have no limit.

You refer to individual fixed array elements with numeric subscripts. For example, Sales[3] is the total sales for March. PAL provides the FOR/ENDFOR loop structure to simplify sums and other such operations. The following example first initializes the variable Yrsales to zero; each time through the loop adds a month's sales to it. The limit of 12 tells Paradox to perform 12 iterations.

```
Yrsales = 0
FOR Mnth FROM 1 TO 12
  Yrsales = Yrsales + Sales[Mnth]
ENDFOR
```

If you must change your script to handle 1000 salespeople, you simply change the values in the ARRAY statement and the loop limit from 12 to 1000. The other logic stays the same.

Paradox uses dynamic arrays to store information about events such as mouse movements. It also uses them to hold current system and error information. Dynamic arrays are particularly valuable in situations in which the number or type of elements is not determined until runtime.

As with a fixed array, you must declare a dynamic array before using it, but you need not specify the number of elements. The following example defines a dynamic array to hold information about a mouse event. GETEVENT waits until the user moves the mouse. Paradox then stores the type of movement (for example, "UP") in the array element with index TYPE.

```
DYNARRAY Mevent[]
GETEVENT
  MOUSE "ALL"
TO Mevent
? Mevent["TYPE"]
```

You can use a PAL array to hold a record and use field names as subscripts. You need not declare its size, as Paradox determines the number of elements from the number of fields automatically.

The COPYTOARRAY command copies the current record from a table on the workspace to an array; COPYFROMARRAY moves the array values to the current record. This is the only way to move a record between tables unless you do it field by field. The following example moves a record from the Customer table to the Oldcust table via array Temp.

```
VIEW "Customer"          ;Load Customer table
COPYTOARRAY Temp         ;Move first record to array
COEDIT "Oldcust"         ;Edit Oldcust
INS                      ;Insert new blank record
COPYFROMARRAY Temp       ;Copy customer data to it
DO_IT!
CLEARALL
```

You need not declare the arrays used in COPYTOARRAY; PAL allocates memory for them automatically.

If the Customer table has a Cust Id field, the command

```
? Temp["Cust Id"]
```

displays the value in the array Temp. Using field names instead of numerical subscripts makes programs easier to read. Besides, the script does not depend on the field's physical location, so you need not change it if you restructure the table.

PAL Operators

You can use operators to combine constants, variables, and array elements in expressions. In the Sales array example, we calculate total annual sales with the expression

```
Yrsales = Yrsales + Sales[Mnth]
```

Yrsales is the cumulative variable and Sales[Mnth] is the current month's amount.

PAL operators fall into five categories: numeric, alphanumeric, date, logical, and comparison. Table 2-6 contains a complete list.

Table 2-6. PAL Operators

Operator	Function	Operator	Function
Numeric		**Alphanumeric**	
+	Addition	+	Concatenation
-	Subtraction		
*	Multiplication	**Date**	
/	Division	+	Addition
		-	Subtraction
Comparison			
=	Equal to		
<>	Not equal to	**Logical**	
<	Less than		
<=	Less than or equal	AND	Logical AND
		OR	Logical OR

>	Greater than	NOT	Logical NOT
>=	Greater than or equal		

You use **numeric** operators to perform arithmetic calculations such as accumulating sales. Note that you may have to watch out for the possibility of dividing by zero, as Paradox does not handle the problem on its own.

> **Warning**
>
> Division by zero produces a zero answer, not an error. You must test for it explicitly to report when it happens.

> **Warning**
>
> Mathematical functions with illegal parameters such as SQRT(-16) produce a string containing "Error" rather than a script error.

Plus (+) is the only **alphanumeric** operator. It combines two strings. For example, the following expression creates a string with today's date such as "Today is 2/9/92":

```
Newdate = "Today is " + STRVAL(TODAY())
```

The impressive technical term for the operation is **concatenation**. You can use it to dazzle your boss and coworkers. Be careful—some cat lovers think it's a euphemism for eliminating their favorite animals.

Date operators add or subtract a number of days from a date variable or field. Paradox automatically accounts for months and years. For example, TODAY() - [Invoice Date] calculates the number of days between today and an invoice date for aging.

Logical operators return values based on the following rules (similar to the standard English meanings), where A and B are variables or expressions:

A AND B is True if both A and B are True.

A OR B is True if either A or B is True (or both).

NOT A is True if A is False.

You can use **comparison** operators with all data types. Blank values are above everything else. Alphanumeric comparisons depend on the country group chosen when you installed Paradox. In general, numbers sort lowest, followed by lowercase and capital letters. For example, *smith* is less than *SMITH*. Table 2-7 shows the comparison rules.

Table 2-7. Comparison Rules

Data Type	Comparison Order
Alphanumeric	Selected sort order based on country
Date	Earlier < later
Logical	False < True
Numeric	Lower < higher

When you use operators in expressions, PAL uses precedence rules to decide what to do first. You can use parentheses to override them and establish your own order. Table 2-8 lists the precedence for all PAL operators. (Lowest values indicate the highest precedence).

Table 2-8. PAL Operator Precedence

Precedence	Operators
1	()
2	* /
3	+ -
4	= <> < <= > >=
5	NOT
6	AND
7	OR

Field Specifiers

You can use field specifiers in expressions to refer to a field in an image on the workspace. You must enclose them in brackets ([]). Fields must be in display or query images, and display images may be in table or form view. Table 2-9 lists typical field specifiers.

Table 2-9. Field Specifiers

Specifier	Points to
[]	Current field in current image
[#]	Current record number in current image
[field]	Named field in current image
[table->]	Current field in named image
[table->field]	Named field in named image
[table(Q)->]	Current field in query image of table
[table(Q)->field]	Named field in query image of table
[table(n)->]	Current field in nth image of table
[table(n)->field]	Named field in nth image of table

You can use field specifiers in expressions just like constants and variables, but only in Edit and Coedit mode. The following examples show valid combinations:

```
Aging = [Invoice Date] + 30

[Lname] = "Smith"

InvTotal = [Subtotal] + [Sales Tax]
```

Figure 2-1 displays a Customer table with field specifiers. You refer to a field in the current image by putting its name inside brackets. Note that you can refer to one elsewhere using the syntax [tablename->fieldname]. You can assign values only to ones in the current image.

```
Viewing Customer table
Record 1 of 1000                                Current Record

Customer    Cust Id     Name       State
1           926         Heep       CT
            928         Twist      CT
3           935         Pickwik    NY

[State]               is equal to     "CT"
[Customer->Name]      is equal to     "Heep"
[Cust Id]             is equal to     926
[#]                   is equal to     1
```

Figure 2-1. *Customer table field specifiers.*

To assign values to fields in other tables on the workspace, you must move to them first. Paradox remembers the record position (but not always the field) when you move back.

The MOVETO command moves the cursor to a specified image, field, or record on the workspace. You can refer to any field, but you can assign values only to ones in the current image. The following are valid MOVETO commands.

MOVETO "Customer" moves to the Customer image.

MOVETO [Name] moves to the Name field in the current record.

MOVETO RECORD 1 moves to record 1 in the current image.

PAL Functions

Functions consist of keywords and optional arguments; they may return a single value. PAL has a large library of built-in functions that fall into eight general categories: date/time, information, input/output, mathematical, statistical, string, system status, and workspace/canvas.

As with PAL commands, we discuss individual functions in more detail as we need them. For example, we consider workspace and canvas functions when describing the user interface. The following is a brief explanation of each type with an example.

- Date and Time

```
Thirty = TODAY() + 30
```

Add thirty days to today's date.

- Information

```
IF ISEMPTY("Answer") THEN
  MESSAGE "Answer table has no records"
ENDIF
```

Display a message if the Answer table is empty.

- Input/Output

```
ACCEPT "A2" TO State
```

Accept a two-character state abbreviation entered by the user.

- Mathematical

```
Sqrroot = SQRT(ABS(Numbr))
```

Find the square root of the absolute value of Numbr.

- Statistical

```
MOVETO FIELD "Sales"
Big = IMAGECMAX()
```

Find the largest sales amount and assign it to Big.

- String

```
Client = UPPER([Lname])
```

Convert Lname to uppercase and assign it to Client.

- System Status

```
Howmuch = MEMLEFT()
```

Determine how much RAM is available.

- Workspace and Canvas

  ```
  Curtable = TABLE()
  ```

  Determine which table is current.

PAL Key Codes

Programs often must perform PAL commands and functions based on the key a user presses in response to a prompt, menu, or message. PAL also uses single **key codes** to control printer actions such as form feed and line feed. You can use extended codes in PAL programs to access Alt and Ctrl keys or include special characters such as √ in messages and prompts.

PAL key codes represent keys or key combinations in the ASCII and IBM extended character set. They can take four forms: single character strings, function keys, ASCII characters, and extended codes.

Single Character Strings

Single character strings represent all keyboard letters, numbers, and symbols. You can also use the Alt key plus a number to access non-keyboard characters. The number comes from the ASCII character set. For example, Alt-251 puts a check mark in the following message.

```
MESSAGE "Press √ to select a field"
```

Backslash codes replace the following keys:

"\\"	for backslash (\)
"\""	for double quotation mark (")
"\f"	for form feed (Ctrl-L)
"\n"	for newline (Ctrl-J)
"\r"	for carriage return (Ctrl-M)
"\t"	for tab (Ctrl-I)

I use backslash codes mainly to control the printer, bypassing the report facility. The following commands send the setup string to start compressed print on a Hewlett-Packard LaserJet printer:

```
PRINT "\027(s0p16.66H"
PRINT "\f"
```

Function Keys

Another class of key codes lets you refer to function keys by name. A script is much easier to read if it refers to "F2" rather than -60.

Table 2-10 shows how the strings "F1" through "F40" represent function key combinations.

Table 2-10. Function Key Combinations

Keys	Represent
F1 - F10	Function keys F1 through F10
F11 - F20	Shift functions (Shift-F1 through Shift-F10)
F21 - F30	Ctrl functions (Ctrl-F1 through Ctrl-F10)
F31 - F40	Alt functions (Alt-F1 through Alt-F10)

Warning

Paradox cannot use the F11 and F12 keys available on some keyboards.

The following example puts the Customer table on the workspace in Coedit mode. Pressing F2 ends the editing session and returns Paradox to Main mode.

```
COEDIT "Customer"
WAIT TABLE
  PROMPT "Press F2 to finish editing"
UNTIL "F2"
DO_IT!
```

ASCII Values

If a key lacks an equivalent PAL name, you can refer to it by its ASCII value. In this example, the user would press Ctrl-P (code 16) to print the current invoice.

```
COEDIT "Openinv"
WAIT TABLE
  PROMPT "Press F2 to finish, Ctrl-P to print invoice"
UNTIL "F2", 16
IF Retval = 16 THEN
  PLAY "Printinv"
ENDIF
DO_IT!
```

Extended Codes

Negative values from -1 through -132 refer to keys and keystroke combinations not represented by the 256 ASCII characters. For example, the following SETKEY command defines Alt-S as a "hot key" combination. Pressing it brings the State table into view.

```
SETKEY -31 VIEW "State"
```

Control Structures

Scripts generally execute sequentially, but they, like us, sometimes must deviate from the straight and narrow path. Programs must take different actions based on user input and the availability of resources such as tables and printers. Menus should display in loops until the user decides to exit. PAL provides six control structures that change the flow of control in scripts: IF, SWITCH, FOR, FOREACH, WHILE, and SCAN.

IF—Two-Way Branch

The IF statement provides an either-or branch. If the condition is True, the THEN statements execute; otherwise, the ELSE ones do. The ELSE may be omitted. The following example displays a message if the Answer table is empty.

```
IF ISEMPTY("Answer") THEN
  MESSAGE "Answer is empty"
  SLEEP 1500
ENDIF
```

You can nest IF statements, but each must have a matching ENDIF. The following example reports the states of two related tables (Customer and Orders). If either is empty, the script displays a message.

```
IF ISEMPTY("Customer") THEN
  MESSAGE "There are no customers"
ELSE
  IF ISEMPTY("Orders") THEN
    MESSAGE "There are customers but no orders"
  ELSE
    MESSAGE "There are customers and orders"
  ENDIF
ENDIF
```

SWITCH—Multiway Branch

SWITCH provides a multiway branch. Program 2-5 displays a popup menu with three choices. Moption contains the user's choice, and SWITCH determines from it which script to play.

```
;Showmenu.sc
;Display a menu with three choices and accept user
; selection

SHOWMENU
  "Maint"   :  "Customer Maintenance",
  "Reports" :  "Customer Reports",
  "Return"  :  "Return to Operating System"
TO Moption
SWITCH
  CASE Moption = "Maint"   :
    PLAY "TblMaint"
  CASE Moption = "Reports" :
    PLAY "TblRept"
  CASE Moption = "Return"  :
    EXIT
ENDSWITCH
```

Program 2-5. *Popup Menu with a Switch*

SWITCH may have any number of CASEs. PAL executes the first true one. The CASE condition may be compound as in:

```
CASE Retval = "PgUp" OR Retval = "PgDn":
```

This allows several values to produce the same result. You can include an optional OTHERWISE that executes if no CASE is true. The structure must end with ENDSWITCH.

> **Warning**
>
> The SWITCH command is case sensitive. The following cases are not the same:
>
> ```
> CASE Option = "Add":
> CASE Option = "ADD":
> ```

FOR—Counting Loop

FOR loops execute a specific number of times based on a counter. Program 2-6 uses the number of records in the Customer table to determine the limit for loading the array Cust.

```
;Loadcust.sc
;Use number of records in Customer table to
; control a FOR loop that loads an array


Ncust = NRECORDS("Customer")      ;Number of records in table
ARRAY Cust[Ncust]                 ;Dimension array same size
VIEW "Customer"                   ;Load table on workspace
FOR Ctr FROM 1 TO Ncust           ;Load array from table
  Cust[Ctr] = [Cust Id]
ENDFOR
CLEARALL
```

Program 2-6. *Load Customer Array from a Table*

Ctr is the counter here. PAL initializes it to 1 when the loop starts and increases it by 1 each time through. The loop ends when Ctr exceeds Ncust.

An optional STEP clause can specify how much to increment the counter after each iteration. The following example assumes two arrays contain numbers and dates from a customer's open invoices. The latest one is the last (highest numbered) entry. The FOR loop displays them in reverse chronological order.

```
FOR Numbr FROM Ctr TO 1 STEP -1
  ? Invoice[Numbr]," ",Invoice_Date[Numbr]
ENDFOR
```

FOREACH—Dynamic Array Loop

FOREACH loops perform a set of commands for each element in a dynamic array. Because Paradox does not store the elements sequentially, the order in which it will process them is unpredictable. In the following example, Paradox stores information about the latest script error in the dynamic array Scripterr and then displays elements such as script name, problem line number, and error code.

```
DYNARRAY Scripterr[]
ERRORINFO TO Scripterr
FOREACH Element IN Scripterr
  ? Scripterr[Element]
ENDFOREACH
```

WHILE—Conditional Loop

A WHILE loop repeats until its condition becomes False or PAL executes a QUITLOOP. It must end with an ENDWHILE. The following example empties the keyboard buffer.

```
WHILE CHARWAITING()
  Ch = GETCHAR()
ENDWHILE
```

SCAN—Search and Loop

SCAN moves through the current table sequentially, executing a group of commands for each record that meets an optional condition. For example, Program 2-7 increases the credit limit for each Connecticut customer by

10 percent. There should be some compensation for living in Connecticut! (My editor made me say that! I like living there on alternate Tuesdays.)

```
;Scanloop.sc
;Scan Customer table and increase credit limit for
; Connecticut customers by 10 percent

COEDIT "Customer"
SCAN FOR [State] = "CT"
  [Credit_Limit] = [Credit_Limit] * 1.1
ENDSCAN
DO_IT!
```

Program 2-7. *Scan Table and Increase Credit Limit*

Interrupting a Loop

The LOOP command transfers control immediately to the top of a FOR, FOREACH, SCAN, or WHILE loop. It skips the rest of the iteration.

QUITLOOP ends a loop, regardless of the condition. Execution continues with the command following ENDFOR, ENDFOREACH, ENDWHILE, or ENDSCAN.

> **Tip**
>
> Multiple QUITLOOP commands make loops difficult to follow or understand, so use them sparingly. They are contrary to the structured programming maxim of single-entry, single-exit modules.

Paradox Modes

All Paradox programming commands and functions execute in a mode. It determines which actions are legal. For example, queries occur in Main mode; you cannot use arithmetic expressions in a query form. A script error occurs if you put the following statement in one.

```
[Cust Id] = Old_Id + 1
```

Table 2-11 lists the 15 major Paradox modes.

Table 2-11. Paradox Major Modes

Mode	Description
Coedit	Modify table with Coedit
Create	Create a new table
DataEntry	Batch table maintenance
Edit	Modify table with Edit
File Editor	Edit ASCII files (scripts)
Form	Design or change forms
Graph	Create graph specifications
Index	Create secondary indexes
Main	Default mode
Password	Define or change passwords
Preview	Examine reports on screen
Report	Design or change reports
Restructure	Restructure a table
Script	Edit or write scripts
Sort	Sort a table

Paradox always starts in Main mode. The mode changes when you select menu options and while some commands execute. The SORT command, for example, switches Paradox from Main to Sort mode when the sort begins and back to Main mode when it finishes.

How to DO_IT!

This section contains three scripts that demonstrate common Paradox techniques. Program 2-8 loads three arrays with menu information. It makes an application flexible because you can change the menu without changing the display program.

Program 2-9 coedits a table and traps the Del key. It asks the user for confirmation before deleting the record. Normally, if he or she mistakenly presses Del instead of backspace to erase a character, Paradox simply deletes the record. That could be both surprising and annoying! I call Del the "Oh My Deity" key. A user often invokes a deity's name when he or she presses it by mistake.

> **Tip**
>
> The user can press Ctrl-U to undo the last action, such as pressing Del in Coedit mode.

Program 2-10 does a wildcard search on a customer's last name and displays all matches regardless of capitalization. This is particularly helpful for names such as MacDonald (or Macdonald), Levine (or LeVine), and Devere (or DeVere).

```
;Loadmenu.sc
;Loads three arrays with values stored in Menu table.
;Items contains tags to display in a Paradox popup
; menu. Descs contains matching descriptions,
; and Scripts holds script to play when user
; picks an item.

;Arrays are sized based on number of entries in
; table

Nrecs = NRECORDS("Menu")
ARRAY Items[Nrecs]
ARRAY Descs[Nrecs]
ARRAY Scripts[Nrecs]

;Load arrays from Menu table. Use RECNO() as array
; index
VIEW "Menu"
SCAN
  Items[RECNO()]   = [Menu Item]
  Descs[RECNO()]   = [Description]
  Scripts[RECNO()] = [Script]
ENDSCAN
CLEARIMAGE
```

```
;Use Showarray to display Paradox menu. User may press
; F1 for help with Keyto option. User exits with
; Esc key.
WHILE True
  CLEAR
  Mkey = ""
  SHOWARRAY
    Items Descs
      UNTIL "F1" KEYTO Mkey
  TO Moption

  ;Test for help key
  IF Mkey = "F1" THEN
    MESSAGE "Here is some help - Never trust a "+
      "surgeon who offers 2-for-1 twilight specials!"
    SLEEP 2000
    LOOP
  ENDIF

  ;Test for Esc key
  IF Retval = False THEN
    QUITLOOP
  ENDIF

  ;User must have selected a menu option. Find out
  ; which one and play corresponding script
  FOR Choice FROM 1 TO Nrecs
    IF Items[Choice] = Moption THEN
      PLAY Scripts[Choice]
      QUITLOOP
    ENDIF
  ENDFOR
ENDWHILE
```

Program 2-8. *Table-Driven Menu Display*

Adding records to the Menu table changes the menu without requiring a program change. This saves time because you can test a new script by itself and add it to your application quickly. The SHOW commands include a KEYTO option that traps a list of keys besides the options on the menu. This program uses F1 in SHOWARRAY to display help. Note that you cannot use dynamic arrays with SHOWARRAY because Paradox does not organize them sequentially.

Program 2-9 traps the Del key while Coediting a Customer table. Users often forget that Del deletes the current record, not the character under the cursor! The program asks for confirmation, and deletes the record only if the user presses y or Y.

```
;Trapdel.sc
;Coedit a Customer table and trap Del key.
;Ask for confirmation before deleting current
; record. All other keys work as usual in Coedit mode.

;Put Customer table on Workspace
COEDIT "Customer"
WHILE True
  ;Allow user to Coedit table
  WAIT TABLE
    PROMPT "F2-Quit, Del-Delete Record"
  UNTIL "F2","Del"
  ;Trap F2 and Del keys. All others work normally.
  SWITCH
    CASE Retval = "F2":
      QUITLOOP
    CASE Retval = "Del":
      MESSAGE "Do you want to delete this record? (Y/N) "
      Ans = GETCHAR()
      ;Erase message
      MESSAGE ""
      ;Test for y or Y
      ;GETCHAR returns ASCII value for a keypress
      ; 89 = Y and 121 = y
      IF Ans <> 89 AND Ans <> 121 THEN
        LOOP
      ELSE
        DEL
      ENDIF
  ENDSWITCH
ENDWHILE
DO_IT!
CLEARALL
```

Program 2-9. *Trap Del Key during Coedit*

Paradox traps keys you list in the UNTIL part of your WAIT commands. Remember that the prompt only displays information to the user; it does not tell Paradox anything. Paradox puts the last key pressed in the system variable Retval, so you can determine what ended the WAIT.

Program 2-10 lets the user search a Customer table by last name. He or she can enter a partial name such as Sm, and the pattern option on the LOCATE INDEXORDER command does a wildcard search. Names such as Smith, SMITH, Smythe, and Smithe will match. Of course, so will Smart and Smucker. If the search succeeds, Paradox sets Retval to True. The program assumes a secondary index on Name. If it does not exist, LOCATE INDEXORDER on that field causes a script error.

```
;Wildsrch.sc
;Wild card search of last name field for user specified value.
;Moves cursor to record with matching value.
;Alt-S starts search, Alt-D looks for duplicates

VIEW "Customer"
;Make sure search name is empty initially
RELEASE VARS Mname
;-31 is extended code for Alt-S
;-32 is extended code for Alt-D
WHILE True
  WAIT TABLE
    PROMPT "F2-Quit, Alt-S/D to search by last name"
  UNTIL "F2",-31,-32
  SWITCH
    CASE Retval = "F2":
      QUITLOOP

    ;Alt-S to start search
    CASE Retval = -31:
      @ 0,0 CLEAR EOL
      @ 0,1 ?? "Enter Name==>"
      ACCEPT "A10" TO Mname
      ;Quit if user presses Esc
      IF NOT Retval THEN
        LOOP
      ENDIF

      ;Use pattern option of LOCATE INDEXORDER to do
      ; wildcard search
      MOVETO [Name]
      LOCATE INDEXORDER PATTERN Mname + ".."
```

```
      ;See if match found. If not, display a message
      ; for 2 seconds. SLEEP pauses script action.
      IF NOT Retval THEN
        MESSAGE "No match found"
        SLEEP 2000
        ;Remove message
        MESSAGE ""
        RELEASE VARS Mname
        LOOP
      ENDIF
    ;Alt-D to search for duplicates
    CASE Retval = -32:
      ;Make sure search criteria is assigned
      ;ISASSIGNED checks whether a variable has
      ; been assigned a value
      IF NOT ISASSIGNED(Mname) THEN
        MESSAGE "Enter original name with Alt-S please"
        SLEEP 2000
        MESSAGE ""
        LOOP
      ENDIF

      ;Look for duplicate.
      ;ATLAST tests for last table record.
      IF NOT ATLAST() THEN
        LOCATE INDEXORDER NEXT PATTERN Mname + ".."
      ELSE
        MESSAGE "No more matches"
        SLEEP 2000
        MESSAGE ""
        RELEASE VARS Mname
        LOOP
      ENDIF

      ;See if match found
      IF NOT Retval THEN
        MESSAGE "No more matches"
        SLEEP 2000 MESSAGE ""
        RELEASE VARS Mname
        LOOP
      ENDIF
  ENDSWITCH
ENDWHILE
CLEARALL
```

Program 2-10. *Wildcard Search by Name*

Releasing the variable Mname indicates that no search criteria has been selected. If Mname is assigned, Paradox does a duplicate search with LOCATE INDEXORDER NEXT. The code need not move off each match as it would with the LOCATE command to avoid creating an infinite loop, finding the same record forever.

Summary

You already know more PAL than you might think! Recording keystrokes, saving queries, and using the Value and Miniscript options are good stepping stones to using the full language.

This chapter described the basic PAL building blocks, including commands, expressions, arrays, and functions. It also showed how to use the IF, FOR, FOREACH, WHILE, SWITCH, and SCAN structures to change the flow of control in scripts. It presented examples of PAL commands for creating windows and dialog boxes.

The DO_IT! section illustrated three common programming techniques: loading menu arrays from tables to make programs more flexible, trapping troublesome keys during data entry, and doing wildcard searches using secondary indexes.

3

Procedures and Libraries

From a little distance one can perceive an order in what at the time seemed confusion.

—F. Scott Fitzgerald

Introduction

If you write applications for others, you must convert your scripts into procedures and store them in libraries. Paradox parses (precompiles) them as it loads them into memory, so they run faster.

Procedures accept arguments and return values just like PAL functions. You can write general-purpose routines to do jobs such as display menus, then change the result by changing the values passed. You can develop your own error handling procedures, and users need never see Paradox's cryptic and ominous Cancel/Debug menu when a runtime error occurs. Note that I said "When", not "If"!

Since Paradox encrypts library procedures, you can remove the source code to prevent adventurous users from making changes. If you define an Autolib path with a list of library names, PAL searches them automatically for a procedure when you call it. Closed procedures, which must be stored in libraries, release all memory used for variables, arrays, and called procedures when they end. So you do not have to release it explicitly.

This chapter describes how to convert scripts into procedures and pass arguments to them. In a program containing procedures, there are several places where you can declare variables: in the startup script, in the argument list passed to a procedure, or in a procedure's variable list. The part of the program in which a variable is accessible and can be used is called its **scope**. We explain the difference between global and private variables and discuss how to avoid scoping errors that may cause you to use or change the wrong value inadvertently.

We show how to write two special types of procedures: errorprocs and closed procedures. Paradox sends users to your errorproc rather than displaying the Cancel/Debug menu when a runtime error occurs. Closed procedures allow Paradox to manage memory for you.

We show how to combine procedures into libraries, list information in them, and autoload procedures from them. We also show how to call procedures to minimize memory usage.

Lastly, we show how to package an application into an efficient combination of scripts and libraries for distribution.

How to DO_IT!

This section illustrates table-driven programming and recursive procedure calls. If you store information such as options in tables, you can display different menus by passing different table names to a procedure.

Recursion means that a procedure calls itself (presumably with different parameters!). This saves you from having to write a new one for each submenu.

Using Procedures

Procedures, like scripts, bundle a sequence of instructions into a package. However, they are more powerful in several ways. First, they can accept arguments and return values like PAL functions. Because Paradox parses them as it loads them into memory, they execute faster than scripts. Procedures can also declare private variables, thus avoiding side effects.

Creating Procedures

You convert a script into a procedure by adding a header and a footer. The header starts with the keyword PROC, followed by the procedure name and a parameter list (possibly empty) in parentheses. The body is the same as the script; it ends with the odd-sounding ENDPROC.

Program 3-1 shows a script to display a dialog box at screen position 5,5 with height 10 and width 50. It would be a good utility if we rewrote it to accept parameters for the message, box coordinates, height, and width. It could then display a dialog box anywhere.

```
;Msgbox1.sc
;Display a message in a box with an Accept button
;Top left corner at coordinates 5,5
;Height 10 and width 50

SHOWDIALOG ""
  @ 5,5 HEIGHT 10 WIDTH 50
  @ 2,10 ?? "Press any key to continue..."

  PUSHBUTTON @ 5,18 WIDTH 10
    "Accept"
    OK
    DEFAULT
    VALUE "OK"
    TAG "Yes"
    TO Button

ENDDIALOG
```

Program 3-1. *Display Dialog Box (Script Version)*

Program 3-2 is the procedure version. The header consists of PROC followed by the name and parameters for the message, coordinates, height, and width. The last line is ENDPROC.

```
;Msgbox.sc
;Display a message in a box with an Accept button
;Top left corner at coordinates Tlr,Tlc
;Height Hgt (must be at least 6 to accommodate message
;and button)
;Width Wdth (must be at least message length + 5)

PROC Msgbox(Msg,Tlr,Tlc,Hgt,Wdth)
PRIVATE ButtonMargin,MsgMargin,Msglen

;Calculate left margin to center message
Msglen = LEN(Msg)
MsgMargin = INT((Wdth-Msglen)/2)

;Calculate left margin to center
; Accept button
ButtonMargin = INT((Wdth-10)/2)

SHOWDIALOG ""
  @ Tlr,Tlc HEIGHT Hgt WIDTH Wdth
  @ 2,MsgMargin ?? Msg

  PUSHBUTTON @ 5,ButtonMargin WIDTH 10
    "Accept"
    OK
    DEFAULT
    VALUE "OK"
    TAG "Yes"
    TO Button

ENDDIALOG
ENDPROC
```

Program 3-2. *Display Dialog Box (Procedure Version)*

When you play Msgbox, nothing happens! Paradox loads its definition into memory, but does not run it immediately as it does Msgbox1. Instead, you must call it. For example, the following command displays a dialog box at coordinates 5,5 with height 10 and width 50.

```
Msgbox("Press any key to continue..",5,5,10,50)
```

The procedure definition stays in memory until all script play ends or you release it with RELEASE PROCS. (Sounds like the command you give when you see Captain Hook approaching! Sorry about that.)

Passing Arguments and Returning Values

The values "Press any key to continue..", 5, 5, 10, and 50 are arguments passed to procedure Msgbox; Msg, Tlr, Tlc, Hgt, and Wdth are its parameters. Arguments can be constants, variables, field values, array elements, or entire arrays.

PAL passes arguments (except arrays) using **call by value**. That is, it moves their current values into the parameter locations before calling a procedure. Any changes that occur during the procedure affect only the parameters, not the original arguments. They retain their old values.

PAL passes an array to a procedure using **call by reference**. That is, it passes the array's memory address instead of the element values. The procedure can change the elements, and they keep their new values when it ends.

For example, Program 3-3 accepts a rectangle's length and width and returns its area.

```
;Calcarea.sc
;Calculate a rectangle's area given its length and width
;Be careful not to use Width as a variable; It is a
;reserved word!

PROC Calcarea(Length,Wdth)
Area = Length * Wdth
RETURN Area
ENDPROC
```

Program 3-3. *Calculate Area of a Rectangle*

You must assign Calcarea's result to a variable because it returns a value. The following statement calculates the area of a rectangle 10 units long by 15 wide.

```
Recarea = Calcarea(10,15)
```

The order is important here—length first, then width.

Scope of Control

You create a call chain when one script or procedure calls another. The called procedure is lower on the chain than the caller. Once you assign global variables, any script or procedure (except closed ones) below it on the call chain can use or change them. Private variables are available only to the procedure that declares them and other scripts or procedures it calls.

Program 3-4 shows the scope of global and private variables for a credit limit update. It asks the user to enter a customer number and new limit, finds the customer record, and updates the limit.

Paradox loads procedures New_Limit and Update_Cust into memory when the script plays, but does not execute them. The action starts when the script asks the user to enter a customer number. Variable Cust_Id is global, so both procedures can access it. Procedure New_Limit asks the user to enter a credit limit as a private variable and calls Update_Cust to perform the update. Procedure Update_Cust knows the values of Cust_Id (global) and Crd_Limit (private to procedure New_Limit above it on the call chain). Figure 3-1 shows the chain and the scopes of all variables.

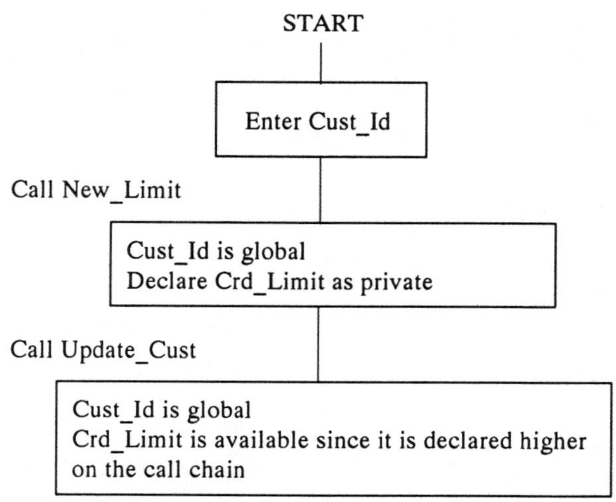

Figure 3-1. *Call chain for credit limit update.*

```
;Credadj.sc
;Update customer's credit limit.

;Ask user for new credit limit amount. Cust_Id is
; a global variable.
PROC New_Limit()
PRIVATE Crd_Limit
CLEAR
@ 5,3 ?? Cust_Id
@ 7,3 ?? "Enter new credit limit==>"
ACCEPT "$" TO Crd_Limit
Update_Cust()
ENDPROC

;Update customer's credit limit. Cust_Id is a
; global variable. Crd_Limit is private to
; proc New_Limit above it on call chain
PROC Update_Cust()
COEDIT "Customer"
MOVETO [Customer Id]
LOCATE Cust_Id
[Credit Limit] = Crd_Limit
DO_IT!
CLEARALL
ENDPROC

;Main part of script starts action. Cust_Id
; is global to all procedures
CLEAR
@ 5,3 ?? "Enter customer id==>"
ACCEPT "N" TO Cust_Id
New_Limit()
```

Program 3-4. *Credit Limit Adjustment*

Special Procedures

Paradox has two special types of procedures: errorprocs and closed procedures. If you assign a procedure name to the reserved variable

Errorproc, control transfers there when a runtime error occurs rather than to the dreaded (and confusing) Cancel/Debug menu.

A closed procedure is a self-contained unit that knows only about variables passed through the parameter list or imported via the USEVARS statement. This self-containment or **encapsulation** (a word to impress your friends with!) reduces the chance of causing side effects in other routines.

Using Errorprocs

If an errorproc is in memory when a runtime error occurs, Paradox transfers control to it automatically instead of to the Cancel/Debug menu. It must return one of the following values:

- 0 to rerun the statement that triggered the error. Useful for easily correctable problems such as off-line printers, open disk doors, or empty drives.
- 1 to continue execution with the line after the one that triggered the error. Useful for breakpoints or confirmations.
- 2 to display the Cancel/Debug menu. Useful during debugging, testing, and maintenance.

Anything else has the same effect as 2. I use a combination of two error procedures to handle runtime problems. This approach uses less memory and saves environment information in files I can review later. The ErrorHandler procedure (Program 3-5) is very small since it must stay resident in memory during the entire application. It calls a much larger procedure Errormenu (Program 3-6) that actually handles error processing. If the user decides to exit the application, it saves system information in one script and variable assignments in another.

The following command assigns ErrorHandler to Errorproc at the beginning of the application:

```
Errorproc = "ErrorHandler"
```

ErrorHandler deassigns Errorproc to avoid creating an infinite loop if the error procedure has an error. “Physician, heal thyself!”

```
;Ehandle.sc
;Small error handling procedure always in memory
;during an application
PROC ErrorHandler()
PRIVATE Errorproc,    ;Don't call this if it has an error!
        ReturnCode    ;Return code of 0, 1, or 2

Errorproc =  ""
;Read ErrorMenu procedure from
; Utility library
READLIB Ulib ErrorMenu
;Call larger ErrorMenu procedure
ReturnCode = ErrorMenu()
RETURN ReturnCode
ENDPROC
```

Program 3-5. *Memory Resident Error Handler*

ErrorMenu displays a menu to let the user retry the operation that caused the problem or exit to the operating system. It treats Ctrl-D (ASCII 4) as a secret key that transfers control to the Cancel/Debug menu. This lets you access the Paradox debugger, but hides it from users.

```
;EMenu.sc
;Handles runtime errors. Allows user to
;retry operations such as fixing off-line
;or jammed printers. If user exits to
;operating system, it saves system information
;in two scripts.
PROC ErrorMenu()
PRIVATE
        Debugkey,   ;Hidden Cancel/Debug key choice
        Efile,      ;Error file, no extension
        Errfile,    ;Error file (script)
        Errormsg,   ;Error message line
        Mchoice,    ;User's menu choice
        Whandles    ;Counter for window handles
```

```
;Display system error message and error code.
;Use dynamic array to get error information
ERRORINFO TO Error
IF NOT ISBLANK(Error["Code"]) THEN
  Errormsg = Error["Message"] + "(" + Error["Proc"] +
    ":" + STRVAL(Error["Code"]) + ")"
ELSE
  Errormsg = ERRORMESSAGE() + "(" +
    STRVAL(ERRORCODE()) + ")"
ENDIF

;Roadrunner lives!
BEEP BEEP
MESSAGE Errormsg

;Get user's choice
;Use hidden key Ctrl-D to reach Cancel/Debug menu
Debugkey = ""
SHOWMENU
  "Stop"  :  "Return to DOS",
  "Retry" :  "Try this operation again"
    UNTIL 4 KEYTO Debugkey
TO Mchoice

;If user pressed Esc, assume he or she wants to Stop
IF NOT Retval THEN
  Mchoice = "Stop"
ENDIF

;If user pressed Ctrl-D, return 2 to enter debugger

IF Debugkey = 4 THEN
  RETURN 2
ENDIF

SWITCH
  ;Stop processing, save values, return to DOS
  CASE choice = "Stop" :
    ;If mode not main, then editing
    IF SYSMODE() <> "Main" THEN
      RESET
    ENDIF

    ;Define file to hold all error information in
    ; user's private directory
    Errfile = PRIVDIR() + "Errfile.sc"
    Efile = PRIVDIR() + "Errfile"
```

```
;Delete old error file if one exists
IF ISFILE(Errfile) THEN
  Menu {tools} {Delete} {Script} SELECT Efile {Ok}
ENDIF
;Create error file
MESSAGE "Writing error information to file ",Errfile
PRINT FILE Errfile "Date = ",TODAY(), "\n"
PRINT FILE Errfile "Directory = ",DIRECTORY(), "\n"
PRINT FILE Errfile "Errormessage = ",Error["Message"], "\n"
PRINT FILE Errfile "Errorcode = ",Error["Code"], "\n"
PRINT FILE Errfile "IsBlankZero = ",ISBLANKZERO(), "\n"
PRINT FILE Errfile "IsRunTime = ",ISRUNTIME(), "\n"
PRINT FILE Errfile "Memleft = ",MEMLEFT(), "\n"
PRINT FILE Errfile "Menuchoice = ",MENUCHOICE(), "\n"
PRINT FILE Errfile "Monitor = ",MONITOR(), "\n"
PRINT FILE Errfile "Nettype = ",NETTYPE(), "\n"
PRINT FILE Errfile "Nimages = ",NIMAGES(), "\n"

IF NIMAGES() > 0 THEN
  PRINT FILE Errfile "Table = ",TABLE(), "\n"
  PRINT FILE Errfile "Imageno = ",IMAGENO(), "\n"
  PRINT FILE Errfile "Imagetype = ",IMAGETYPE(),"\n"
ENDIF

PRINT FILE Errfile "Privdir = ",PRIVDIR(),"\n"

IF NOT ISBLANK(Error["Proc"]) THEN
  PRINT FILE Errfile "Procname = ",Error["Proc"],"\n"
ENDIF

PRINT FILE Errfile "QueryOrder = ",QUERYORDER(),"\n"
PRINT FILE Errfile "RetryPeriod = ",RETRYPERIOD(),"\n"
PRINT FILE Errfile "Sdir = ",SDIR(),"\n"
PRINT FILE Errfile "SortOrder = ",SORTORDER(),"\n"
PRINT FILE Errfile "Sysmode = ",SYSMODE(),"\n"
PRINT FILE Errfile "Time = ",TIME(),"\n"

PRINT FILE Errfile "UserName = ",Error["User"],"\n"
PRINT FILE Errfile "Version = ",VERSION(),"\n"

;Save open window information
PRINT FILE Errfile "Open Windows:","\n"
WINDOW LIST TO WindowHandles
FOR Whandles FROM 1 TO ARRAYSIZE(WindowHandles)
  PRINT FILE Errfile "Window = ",
    WindowHandles[Whandles],"\n"
ENDFOR
```

```
    ;Use Savevars last. It will not work if a current
    ; variable is a string with control characters or graphics
    SAVEVARS ALL
    EXIT

  ;Fix problem and retry
  CASE Mchoice = "Retry":
    RETURN 0
ENDSWITCH
ENDPROC
```

Program 3-6. *Complete Error Handler (Saved on Disk)*

ErrorMenu creates two scripts if the user leaves Paradox. The first, Errfile, contains the current state of all Paradox status functions. The second, Savevars, contains all current variables. You can review them to determine what went wrong. Figure 3-2 shows a sample Errfile; Figure 3-3 shows the corresponding Savevars script.

```
Date = 7/18/92
Directory = C:\APPLIB\
Errormessage = Run error: Variable CUSTTBL has not been
  assigned a value
Errorcode = 34
IsBlankZero = True
IsRunTime = False
Memleft = 872448
Menuchoice = Error
Monitor = Color
Nettype = Other
Nimages = 0
Privdir = C:\PDOX4386\
Procname = MAINMENU
QueryOrder = TableOrder
RetryPeriod = 0
Sdir = C:\APPLIB\
SortOrder = ascii
Sysmode = Main
Time = 08:54:12
UserName =
Version = 4
Open Windows:
```

Figure 3-2. *Sample listing of Paradox status functions.*

```
; Variables Saved Using Savevars Command
ERRORMSG = "Run error: Variable CUSTTBL has not been
  assigned a value(MAINMENU:34)"
Dynarray ERROR[]
ERROR["PROC"] = "MAINMENU"
ERROR["SCRIPT"] = "MAINTLIB"
ERROR["MESSAGE"] = "Run error: Variable CUSTTBL has not been
  assigned a value"
ERROR["SQLERRORMESSAGE"] = ""
ERROR["LINE"] = 21
ERROR["POSITION"] = 551
ERROR["SQLERRORCODE"] = 0
ERROR["CODE"] = 34
ERROR["USER"] = ""
ULIB = "Utillib"
PROCNAME = "Mainmenu"
AUTOLIB = "Maintlib,Utillib,Rptlib"
ERRORPROC = ""
EFILE = "C:\\PDOX4386\\Errfile"
ERRFILE = "C:\\PDOX4386\\Errfile.sc"
```

Figure 3-3. *Sample listing of current variables.*

Using Closed Procedures

A closed procedure does not know about global variables or private ones further up the call chain. You must pass values through an argument list or provide access to globals through the USEVARS statement. Closed procedures have the following advantages:

- All memory used for variables, arrays, and procedures returns to the central memory pool when they end. You need not use RELEASE PROCS or RELEASE VARS to recover it.
- You have complete control over what variables are available. This reduces the chances of side effects.
- They take advantage of extended and expanded memory automatically.

Paradox saves the current states of all application procedures and variables when a closed procedure begins and restores them when it ends. You pay a performance penalty of half a second to load a closed procedure and the same to release memory when it ends.

> **Warning**
>
> You must reload the error procedure explicitly at the beginning of each closed procedure, or Paradox will not know about it when a runtime error occurs.

Program 3-7 shows a menu in a closed procedure. Note that it imports Errorproc in the USEVARS statement. I assign it (Errorproc = "Errorhandler") as a global variable and import it into closed procedures to simplify maintenance. Changing the top level assignment changes all references to it automatically. The script reloads Errorhandler from a procedure library so it will be available when a runtime error occurs. Paradox knows this is a closed procedure from the keyword CLOSED in the header. How subtle!

```
;Apmenu.sc
;Display main application menu. Read Errorhandler from
;a library so it is available for runtime errors.
PROC CLOSED Mainmenu()
USEVARS Errorproc
PRIVATE
        Moption,   ;User's menu choice
        Procname   ;Save procedure name for error
                   ; handler

Procname = "Mainmenu"
;Load Errorhandler from Utility library
READLIB "Utility" Errorhandler

SHOWMENU
  "Maint"   :  "Customer maintenace",
  "Reports" :  "Print reports",
  "Exit"    :  "Leave the system"
TO Moption

SWITCH
  CASE Moption = "Maint":
    PLAY "Maint"
  CASE Moption = "Reports":
    PLAY "Reports"
  OTHERWISE:
```

```
    EXIT
ENDSWITCH
ENDPROC
```

***Program 3-7.** Main Menu in a Closed Procedure*

You must store closed procedures in libraries; you cannot play a script that contains one to load it into memory as you can a regular procedure.

Procedure Libraries

You gain the following benefits by storing a set of procedures in a library:

- Paradox tracks available memory and swaps procedures out automatically as required.
- It stores swapped procedures in a cache to take advantage of extended and expanded memory.
- It preparses and encrypts procedures stored in libraries. You can then remove source code to protect it when distributing an application.

Creating a Library

The CREATELIB command creates a procedure library. It can hold up to 320 procedures, but 50 is the most allowed without incurring an overhead penalty. (Each group of 50 takes approximately 2K of disk space for housekeeping besides their actual size). There is no limit to how many libraries a single application can include.

You cannot remove procedures from a library, and it never shrinks even if you replace a procedure with a smaller version. If you write a new version, Paradox simply marks the original as obsolete (but without deleting it) and adds the new one.

> **Tip**
>
> Recreate a library every time you change one of its procedures to keep it compact.

Program 3-8 creates a library Lib1 with procedures Mickey and Minnie. Playing the script loads each procedure into memory, writes it to the library, and releases it from memory. You will not see anything while the script plays. All the action is off-stage or behind the curtain! When it finishes (if there are no syntax errors), Paradox creates a new file with the library name and the extension LIB.

```
;Lib1.sc
;Create a library Lib1 with procedures Mickey and Minnie
;Use a variable for library name to simplify maintenance
Applib = "Lib1"
CREATELIB Applib


PROC Mickey()
  ***  procedure statements  ***
ENDPROC
WRITELIB Applib Mickey
RELEASE PROCS Mickey

PROC Minnie()
  ***  procedure statements  ***
ENDPROC
WRITELIB Applib Minnie
RELEASE PROCS Minnie
```

Program 3-8. *Create a Procedure Library*

> **Tip**
>
> Give the script that creates a library the same name as the library itself. It will then be easy to remember or spot in a directory listing.

Listing Library Information

The INFOLIB command with a library name creates a temporary List table that contains each procedure name and its approximate size in bytes. For example, the following command creates a List table for Lib1:

```
INFOLIB("Lib1")
```

Figure 3-4 shows the result. The sizes are in bytes.

LIST	Procedure	Size
	Mickey	54
	Minnie	54

Figure 3-4. *Temporary list table for a library.*

Executing Library Procedures

You can execute a library procedure by loading it explicitly with READLIB, or you can let Paradox find it and load it if its library is included on an Autolib path. For example, you load and execute Mickey from Lib1 with the command sequence:

```
READLIB "Lib1" Mickey
Mickey()
```

You can load several procedures with READLIB by separating their names with commas. They stay in memory until you remove them with RELEASE PROCS or Paradox swaps them out.

If you use an Autolib path, Paradox searches listed libraries automatically. The following example assigns libraries Lib1 and Lib2 to Autolib. If your application calls Mickey, Paradox searches Lib1 and then Lib2, if required, to find it, loads it into memory, and executes it.

```
Autolib = "Lib1,Lib2"
Mickey()
```

Paradox searches libraries sequentially, so put the most frequently used ones first. Remember that Autolib is a variable and is not available to closed procedures unless you import it via USEVARS.

Warning

Do not leave any space between library names in the Autolib statement. Otherwise, Paradox will include only the first one and ignore the rest (with no warning whatsoever!)

Swapping Procedures

Paradox assigns memory from a central pool to variables, procedures, forms, and other objects. It has a default swap point. If the amount of free memory falls below that value, Paradox swaps procedures to other areas or removes them completely to accommodate requests.

You may want to change the default swap point with the SETSWAP command to improve performance or prevent your application from running out of memory. The larger SETSWAP is, the slower programs run, as Paradox spends more time swapping. If it is too low, your application may abort for lack of resources. For example, there may not be enough memory left to complete a query. The optimum value is usually between 25K and 35K. The MEMLEFT function returns the amount of available memory.

Paradox's memory management scheme swaps efficiently if you restrict procedures to 10K. Paradox can then swap completed procedures and ones that will be recalled (that is, ones up the call chain from the current one).

Paradox cannot swap embedded procedures, ones called within others. In the following example, it suspends procedure Locatecust while it executes Getcustnum but cannot swap it.

```
Found = Locatecust(Getcustnum())
```

We can rearrange the calls as follows to allow swapping.

```
Custnum = Getcustnum()
Found = Locatecust(Custnum)
```

Debugging Procedures in Libraries

If you keep the original script that created the library in the directory with it (and do not password protect it), the source code is available to the debugger. When a runtime error occurs, Paradox transfers control to the Cancel/Debug menu. If you select Debug and press Ctrl-E, Paradox transfers control to the editor at the problem line.

Paradox stores the script's original pathname as part of the library header. The debugger will look for the source code there, not in the working directory, when an error occurs.

> **Tip**
>
> If you port an application to another machine or copy libraries to another directory, play the scripts to recreate the libraries. The library headers then always contain the correct source code path.

Packaging Applications

An application must include at least one startup script. The reason is that Paradox cannot play a procedure; it can only call one. The Paradox menu has a Scripts/Play option, but nothing that calls a procedure.

The startup script should be as small as possible because the memory it uses cannot be recovered during the current session. Use it to assign an Autolib path, Errorproc, and SETSWAP level, and call the first menu procedure. Program 3-9 is a typical example.

```
;Startup.sc
;Set up system defaults and call first menu
Autolib = "Lib1,Lib2"
SETSWAP 32000
Errorproc = "Errorhandler"
Mainmenu()
```

Program 3-9. *Application Startup Script*

Store all procedures in libraries so Paradox can handle memory management and RELEASE you (get the connection) from having to remember to release procedures and variables explicitly. Close the top level procedure that contains the first menu and the first procedure of each option. Paradox then releases all memory after it completes so its successor starts with the maximum amount.

Do not close any other procedures. Remember that you pay a half second penalty to load a closed procedure or release memory.

How to DO_IT!

Large applications often have many menu levels. I prefer to store the data in tables rather than hard code it into procedures. This reduces the amount of code I must write, and makes my applications more flexible. If I must add a menu choice or change a description, I edit a table rather than the source code. Figure 3-5 shows my generic table structure and a small menu tree with sample data. This approach is a typical example of table-driven programming (see Chapter 9 for more).

Program 3-10 displays menus. The table argument contains menu choices, descriptions, procedure names, and argument lists. The procedure is recursive because it calls itself with a new table name if the option calls a submenu.

If the user selects an option that is not itself a menu, Program 3-10 calls the working procedure with the corresponding argument list. Choosing the Return option from a menu unloads the system stack and recalls the menu one level higher.

> **Warning**
>
> The amount of system memory limits the number of recursion levels you can use. If you exceed the limit, you will get an error indicating lack of memory or stack space.

Menu Table Structure

Field Name	Field Type	Description
Item	A15	Menu choice
Desc	A50	Description
Proc	A15	Procedure to call
Args	A25	Argument list

Sample Menu Tree

```
Maint—Report—Utility—Exit
|
├────────┬─────────┐
Add   Edit   Return
```

Data for Sample Menu Tree

Mainmenu	Item	Desc	Proc	Args
1	Maint	Customer Maintenance	Domenu	Maint
2	Report	Print Reports	Domenu	"Report"
3	Utility	System Utilities	Domenu	"Utility"
4	Return	Return to DOS		

Maint	Item	Desc	Proc	Args
1	Add	Add Customers	Addit	
2	Edit	Edit Customers	Chgit	
3	Return	Return to Main Menu		

Figure 3-5. Sample menu information for tables.

```
;Domenu.sc
;Display a menu with options stored in table Tbl
PROC Domenu(Tbl)
PRIVATE
         Arglist,      ;Argument list for procedure
         Mchoice,      ;User's menu choice
         Numrecs,      ;Number of records in menu table
         Procname,     ;This procedure's name
         Procnm,       ;Procedure to execute
```

```
          Tblchoice,    ;Array of menu choices
          Tbldesc       ;Array of menu choice descriptions

Procname = "Domenu"

;Set library path
Autolib = "Lib1,Lib2"

WHILE True
;Load menu arrays from table
Numrecs = NRECORDS(Tbl)
ARRAY Tblchoice[Numrecs]
ARRAY Tbldesc[Numrecs]
VIEW Tbl
SCAN
  Tblchoice[RECNO()] = [Item]
  Tbldesc[RECNO()] = [Desc]
ENDSCAN

;Display menu, get user's choice
CLEAR
SHOWARRAY
  Tblchoice Tbldesc
TO Mchoice

;If user did not press Esc or choose Return,
; execute procedure that matches menu choice
IF Retval AND (Mchoice <> "Return") THEN
  ;Look up menu choice to get procedure name
  ; and argument list
  MOVETO [Item]
  LOCATE Mchoice
  Procnm  = [Proc]
  Arglist = [Args]
  CLEARALL
  ;Recursive call if one menu calls another
  EXECUTE Procnm + "(" + Arglist + ")"
ENDIF
ENDWHILE
ENDPROC
```

Program 3-10. *Recursive Menu Procedure*

A small startup script calls Domenu with the name of the first menu table. In this example, it would be

```
Domenu("Mainmenu")
```

You can add items to a menu by editing the corresponding table. You need not change the code. This saves time and, heavens knows, none of us is getting any younger.

CheckPoint **3-1.** Add a Menu Option

Objective: Edit the Maint table and add an option to delete customers. Item is "Delete", Desc is "Delete Customer", and Proc is "Delit". Play Domenu to confirm that the new option appears on the menu.

Adding submenus is also easy. You must create a new table with the same structure as Mainmenu and Maint and insert a record for each option. You must also edit an existing table to call procedure Domenu with the new table name.

CheckPoint **3-2.** Add a Submenu

Objective: Change the Edit option on the maintenance menu to call a submenu with options to change a customer name or search for customers by city. The first procedure name is Chgname and the second is Srchcust. Store submenu options in table Editcust.

Summary

You should package your application's source code into procedures and libraries. This approach lets you write general purpose routines you can reuse by passing different arguments.

You can assign a custom procedure to the reserved variable Errorproc. If the error procedure is in memory, Paradox transfers control to it instead of to the Cancel/Debug menu when a runtime error occurs. You can thus provide more flexible and more comprehensive error handling.

Paradox handles memory management when you collect procedures into libraries. Closed procedures, which must be stored in a library, release all memory used for variables, arrays, and called procedures when they end. This frees you from having to manage memory explicitly. When you provide an Autolib path with a list of library names, Paradox searches them for procedures automatically.

The How to DO_IT! section showed a table-driven technique for generating menus. A general purpose procedure reads the table, displays the menu, accepts a user's choice, and executes the corresponding procedure. By changing the table, you can change an application without modifying the program. This saves time, and avoids the possibility of introducing errors while editing application code. It also simplifies software management and maintenance.

4

Arrays

With silver bells, and cockle shells, and pretty maids all in a row.

—Mother Goose

Introduction

Arrays are the most important PAL building blocks after tables. We use them to copy records between tables and to hold system information such as menu options and printer setup strings. Since they are kept in memory, Paradox can access their elements quickly.

This chapter shows how to declare and use arrays, including how to load them from tables. It presents routines to copy them, delete and find elements, and store table structure information. Paradox has only one-dimensional arrays, but you can simulate two-dimensional ones by calculating subscripts explicitly.

How to DO_IT!

This section contains examples of the following PAL techniques:

- Place all matching records for a wildcard search in a new table and allow users to select their choice. Includes a technique for displaying a highlight bar in a multi-record form to help them locate the record they want.
- Search a string containing a name such as Jesse R. James III and separate out the first name, middle initial, last name, and any optional ending.

Defining Arrays

As noted in Chapter 2, Paradox arrays are sets of related memory variables. There are two types: fixed and dynamic. All arrays are one-dimensional, and the elements may be of different types.

In a fixed array, each element has a numerical subscript. In a dynamic one, a number or string can identify an element. The subscript always appears in square brackets after the array name.

You must indicate the size (**dimension**) of a fixed array when you declare it. The dimension can be a variable if you assign it first. You need not specify the size of a dynamic array.

You declare an array with the keyword ARRAY followed by its name and dimension (fixed only) in square brackets. For example, the following statement declares a fixed array States with 50 elements:

```
ARRAY States[50]
```

Fixed array subscripts start at 1 as in dBASE, BASIC, and Pascal, not at 0 as in C. For example, you refer to element 4 of States as:

```
States[4]
```

You assign values to array elements just like single memory variables. For example, to assign the string *CT* to element 4 of States, use:

```
States[4] = "CT"
```

The ISASSIGNED function checks whether a variable or array element has a value. It returns True if it does and False if not.

A dynamic array describes an event such as a mouse action or script error. Paradox creates different elements based on the event. In the following example, ErrorInfo is a dynamic array containing information about the latest script error. ErrorInfo["PROC"] contains the name of the procedure with the runtime error.

```
DYNARRAY ErrorInfo[]
? ErrorInfo["PROC"]
```

Array scope follows the same rules as for ordinary memory variables. You can include array names in a PRIVATE list, giving them private scope. They are then available to all procedures and scripts called after you declare them.

Using Arrays

I use arrays to hold temporary sets of data, such as customer ids for a report. For example, Program 4-1 asks the user to enter ids. The loop stops after 10 entries or when he or she presses Esc. Note that the program accepts the value in a variable and then assigns it to the array element.

> **Tip**
>
> Use a temporary variable to ACCEPT array values. Paradox cannot ACCEPT them directly.

```
;Custarry.sc
;Accept up to 10 customer ids and store them
; in an array

;Allow up to 10 customer entries
ARRAY Cust[10]
FOR Ctr FROM 1 TO 10
  ;Clear line for new entry
  @ 2,1 CLEAR EOL
  @ 2,1 ?? "Enter Customer Id, or Esc to stop==>"
  ;Accept value in a variable. Paradox does not
  ; allow direct entry into an array element
  ACCEPT "S" TO Cust_Id
  ;Exit if user pressed Esc rather
  ; than entering a value
  IF NOT Retval THEN
    QUITLOOP
  ENDIF
  ;If user entered a value, assign it to
  ; array element
  Cust[Ctr] = Cust_Id
ENDFOR
```

Program 4-1. Accept Customer Ids into an Array

Similarly, I can set up an array of messages and center them on the screen. The LEN function returns the number of characters in a string. Here is the array definition and a sample message:

```
ARRAY Msgs[10]
Msgs[1] = "Loading..."
```

Program 4-2 displays a blinking message centered in a row until the user presses a key. It accepts a string and a row number. For example, you can use Arcenter(Msgs[1],20) to center "Loading..." on row 20.

```
;Arcenter.sc
;Accept message less than 80 characters long and center
; it on given row. Display it until user presses
; a key.

PROC Arcenter(Msg,Rownum)
PRIVATE
        Colnum,  ;Column to display message
        Keypr    ;Wait for user keypress

Colnum = INT((80 - LEN(Msg))/2)
;Display message in white on red and blink
STYLE ATTRIBUTE 207
@ Rownum,Colnum ?? Msg
Keypr = GETCHAR()
;Restore original style
STYLE
ENDPROC
```

Program 4-2. *Display a Centered Message*

ARRAYSIZE returns the number of elements in an array, but Paradox provides no direct way to determine how many are actually occupied. For example, ARRAY Country[4] declares a four element array of names. Country[1] = "Italy" puts a value in the first one, leaving the last three empty. However, ARRAYSIZE(Country) returns 4 anyway.

How can we find the last occupied element, assuming the array is filled in normal consecutive sequence? Arlen (Program 4-3) uses a binary search to do the job. It splits the array in half and checks the midpoint.

That element is the one being sought if it is occupied and its successor is not. Arlen discards the bottom half of the array if the two are both occupied and the top half if they are both empty. As a binary search eliminates half the remaining array during each iteration, it is much faster than a sequential method.

The procedure accepts the array to check and returns the position of the last occupied element.

```
;Arlen.sc
;Use a binary search to locate the last occupied
;element. Examine the middle element among the
;remaining ones. If it is occupied and its
;successor is not, it is the element being
;sought. Otherwise, drop the half known to
;be occupied or empty and repeat the process.

;ISBLANK returns True for null string(""),
;BLANKNUM, or BLANKDATE.

PROC Arlen(Sarray)
PRIVATE
        Arsize,  ;Size of array
        High,    ;Highest subscript in remaining part
        Low,     ;Lowest subscript in remaining part
        Mid,     ;Midpoint
        Slast    ;Subscript of last occupied element

Low = 1
High = ARRAYSIZE(Sarray)

;Test last element to avoid looping if possible
Arsize = ARRAYSIZE(Sarray)
IF ISASSIGNED(Sarray[Arsize]) AND
  NOT ISBLANK(Sarray[Arsize]) THEN
    Mid = Arsize
    RETURN Mid
ENDIF

WHILE True
  Mid = INT((Low+High)/2)
  IF (ISASSIGNED(Sarray[Mid])) AND
    (NOT ISBLANK(Sarray[Mid])) THEN
      ;Found end of array
```

```
        IF NOT (ISASSIGNED(Sarray[Mid + 1])) OR
              (ISBLANK(Sarray[Mid + 1])) THEN
           QUITLOOP
        ELSE
           ;If midpoint occupied, drop lower half
           Low = Mid
        ENDIF
   ELSE
      ;If midpoint unoccupied, drop upper half
      High = Mid
   ENDIF
ENDWHILE
Slast = Mid
RETURN Slast
ENDPROC
```

Program 4-3. *Find Last Occupied Array Element*

CheckPoint **4-1.** Find Largest Array Element

Objective: Write a procedure MaxElement that finds the largest value in an array of numbers.

Array Handling Routines

This section shows routines that delete, copy, and fill elements; search for values; and convert two-dimensional subscripts to one-dimensional. Paradox passes arrays to procedures by reference. This means a procedure can change elements or even delete them, and the effects remain in force after it ends.

Deleting an Array Element

Ardel (Program 4-4) deletes an element from an array. It shifts everything above it down one position and blanks the last element. It verifies that the selected position is valid. I use it after loading menu arrays from tables to delete options based on a user's password. For example, an ordinary user may not be able to change, remove, or restructure tables, whereas an administrator can.

```
;Ardel.sc
;Deletes element at Spos from array. Shifts all
;elements past it down one position, and gives
;last element a blank value. Checks whether
;indicated position is within array bounds.
;Spos <= ARRAYSIZE(Sarray)
;If deleting last element, make it blank and quit.
;Slast is last occupied element. Use Arlen to obtain it.
PROC Ardel(Sarray,Spos,Slast)
PRIVATE
        Arsize,     ;Size of array
        Sloop       ;Loop variable


Arsize = ARRAYSIZE(Sarray)
IF Spos <= Arsize HEN
  IF Spos = Arsize THEN
    ;Just blank element if last one specified
    Sarray[Arsize] = ""
  ELSE
    ;Shift elements up one position
    FOR Sloop FROM Spos + 1 TO Slast
      Sarray[Sloop-1] = Sarray[Sloop]
    ENDFOR
    ;Blank last element
    Sarray[Slast] = ""
  ENDIF
ELSE
  MESSAGE "Position ",STRVAL(Spos), " is not in the array"
  SLEEP 1500
ENDIF
ENDPROC
```

Program 4-4. *Delete Array Element*

CheckPoint 4-2. Inserting an Array Element

Objective: Write a procedure Arinsert to insert an item at a specified position in an array. Its arguments should include the value to insert and the position.

Hint: Use the same procedure as in Ardel (Program 4-4), but move the items up one position instead of down.

Copying an Array

Arcopy (Program 4-5) copies elements from one array to another, starting at a given position. It performs bounds checking. If an array holds a data record, you can copy a selected part of it that you can then store in a table with a different structure. This is a good way to move information between tables without doing it field by field.

```
;Arcopy.sc
;Copy one array to another
; Sarray  = Source array
; Tarray  = Target array
;   Spos  = Starting cell in source array
;   Tpos  = Starting cell in target array
;    Num  = Number of elements to copy
;Copies Num elements from one array starting at
;Spos to a second starting at Tpos.
;It ensures that
; 1) You do not go outside source array.
;      Spos + Num - 1 > ARRAYSIZE(Sarray)
; 2) You do not overrun target array.
;      Tpos + Num - 1 > ARRAYSIZE(Tarray)
PROC Arcopy(Sarray,Tarray,Spos,Tpos,Num)
PRIVATE
        Sloop  ;Loop variable
WHILE True
  ;Make sure first array has enough elements
  IF Spos + Num - 1 > ARRAYSIZE(Sarray) THEN
```

```
    MESSAGE "Too many source elements specified -"+
      " Cannot copy"
    SLEEP 1500
    QUITLOOP
  ENDIF
  ;Make sure second array is big enough for copy
  IF Tpos + Num - 1 > ARRAYSIZE(Tarray) THEN
    MESSAGE "Not enough room in target array"
    SLEEP 1500
    QUITLOOP
  ENDIF
  ;Copy array
  Tpos = Tpos - 1
  FOR Sloop FROM Spos TO (Spos + Num - 1)
    Tpos = Tpos + 1
    Tarray[Tpos] = Sarray[Sloop]
  ENDFOR
  QUITLOOP
ENDWHILE
ENDPROC
```

Program 4-5. *Copy an Array*

Filling Arrays with Table Structure Information

Arstruc (Program 4-6) fills array Fnames with field names and Ftypes with field types for a given table. You could use Ardel to limit the fields included and SHOWARRAY to let a user select a field to search on. You can thus remove sensitive fields, such as Pay_Rate, from the list if the user lacks authorization to view them.

```
;Arstruc.sc
;Load a table structure into two arrays
;     Tbl    = Table name passed to procedure
;     Fnames = Array of table field names
;     Ftypes = Array of table field types
;
;Accepts a table name and fills array Fnames with its
;field names and Ftypes with its field types
```

```
PROC Tblstruc(Tbl)
PRIVATE
       Num   ;Number of elements in arrays

;Make sure table exists
IF ISTABLE(Tbl) THEN
  ;Create a temporary table called Struct
  ; available on workspace
  {Tools} {Info} {Structure} TYPEIN Tbl ENTER
  Num = NRECORDS(Tbl)
  ARRAY Fnames[Num]
  ARRAY Ftypes[Num]
  SCAN
    ;Fill arrays with table data
    Fnames[RECNO()] = [Field Name]
    Ftypes[RECNO()] = [Field Type]
  ENDSCAN
  CLEARIMAGE
ELSE
  MESSAGE "Table ",Tbl, " is not in this directory"
  SLEEP 1500
ENDIF
ENDPROC
```

Program 4-6. *Fill Arrays with Table Information*

Finding an Element in an Ordered Array

Arscan (Program 4-7) uses a binary search to locate a value in an array. The array should be large and ordered; otherwise, you must use a sequential method. If Arscan finds the value, it sets Pos to its position in the array; otherwise, it sets Pos to zero. I store menu choices in one array and procedure names in another. I use Arscan to locate the option in the first, and execute the procedure from the second.

```
;Arscan.sc
;Find position of element in a large ordered
;array
;   Sarray    = Source array
;   Searchfor = Item to search for
```

```
;       Low  = Low bound for search
;       High = High bound for search
;       Mid  = Midpoint for search
;       Pos  = Position of found element, 0 if not found

;Does a binary search to locate Searchfor in an array.
;If array is not large and ordered, use sequential
;method instead. If item is found, set Pos to its
;position. Otherwise, set Pos to zero.

;Start search with low bound at first position
;and high bound at last one
PROC Arscan(Sarray,Searchfor)
PRIVATE
       High, ;High bound for search
       Low,  ;Low bound for search
       Mid,  ;Midpoint for search
       Pos   ;Position of found element,
             ; 0 if not found

Low = 1
High = ARRAYSIZE(Sarray)

Mid = INT((Low+High)/2)
WHILE (Sarray[Md] <> Searchfor) AND (Low <= High)
  ;Check midpoint of array
  IF Searchfor > SARRAY[Mid] THEN
    ;Move to upper half of array
    Low = Mid + 1
  ELSE
    ;Move to lower half of array
    High = Mid - 1
  ENDIF
  ;Find new midpoint
  Mid = INT((Low+High)/2)
ENDWHILE
;If value sought is found, it is
; at midpoint
IF Sarray[Mid] <> Searchfor THEN
  Pos = 0
ELSE
  Pos = Mid
ENDIF
RETURN Pos
ENDPROC
```

Program 4-7. Find Element Position in an Array

Using Arrays with Records

As described in Chapter 2, you can store a record in an array and use either numbers or field names as subscripts. The COPYTOARRAY command moves the current record to an array; COPYFROMARRAY does the opposite. PAL allocates memory for the arrays automatically, so you need not declare them.

Using field names is especially handy when adding fields to a table or deleting them from it. You can access them independently of where they are in the table, unlike the alternative of using numeric subscripts. Furthermore, changes in table structure do not require any code changes, and programs are more readable as well.

> **Tip**
>
> I use array copying commands with a custom printer table so users can change report destinations at run time. They can also select paper size, orientation, and pitch. They can thus switch between a dot matrix printer and a laser printer, depending on whether they need draft or presentation quality output.

The Printsel procedure (Program 4-8) replaces the interactive Paradox menu path Report/Output. Its arguments are a table to report on, the report number, and the printer table. The printer table (Table 4-1) contains printer descriptions, setup strings, and port information. Fields Printer and Prt Desc are descriptive information used in the popup selection box. Portrait mode is the usual one with printing along the shorter dimension; landscape mode prints along the longer dimension (sideways).

Printsel displays a popup menu with either Screen or Printer as the output destination. If the user selects Printer, it loads printer names and descriptions from the configuration table into two arrays. The user selects the printer with SHOWARRAY and then selects the orientation, paper size, and print size.

Table 4-1. Custom Printer Configuration

Field Name	Type	Sample Data
Printer	A15	HP LaserJet
Prt Desc	A30	HP LaserJet II,IIP,III,IIIP
Port Letter Normal	A40	\027(s0p10H
Port Letter Compress	A40	\027(s0p16.66H
Port Legal Normal	A40	\027&l84P\027(s0p10H
Port Letter Compress	A40	\027&l84P\027(s0p16.66H
Land Letter Normal	A40	\027&l1O\027(sp10H
Land Letter Compress	A40	\027&l1O\027(s0p16.66H
Land Legal Normal	A40	\027&l84p1O\027(s0p10H
Land Legal Compress	A40	\027&l84p1O\027(s0p16.66H
Resetptr	A40	\027E
Port	A4	LPT1

Note: Land means "Landscape", Port means "Portrait"

Printsel sets the port and tests whether the printer is ready. If it is not after three tries, the routine changes the output destination to Screen. After printing the report, it resets the printer. The next user thus finds it in a normal startup state rather than customized.

```
;Printsel.sc
;Select print destination and assign setup string.
;Choices are Printer and Screen. If users choose
;Printer, they can also choose a setup string
;to override default.


PROC PrintSel(Tbl,Rn,Ptbl)
PRIVATE
        Choice,     ;User output choice,
                    ; Printer or Screen
        Ct,         ;Number of tries for printer status
        Key,        ;User keypress
```

```
        Num,        ;Number of records in printer table
        Orstr,      ;Orientation string
        Parray,     ;Array to hold printer record
        Pdesc,      ;Array of printer descriptions
        Porient,    ;Printer orientation
        Prtrs,      ;Array of printer choices
        Ptbl,       ;Printer table
        Setupstr,   ;Printer setup string
        Uprtr       ;Printer selection

MESSAGE "Select Output Destination for report"
SHOWMENU
   "Printer" : "Send report to printer",
   "Screen"  : "Send report to screen"
TO Pchoice

IF Pchoice = "Printer" THEN
   ;Load tables with printer names and
   ; descriptions
   Num = NRECORDS(Ptbl)
   ARRAY Prtrs[Num]
   ARRAY Pdesc[Num]
   VIEW Ptbl
   SCAN
     Prtrs[RECNO()] = [Printer]
     Pdesc[RECNO()] = [Prt Desc]
   ENDSCAN
   ;Display available printers
   SHOWARRAY
     Prtrs Pdesc
   TO Uprtr
   MOVETO Ptbl
   ;Locate selected printer in array
   ; to get setup string
   MOVETO FIELD "Printer"
   LOCATE Uprtr
   COPYTOARRAY Parray
   CLEARIMAGE
   MESSAGE "Select Printer Orientation"
   ;Determine setup string
   SHOWMENU
     "PLTN" : "Portrait/Letter/Normal",
     "PLTC" : "Portrait/Letter/Compress",
     "PLGN" : "Portrait/Legal/Normal",
     "PLGC" : "Portrait/Legal/Compress",
     "LLTN" : "Landscape/Letter/Normal",
     "LLTC" : "Landscape/Letter/Compress",
     "LLGN" : "Landscape/Legal/Normal",
     "LLGC" : "Landscape/Legal/Compress"
```

```
  TO Porient
  ;Select setup string based on user choice
  SWITCH
    CASE Porient = "PLTN" :
      Setupstr = Parray["Port Letter Normal"]
    CASE Porient = "PLTC" :
      Setupstr = Parray["Port Letter Compress"]
    CASE Porient = "PLGN" :
      Setupstr = Parray["Port Legal Normal"]
    CASE Porient = "PLGC" :
      Setupstr = Parray["Port Legal Compress"]
    CASE Porient = "LLTN" :
      Setupstr = Parray["Land Letter Normal"]
    CASE Porient = "LLTC" :
      Setupstr = Parray["Land Letter Compress"]
    CASE Porient = "LLGN" :
      Setupstr = Parray["Land Legal Normal"]
    CASE Porient = "LLGC" :
      Setupstr = Parray["Land Legal Compress"]
  ENDSWITCH
  ;Make sure printer is ready, allow three tries,
  ; then switch to screen
  SETPRINTER(Parray["Port"])
  Ct = 0
  WHILE True
    IF Ct > 2 THEN
      BEEP
      MESSAGE "Printer not ready after 3 tries - " +
        "destination changed to screen"
      SLEEP 1500
      Pchoice = "Screen"
      QUITLOOP
    ENDIF
    ;If printer is available, send setup information
    IF PRINTERSTATUS() THEN
      {Report} {Setprinter} {Override} {Setup}
        CTRLBACKSPACE TYPEIN Setupstr Enter
      QUITLOOP
    ELSE
      BEEP
      MESSAGE "Fix printer - press any key"
      Key = GETCHAR()
      MESSAGE "Checking printer..."
      Ct = Ct + 1
    ENDIF
  ENDWHILE
ENDIF
```

```
;Print report
{Report} {Output} TYPEIN Tbl ENTER
  SELECT Rn SELECT Pchoice
;Send reset code to printer
IF Pchoice = "Printer" THEN
  {Report} {Setprinter} {Override} {Setup}
    CTRLBACKSPACE TYPEIN Parray["Resetptr"] ENTER
  PRINT "\f"
ENDIF
;Reset port to default
SETPRINTER("LPT1")
ENDPROC
```

Program 4-8. *Select Output Destination and Setup*

Simulating Two-Dimensional Arrays

Paradox supports only one-dimensional arrays. Arindex (Program 4-9) lets you simulate two-dimensional ones, thus avoiding the need for parallel arrays for related information.

For example, suppose two parallel arrays hold three menu choices. Letters holds the first letter, and Desc the corresponding menu description. The logical picture of an equivalent two-dimensional array has menu letters in column 1 and descriptions in column 2.

To simulate the structure in Paradox, declare a one-dimensional array with six elements. Figure 4-1 shows the Choices array and the corresponding one- and two-dimensional subscripts.

Arindex converts row and column subscripts into their one-dimensional equivalent. You call it to access an element, passing the row and column, along with the number of logical columns in the array. It returns the one-dimensional subscript.

Logical two-dimensional subscripts

	1,1	1,2	2,1	2,2	3,1	3,2
Choices	A	Add	C	Change	D	Delete
	1	2	3	4	5	6

Paradox one-dimensional subscripts

Figure 4-1*. Simulation of a two-dimensional array.*

```
PROC Arindex(Rownum,Colnum,Ncols)
  RETURN (Rownum - 1) * Ncols + Colnum
ENDPROC
```

Program 4-9*. Indexing a Two-Dimensional Array*

The following example displays the menu description stored in element (3,2):

```
Menuch = Arindex(3,2,2)
? Choices[Menuch]
```

How to DO_IT!

Program 4-10 shows a PAL technique for displaying all wildcard matches in a multi-record form with a scrolling bar. Program 4-11 shows how to place the first name, last name, and middle initial into separate array elements.

Chapter 2 showed a wildcard search for a field in the active table (Program 2-10). It locates the first matching record and allows the user to search selectively for duplicates. Program 4-10 employs a similar technique to find all duplicates and display them in a multi-record form.

It uses a highlight bar instead of the standard Paradox arrow to indicate the current record, thus making it easier to find. The program uses the array copying commands to move records from the original table to the dummy.

Figure 4-2 shows the multi-record form with data for all customers whose names start with "Sm". The search ignores capitalization and endings. The program traps the up and down arrows and repaints the highlight bar on the canvas for the new record.

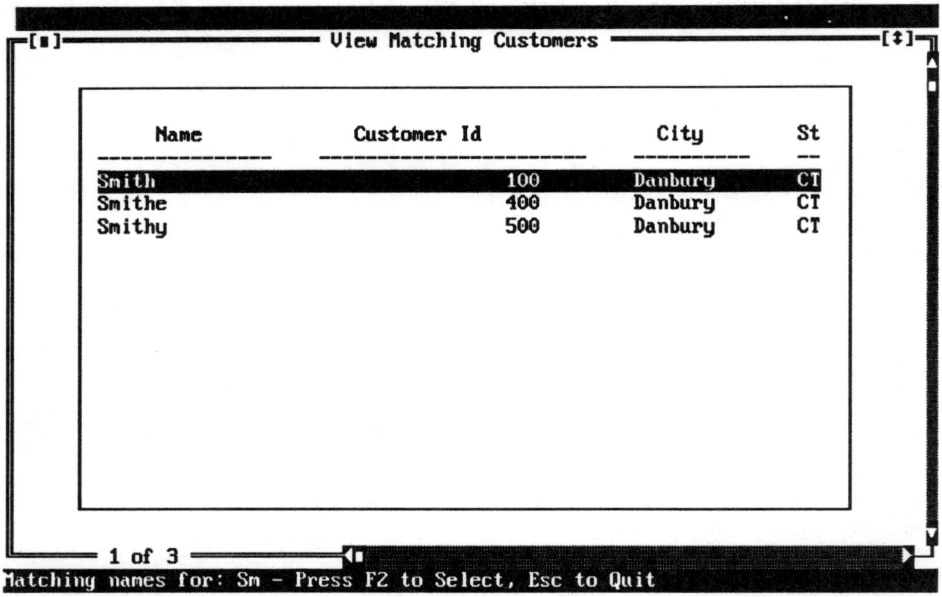

Figure 4-2. Customer matches in a multi-record form.

```
;Scrlsrch.sc
;Pass searchname, the partial string to search for.
;Allow wildcard search in Name field for customer database.
;Move all matching records into a dummy table Tempcust.
;Use a multi-record form to view them and select one.
;Display a highlight bar when user moves from record to
;record. Paradox would normally display only a left arrow.
;Return either the customer number selected or -1
;indicating no record selection or no match.

PROC Scrlsrch(Searchname)
PRIVATE
       Keyval,  ;Key value returned. Could be -1
                ; if no match or none selected
       Namectr  ;How many names matched
;Find matching names and insert records into
; Tempcust table
Namectr = 0
;Make sure dummy table is empty initially
EMPTY "Tempcust"
VIEW "Customer"
VIEW "Tempcust"
COEDITKEY
MOVETO "Customer"
MOVETO [Name]
MESSAGE "Searching..."
;Use pattern option for wildcard search
LOCATE PATTERN Searchname + ".."
WHILE Retval
  ;If match found, use array to move record
  ; to dummy table
  COPYTOARRAY Arnames
  MOVETO "Tempcust"
  INS
  COPYFROMARRAY Arnames
  Namectr = Namectr + 1
  MOVETO "Customer"
  ;Check for end of table
  IF (ATLAST()) THEN
    QUITLOOP
  ELSE
    ;Remember to leave record or program
    ; will find it again!
    DOWN
    MESSAGE "Searching..."
    LOCATE NEXT PATTERN Searchname + ".."
```

```
  ENDIF
ENDWHILE
DO_IT!
MESSAGE ""

;No matches, return indicator
IF Namectr = 0 THEN
  RETURN -1
ENDIF

;Must have been matches
CLEARALL
CLEAR
VIEW "Tempcust"
PICKFORM 1
WINMAX

;Clear pulldown
SHOWPULLDOWN
ENDMENU

;Paint screen with highlight bar. Echo commands display
; workspace before Wait Table
ECHO NORMAL
ECHO OFF
@ 24,0 ?? SPACES(80)
@ 24,0 ?? "Matching names for: " + Searchname +
" - Press F2 to Select, Esc to Quit"
PAINTCANVAS ATTRIBUTE 48 7,8,7,69
CURSOR OFF
;Leave bar until user presses a key
WHILE NOT CHARWAITING()
ENDWHILE

;Respond to cursor movement keys, up and down arrows
; to move highlight bar
WHILE True
  WAIT TABLE
    PROMPT "Matching names for: " + Searchname +
           " - Press F2 to Select, Esc to Quit"
  UNTIL "F2","Esc","Down","Up","Dos","DosBig"
  SWITCH
    ;Return with no record selection
    CASE Retval = "Esc":
      Keyval = -1
      QUITLOOP
```

```
    ;Return with customer number selected
    CASE Retval = "F2":
      Keyval = [Cust Id]
      QUITLOOP

    ;Allow cursor movement keys
    CASE Retval = "Down" OR Retval = "Up":
      KEYPRESS Retval
      PAINTCANVAS ATTRIBUTE 48 ROWNO()+6,8,ROWNO()+6,69
      WHILE NOT CHARWAITING()
      ENDWHILE
  ENDSWITCH
ENDWHILE
CLEARALL
STYLE
CURSOR NORMAL
RETURN Keyval
ENDPROC
```

Program 4-10. *Display Matches in a Multi-Record Form*

Once you pick the form, it is on the workspace but not displayed until the program does a WAIT TABLE. We put a copy of it on the canvas using ECHO NORMAL and ECHO OFF so we can show the highlight bar on the first record. The @ and ?? commands duplicate the prompts that appear on the form. When the user selects the up or down arrow, the highlight bar moves to the new record.

Program 4-11 illustrates a method for parsing a text string. It accepts a name string such as "Sam Spade Jr." and separates individual components such as "Sam" into array elements.

```
;Divname.sc
;Assumes different parts are separated by
;spaces. Example: Sam Spade Jr. Separate
;name into array elements as in:
;N[1] = "Sam", N[2] = "Spade", N[3] = "Jr."

PROC DivideName(Name,Arname)
PRIVATE
```

```
        Arsub,     ;Current array subscript
        Char,      ;Individual characters to analyze
        Leng,      ;Length of name left to search
        Loopc,     ;Loop counter
        Maxsize,   ;Maximum number of name elements
        New,       ;True if starting new string,
                   ; False otherwise
        Str        ;String built from name parts

;Find number of array elements
Maxsize = ARRAYSIZE(Arname)

;Initialize all array positions to null
FOR Loopc FROM 1 TO Maxsize
  Arname[Loopc] = ""
ENDFOR

;Start name search
Leng = LEN(Name)
Arsub = 0
Str = ""
New = True
;Build strings for parts of name and store them
; in array elements. Parts can be separated
; by multiple spaces.
FOR Loopc FROM 1 TO Leng
  ;Get a character
  Char = SUBSTR(Name,Loopc,1)
  SWITCH
    ;Ignore spaces
    ;If starting new part of name, this is
    ; first element. Otherwise, add it
    ; to characters already obtained
    CASE Char <> " ":
      IF New THEN
        Str = Char
        New = False
      ELSE
        Str = Str + Char
      ENDIF
    ;If character is a space, put
    ; string into array element and
    ; start a new one
    CASE Char = " ":
      IF Str <> "" THEN
        Arsub = Arsub + 1
        Arname[Arsub] = Str
```

```
            Str = ""
            New = True
        ENDIF
    ENDSWITCH
ENDFOR

;Put last part of name into last array element
IF Str <> "" THEN
    Arsub = Arsub + 1
    Arname[Arsub] = Str
ENDIF
ENDPROC
```

Program 4-11. *Divide Name String into Components*

Summary

Arrays are like memory tables for storing related information such as printer setup strings and menu choices. You can load them from tables and avoid having to change your program when you add or change items. Access is faster because arrays are memory-resident.

You can pass an entire array to a procedure and change any of its elements. This chapter presented five utilities for working with arrays, including ones that copy them and find and delete elements.

Paradox supports only one-dimensional arrays, but you can simulate two-dimensional ones by computing subscripts explicitly.

The DO_IT! section presented a procedure to load matching records from a wildcard search into a dummy table and display them on a multi-record form with a highlight bar. It also showed how to parse text strings and separate their parts into array elements.

5

User Interface

Learn to get used to it [bombing]. Eels get used to skinning.

—Winston Churchill

Introduction

The PAL stage is called the *desktop*. You direct action in its windows much as a director controls scenes on parts of a stage. Workspace windows contain related objects such as tables in form or table view, queries, or report designs. Canvas windows act as curtains for the scenes. Raising them reveals what is happening; lowering them hides the action.

PAL programs are the actors you control. Fortunately, you do not have to contend with huge egos, mind-boggling salary demands, greedy agents, skyrocketing cost overruns, and vindictive critics. You can focus on creating your own masterpiece—*Night of the Living PAL Application, Part 17*. Never do anything new or original if you can avoid it!

When you start an action in a workspace window, you must also paint a canvas; otherwise, the users see a blank screen. You don't want them to think the play is over before it begins and demand their money back! PAL includes commands to manage windows and perform workspace and canvas actions in them.

This chapter discusses how to open windows, control attributes such as size and color, and switch between them. It describes basic commands to control what appears in canvas windows. It also explains how to manipulate tables in workspace windows and presents a complete single table maintenance procedure. It shows how to include Paradox's Query-by-

Example and report editor in applications. It includes a Query-by-Form technique that lets users create queries on a custom form.

We also show how to create dialog boxes with pick lists of files, tables, and array elements. Finally, we present a popup menu that combines the major routines in a customer maintenance system. It may not be *Hamlet* (or even *Attack of the Killer Tomatoes*), but it can satisfy your customers and make you money. Besides, Shakespeare charges too much for writing PAL programs, and his documentation is unreadable.

How to DO_IT!

This section contains a procedure to display help in a popup window during a dialog box interaction. I use this technique to provide more help than is available in the dialog box itself. I store choices and help text in a table so they are easy to change.

Using Windows

A window is a rectangle on the screen with attributes such as color and size. You direct Paradox to open or select one and place objects such as tables in it. They behave just as in interactive Paradox. For example, you can insert and delete records from a table opened in Coedit mode.

Creating Windows

Paradox creates a workspace window automatically when you request a table operation. The following lines make Paradox create one with default attributes and display the Customer table in it.

```
VIEW "Customer"
WINDOW HANDLE CURRENT TO Custwindow
```

Custwindow contains the window's *handle* (surely an odd term if you think about it!). It is a unique number Paradox assigns to a window when you create it. You use the handle to identify the window when selecting or resizing it, or changing its attributes. Paradox uses a window handle just once during a session. Even if you close a window, it does not reuse the handle. Think of it as a stage name, such as Cary Grant, Doris Day, or Madonna. Once you pick one, you become its sole owner (even if a real Cary Grant were to come along!).

You can use the ISWINDOW function to test whether a window is open. IF ISWINDOW(Custwindow) returns True if the one with handle Custwindow is open, and False otherwise.

You must create canvas windows explicitly to perform non-table operations such as displaying text and accepting single values from a user. The following example creates one with its upper left corner at row 2, column 6. It is 10 rows high and 40 characters wide.

```
WINDOW CREATE @ 2,6 HEIGHT 10 WIDTH 40 TO Textwindow
```

Window Attributes

A window has default attributes. You can use a dynamic array to find out what they are and change them. The following example loads the Customer table into a window to view. It gets the handle, stores current attributes in a dynamic array, and displays them in a canvas window.

```
;Open workspace window containing Customer
VIEW "Customer"

;Get window handle
WINDOW HANDLE CURRENT TO Custwindow

;Create dynamic array of attributes
DYNARRAY Custattributes[]
WINDOW GETATTRIBUTES Custwindow TO Custattributes

;Create canvas window to display attributes
WINDOW CREATE @ 1,1 HEIGHT 23 WIDTH 50 TO Dispattributes

;Display attributes in canvas window
FOREACH ELEMENT IN Custattributes
  ? ELEMENT," = ",Custattributes[ELEMENT]
ENDFOREACH
```

Remember, dynamic arrays are not arranged sequentially. The output will resemble the following list, but the order may differ. This adds a little variety to Paradox's usual mechanical sameness.

```
TITLE = Customer
STYLE = 112
MAXIMIZED = False
HASFRAME = True
```

Table 5-1 summarizes available window attributes. I particularly like CANCLOSE and CANMOVE; they sound like steps from formerly naughty Parisian dance shows. Surely respectable citizens would not do the CANCLOSE even in the privacy of their own computers.

Table 5-1. Window Attributes

Attribute	Description
CANCLOSE	True if user can close window, false otherwise
CANMAXIMIZE	True if user can maximize and restore, false if user cannot change window size
CANMOVE	True if user can move window, false if user cannot
CANRESIZE	True if user can resize window, false if user cannot
CANVAS	True if canvas display commands are immediate, false if display is delayed
CANVASHEIGHT	Height of canvas buffer
CANVASWIDTH	Width of canvas buffer
ECHO	True if WINDOW ECHO True, false otherwise
FLOATING	True if window above ECHO layer, false otherwise
HASFRAME	True if window is framed, false otherwise
HASSHADOW	True if window has shadow, false otherwise
HEIGHT	Height including frame
MARGIN	Number for left margin or OFF if none
MAXIMIZED	True if window size maximized, false if not
ORIGINCOL	Upper left column relative to screen
ORIGINROW	Upper left row relative to screen
STYLE	Style attribute number for canvas text
TITLE	Name centered in frame at top of window
WIDTH	Number of columns wide including frame

You can use a dynamic array to change the default attributes for the next window. The following example creates one to change the colors of a canvas window to white on blue (color attribute 31). Attribute 69 is the "rage" this year on fashion-conscious computers!

```
;Create dynamic array
DYNARRAY Windowattributes[]
```

```
;Change default color
Windowattributes["Style"] = 31

;Create canvas window with new color attribute
WINDOW CREATE ATTRIBUTES Windowattributes @ 1,1
  HEIGHT 10 WIDTH 50 TO Textwindow

;Display a message
@ 2,2 ?? "Help! I'm a prisoner in a locked window."
```

You can change an existing window's attributes similarly. In the following example, the array Windowattributes changes the title centered at the top of the frame.

```
;Create workspace window
VIEW "Customer"
WINDOW HANDLE CURRENT TO Custwindow

;Create dynamic array
DYNARRAY Windowattributes[]

;Change title
Windowattributes["Title"] = "New Customers"

;Change title in window
WINDOW SETATTRIBUTES Custwindow FROM Windowattributes
```

Table 5-2 summarizes commands to move and resize windows.

Table 5-2. Commands to Move and Resize Windows

Command	Description
WINDOW MAXIMIZE	Toggles between full screen and original size
WINDOW MOVE	Moves window to specific row and column
WINDOW RESIZE	Resizes window

Selecting Windows

Paradox refers to the entire screen as the *desktop*. You open, stack, and remove windows there. By default, the last one opened is current and appears on top, or you can make one current by selecting it. The following example opens two windows and selects the first.

```
VIEW "Customer"
WINDOW HANDLE CURRENT TO Custwindow
VIEW "Orders"
WINDOW HANDLE CURRENT TO Ordwindow
WINDOW SELECT Custwindow
```

Working in Windows

The user always interacts with a window in a standard way. He or she can, for example, click on the close button (located in the top left of the frame) to close it. The user also can interact with data inside the window at his or her own risk, of course! For example, he or she can insert records in a table, or press a button in a dialog box. The user works with table data in workspace windows and text objects in canvas windows. The following sections discuss the options available in both types.

CheckPoint **5-1.** Introductory Screen in a Window

Objective: Display an introductory (splash) screen in a canvas window for 2 seconds, then close the window. Title is "A LONG DAY'S JOURNEY INTO PAL". Greeting in window is "Life is a journey, not a destination."

Controlling the Canvas

If the medium is the message, users will judge your applications by how professional the interface looks as much as, or maybe more than, how well they work. After all, the user normally does not see what happens behind the scenes, only what you paint on the canvas. Who knows how quickly Rembrandt mixed his colors or how efficiently he drew his figures and settings?

Table 5-3. Canvas Command Summary

Command	Description
?	Display values one line below cursor
??	Display values at cursor
@	Move cursor to a specific row and column
ACCEPT	Collect a value from the keyboard
CLEAR	Clear entire screen
CLEAR EOL	Clear from cursor to end of line
CLEAR EOS	Clear from cursor to bottom right corner of window or screen
CURSOR BAR	Make cursor into a small box ■
CURSOR BOX	Make cursor into a solid block █
CURSOR OFF	Turn cursor off
CURSOR NORMAL	Turn cursor on
CANVAS OFF	Stop immediate text display
CANVAS ON	Start immediate text display
ECHO SLOW, FAST, NORMAL	Show workspace action on canvas
ECHO OFF	Do not show workspace action on canvas
FORMAT	Format text and numbers with picture strings
PAINTCANVAS	Color rectangular screen areas
SETMARGIN	Change left margin
SHOW COMMANDS	Display menus and dialog boxes
STYLE	Change text attributes
SYNCURSOR	Move canvas cursor to workspace location
TEXT/ENDTEXT	Display literal text

You display menus, messages, and dialog boxes as well as accept single input values on the canvas. If you do not specify a window, commands use the entire screen. If you do select one, everything is relative to it.

This section summarizes commands that control the canvas (Table 5-3) and make it look both functional and professional. It explains a way to give users access to built-in Paradox facilities such as the report editor. Why recreate what Paradox already provides?

Canvas commands fall into the following categories: data entry, cursor control, clearing the canvas, text display, and workspace display.

Data Entry Commands

PAL uses the ACCEPT and SHOW commands to enter values on the canvas. ACCEPT collects a value from the keyboard with validity checks. SHOW commands display menus and dialog boxes of strings, arrays, tables, or files. They return the user's choice.

You specify the type of data to ACCEPT with an optional range, default, and table lookup. The following example accepts a due date for customer invoices. The data is of type date with a minimum value of January 1st and a maximum of today's date. Today appears as the default, and the user can accept it by pressing Enter.

```
ACCEPT "D" MIN 01/01/92 MAX TODAY
   DEFAULT TODAY To Duedate
```

If the user presses Esc to end the ACCEPT command, Duedate contains "Esc"; otherwise, it contains a valid date.

You can include a lookup table in an ACCEPT; PAL checks the entry against the first field. In a multiuser environment, Paradox puts a write lock on the table. If another user places an incompatible lock on it first, you get a script error. (Quick, call the writers' union!)

Tip

Place a prevent write lock on lookup tables before using them on a network to avoid script errors.

A prevent write lock guarantees that you can at least view a lookup table. The following example locks the State lookup table before asking the user to enter a value.

```
LOCK State "PWL"
IF Retval THEN
  ACCEPT "A2" LOOKUP State TO Newstate
ELSE
  MESSAGE "State table is locked! - Try again"
  SLEEP 2000
ENDIF
```

The SHOW commands display menus and dialog boxes based on arrays, files, and user-defined menu choices. The user presses arrow keys to navigate or enters the first letter (or more, if necessary) to choose an option. A hidden keycode list can trap keys that do not appear on the menu.

The SHOWFILES and SHOWTABLES commands let you specify the default directory. The next example displays a list of RPT files in the private directory.

```
SHOWFILES NOEXT
  PRIVDIR()+"*.RPT"
  "Select a file and press Enter"
TO Filename
```

SHOWTABLES also lets you specify the directory, but includes only Paradox tables in the list. For example, we can display all tables in the current directory.

```
SHOWTABLES
  ""
  "Select a table and press Enter"
TO Tblname
```

SHOWPOPUP displays a popup menu at user defined coordinates. You can specify a title and submenu for each choice and separators between options. You may also disable options if they are currently inappropriate. For example, you can disable View or Coedit if the user has not selected a table. You can also hide active keys such as F1 for help. The syntax for SHOWPOPUP is:

```
SHOWPOPUP Title {CENTERED | @ Row,Column}
Menuchoice
ENDMENU
[UNTIL Keylist [KEYTO Variable1]]
```

```
TO Variable2
```

You can define Menuchoice in the following three ways:

- Option : Description [DISABLE] Tag
- Option : Description [DISABLE] [Tag]
  SUBMENU
  Menuchoice
  ENDSUBMENU
- SEPARATOR

Figure 5-1 shows an accounting popup menu with options for Daily Work, Customers, and Utilities. Each choice has a submenu, and Utilities is set off with a separator.

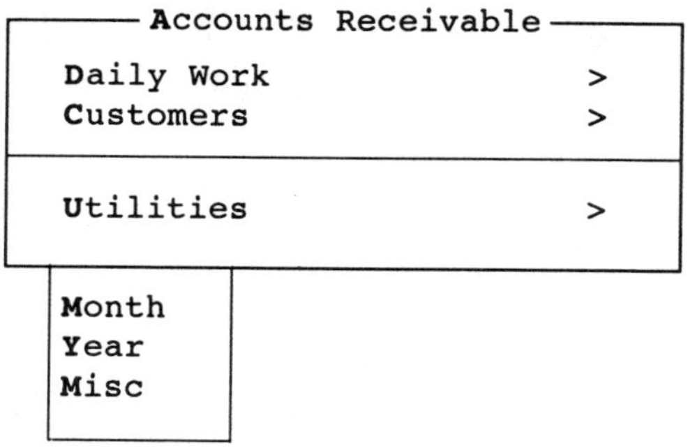

Figure 5-1. *Accounting popup menu.*

Program 5-1 displays the popup menu. It stores the user's choice (menu tag) in Mchoice or returns "Esc" if the user presses Esc to exit without making one. It includes a hidden F1 key to provide help.

```
;Showpop.sc
;Display an accounting menu with three options
;centered on the screen. Each choice has a submenu.
;Mchoice will contain the user's choice or "Esc"
;if none.
;Popup has a hidden F1 key for help
```

```
WHILE True
  Helpkey = ""
  SHOWPOPUP "Accounts Receivable" CENTERED
   "Daily Work   : "Invoices,Receipts,Journals"         : "Rectag"
    SUBMENU
     "Invoices" : "Enter Invoices"                      : "Invtag",
     "Cash"     : "Enter Cash Receipts"                 : "Cashtag",
     "Print"    : "Print Invoices"                      : "Prttag",
     "Post"     : "Post Transactions"                   : "Posttag"

    ENDSUBMENU,
     "Customers": "Maint,Reports,Aging"                 : "Custtag"

    SUBMENU
     "List"     : "List Open Invoices"                  : "Opentag",
     "Trial"    : "Print Trial Balance"                 : "Baltag",
     "Stmts"    : "Print Statements"                    : "Stmttag",
     "Maint"    : "Maintain Customers"                  : "Mainttag"

    ENDSUBMENU,
   SEPARATOR,
   "Utilities"  : "Month/Year End, Misc"                : "Utiltag"

    SUBMENU
     "Month"    : "Month End"                           : "Mntag",
     "Year"     : "Year End"                            : "Yrtag",
     "Misc"     : "Maintain Misc Tables"                : "Misttag"

    ENDSUBMENU
  ENDMENU
UNTIL "F1" KEYTO Helpkey
TO Mchoice

;Test for F1 key
IF Helpkey = "F1" THEN
  MESSAGE "There is one born every minute"
  SLEEP 2000
  MESSAGE ""
  LOOP
ENDIF

;Test for Esc to quit loop
IF NOT Retval THEN
  MESSAGE "Accounts Receivable Finished"
  SLEEP 1000 MESSAGE ""
  QUITLOOP
  ENDIF
```

```
;Display user's choice
  MESSAGE Mchoice
  SLEEP 2000
  MESSAGE ""
ENDWHILE
```

Program 5-1. *Accounting Popup Menu*

SHOWPULLDOWN displays a menu bar at the top of the screen with a pulldown menu for each choice. The following shows the syntax for SHOWPULLDOWN. The Menuchoice and Keylist options resemble SHOWPOPUP.

```
SHOWPULLDOWN
  Menuchoice
ENDMENU [UNTIL Keylist]
```

The GETMENUSELECTION command waits for the user to make a choice.

```
GETMENUSELECTION
  [KEYTO Keyvar]
TO Userchoice
```

If a Keylist is included, Keyvar will contain the key pressed. Userchoice contains the user's menu selection. The pulldown remains until you remove it explicitly with CLEARPULLDOWN. Figure 5-2 shows a pulldown menu with two inventory options: Receipts and Orders.

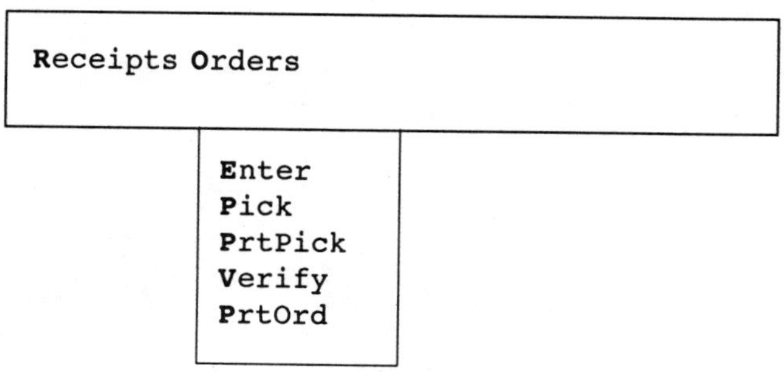

Figure 5-2. *Inventory pulldown menu.*

Program 5-2 displays the pulldown menu and includes the F1 key for help. It clears the pulldown when the user selects an option or presses Esc to exit without selecting anything.

```
;Showpull.sc
;Display a pulldown menu with two choices
;Each choice has a submenu
;Mchoice will contain tag for user's choice
;or "Esc" if no choice.
;Menu has a hidden F1 key for help


WHILE True
  Helpkey = ""
  SHOWPULLDOWN
   "Receipts"   : "Enter,Edit,Post Daily Receipts"   : "Rectag"

     SUBMENU
      "New"     : "Enter New Receipts"                : "Newrectag",
      "Edit"    : "Edit Receipts"                     : "Editrectag",
      "Post"    : "Post Receipts to Inventory"        : "Postrectag"

     ENDSUBMENU,
      "Orders"  : "Enter,Pick,Verify Orders"          : "Ordtag"

     SUBMENU
      "Enter"   : "Enter new orders"                  : "Newordtag",
      "Pick"    : "Pick inventory"                    : "Picktag",
      "PrtPick" : "Print Pick List"                   : "Prtpicktag",
      "Verify"  : "Verify shipments"                  : "Verifytag",
      "PrtOrd"  : "Print Orders"                      : "Prtordtag"

    ENDSUBMENU
 ENDMENU
 UNTIL "F1"

 GETMENUSELECTION KEYTO Helpkey TO Mchoice
   ;Check for F1 key
   IF Helpkey = -59 THEN
   MESSAGE "There is one born every minute"
   SLEEP 2000
   MESSAGE ""
   LOOP
 ENDIF
```

```
;Check for Esc
IF NOT Retval THEN
   MESSAGE "Inventory finished"
   SLEEP 2000
   MESSAGE ""
   ;Remove pulldown menu
   CLEARPULLDOWN
   QUITLOOP
ENDIF

;User must have selected something
;Remove pulldown menu to run script or
;procedure for menu option
CLEARPULLDOWN
CLEAR
MESSAGE Mchoice
SLEEP 2000
MESSAGE ""
LOOP
ENDWHILE
```

Program 5-2. *Inventory Pulldown Menu*

Cursor Control

Paradox uses three symbolic commands to position the cursor on the canvas: ?, ??, and @.

? displays values at the beginning of the line below where the cursor is. You can mix text and values, separated by commas. The following example displays a message and the current date.

```
? "Today's date is ",TODAY()
```

?? displays values where the cursor is. You can combine it with @ to position text. The following example displays the current date at row 10, column 15.

```
@ 10,15 ?? "Today's date is ",TODAY()
```

You can also change the cursor's appearance or remove it. CURSOR BAR changes it to ■, and CURSOR BOX to █. CURSOR OFF turns it off. I use CURSOR OFF when displaying messages to avoid distracting the user. You turn it on again with CURSOR NORMAL (*not* CURSOR ON).

Clearing the Canvas

You can clear the canvas in three ways. CLEAR clears it all. CLEAR EOL and CLEAR EOS both start from the cursor. The former continues to the end of the line, and the latter to the bottom right corner.

There is no command to clear an arbitrary area. But Program 5-3 can do the job, based on top left and bottom right coordinates.

```
;Clearrec.sc
;Clear a rectangle defined by top left corner (Tlr,Tlc)
;and bottom right corner (Brr,Brc)

PROC Clearrec(Tlr,Tlc,Brr,Brc)
PRIVATE
          Blanks,    ;Line of spaces
          Procname,  ;Procedure name
          Rownum     ;Row to clear

Procname = "Clearrec"

Blanks = SPACES(Brc - Tlc + 1)
;Move cursor to row and
; display line of spaces
FOR Rownum FROM Tlr TO Brr
  @ Rownum,Tlc ?? Blanks
ENDFOR
ENDPROC
```

***Program 5-3.** Clear a Rectangle*

Text Display

You can set the left margin to any valid value and display literal text with TEXT/ENDTEXT. The FORMAT command formats numbers and text using picture strings. You can also hide the canvas while painting a complex picture, then redisplay it so your masterpiece pops up in its full glory.

SETMARGIN changes the left margin for later TEXT/ENDTEXT and ? commands. The next example displays a boxed logo starting at column 35.

```
SETMARGIN 35
TEXT
┌──────────────────────────┐
│                          │
│    Werebroke Studios     │
│       Ticket Sales       │
│                          │
└──────────────────────────┘
ENDTEXT
SETMARGIN 0
```

The STYLE command changes the way text displays, and PAINTCANVAS paints rectangular areas. STYLE changes future text, whereas PAINTCANVAS colors what is already there.

Both commands use attributes to select foreground and background colors. To choose a combination, add foreground and background numbers from Table 5-4. Adding 128 makes the text blink. For example, the following sequence displays a blinking white on red message on line 20 for two seconds and then resets the default style. Comments help the reader who may not recognize combination 207 immediately (how ignorant!).

```
@ 20,0
STYLE ATTRIBUTE 207 ;Blinking white on red
?? "Loading..."
SLEEP 2000
STYLE
```

The FORMAT command formats text and numbers for display or printing using a picture string. It handles numeric precision, justification, alignment, case, date formats, and leading blanks. Table 5-5 lists its specifications.

Table 5-4. Text Attributes

Foreground	Number	Color
	0	Black
	1	Blue
	2	Green
	3	Cyan
	4	Red
	5	Magenta
	6	Brown
	7	Light gray
	8	Dark gray
	9	Light blue
	10	Light green
	11	Light cyan
	12	Light red
	13	Light magenta
	14	Yellow
	15	White
Background		
	0	Black
	16	Blue
	32	Green
	48	Cyan
	64	Red
	80	Magenta
	96	Brown
	112	Light gray
Monochrome		
	0	No display
	1	Underline text
	2	Normal text
	9	High intensity + underline
	10	High intensity
	112	Reverse video
Blink	128	Activate blinking

For example, the following command displays the number 346.2 in an 8 character field with 2 decimal places. Remember to count the decimal point (and minus sign) when calculating field width. If the width is too small for the result, Paradox displays asterisks instead.

```
? FORMAT("W8.2",346.2)
```

> **Warning**
>
> Scientific notation displays only one decimal place. PAL rounds the number.

Table 5-5. Format Specifications

Type	Specification		Applies to Data Type
Alignment	AC	Center within width	All
Align left	AL	Align left	All
	AR	Align right	All
Case	CC	Initial caps only	All
	CL	Make lowercase	All
	CU	Make uppercase	All
Date	D1	mm/dd/yy	D
	D2	month dd,yyyy	D
	D3	mm/dd	D
	D4	mm/yy	D
	D5	dd-Mon-yy	D
	D6	Mon yy	D
	D7	dd-Mon-yyyy	D
	D8	mm/dd/yyyy	D
	D9	dd.mm.yy	D
	D10	dd/mm/yy	D
	D11	yy-mm-dd	D
Edit	E$	Floating $ sign	N,S,$

	E*	Use * for leading zeros (for printing checks)	N,S,$
	EB	Use blanks for leading zeros	N,S,$
	EC	Use commas between groups of three digits	N,S,$
	EI	International format	N,S,$
	ES	Scientific notation	N,S,$
	EZ	Print leading zeros	N,S,$
Logical	LO	Use On/Off	L
	LY	Use Yes/No	L
Sign	S+	Print leading sign +/-	N,S,$
	S-	Print leading -	N,S,$
	SC	Print CR after negative	N,S,$
	SD	Print DB or CR	N,S,$
	SP	Print negatives with ()	N,S,$
Width	Wn	Total print width	All
	Wn.m	Width and decimals	N,$

Data types are: D-Date, L-Logical, N-Number, S-Short Number, and $-Currency

Tip

You can use the FORMAT command on reports and forms. Replace a regular field with a calculated one and use FORMAT to change its appearance.

PAL shows canvas commands immediately. You may want to turn CANVAS OFF while painting. CANVAS ON redisplays it. Would Michelangelo seem like such a genius if you had watched him paint or Shakespeare if you had sat through rehearsals?

Workspace Display

The ECHO command lets the user see and interact with what is normally hidden on the workspace during script play. The default is ECHO OFF (no display). You reveal the workspace with ECHO SLOW, FAST, or NORMAL (the options in Scripts/Showplay).

You can use ECHO commands to include such Paradox facilities as the report editor in your applications. This saves time because you need not write or debug them. It also provides a standardized, well-developed interface.

Program 5-4 copies a customer report to a new number and lets the user alter the copy with the Paradox report editor. It passes keystrokes through to Paradox until the mode switches from Report to Main (usually because the user presses F2 to end editing). It is easier to test for the exception than check each keystroke.

```
;Editrpt.sc
;Edit report with Paradox report editor
;Script ends when mode changes from Report to
;anything else

COPYREPORT "Customer" "1" "Customer" "14"
{Report} {Change} {Customer} {14} Enter

;Reveal workspace with report editor
ECHO NORMAL
;Accept keystrokes as long as in Report mode
WHILE SYSMODE() = "Report"
  ;Get key and press it
  Key = GETCHAR()
  KEYPRESS Key
ENDWHILE


;Turn workspace echo off when user
;leaves Report mode
ECHO OFF
```

Program 5-4. *Echo Report Editor*

A similar technique gives users access to other facilities such as the sort and graph editor.

CheckPoint 5-2. Using the Paradox Sort Facility

Objective: Sort the Customer table into a new table, Sortcust. Let the user select the fields to sort on using the Paradox sort facility. Assume Sortcust does not already exist. How could you ask for confirmation before proceeding if it does?

Hint: Use keypress commands to select the Customer and Sortcust tables. Then use the technique shown in Program 5-4 to let the user interact with the sort facility.

Dialog Boxes

You create a dialog box in a canvas window and control its appearance with commands such as STYLE, FORMAT, and PAINTCANVAS. You can use them to present a user with a pick list of files, tables, or array elements. You can also design them to accept inputs such as passwords and search criteria. SHOW commands such as SHOWMENU create simple dialog boxes centered on the screen with default pushbuttons. SHOWDIALOG can produce more complex ones.

You build a dialog box by selecting from a series of options, much as a mason builds a wall by selecting bricks. Options include:

- Title
- Screen placement (row and column)
- Height and width
- Control elements such as buttons and pick lists
- Canvas elements such as frame and color
- Optional procedure for specified events

The format of the SHOWDIALOG command is:

```
SHOWDIALOG Title
[PROC Eventproc Eventlist]
@ Rownum, Colnum HEIGHT Number WIDTH Number
```

```
CanvasElements
ControlElements
ENDDIALOG
```

Title is a string Paradox centers at the top of the dialog box. Eventproc and Eventlist resemble the options in an event-driven WAIT. Paradox transfers control to the event procedure when an event in the list occurs. Rownum and Colnum define the upper left corner of the box, and HEIGHT and WIDTH are its dimensions.

> **Warning**
>
> Paradox does not create a script error if the box is too small to contain all specified options. For example, a button with coordinates outside the box will not display, but the user may still press it! It is in the "Twilight Zone"!

Canvas elements change a dialog box's appearance. They include options such as frames and color. Control elements include buttons, lists, and data entry areas. In the following sections, we introduce canvas choices and explain how to define control elements.

Canvas Elements

The choices for canvas elements are:

- CLEAR EOL or EOS
- FRAME SINGLE or DOUBLE
- PAINTCANVAS
- STYLE
- Text display using @, ?, or ??

Control Elements

Every dialog box must have a control element, usually a pushbutton, to let the user exit. He or she moves through elements using the Tab or arrow keys. The following sections discuss the major varieties including pushbuttons, text boxes, radio buttons, check boxes, and pick lists.

Pushbuttons

Pushbuttons are the most common elements. Most dialog boxes have at least two, one to accept entries and one to cancel them. The general form of a pushbutton is:

```
PUSHBUTTON
  @ Rownum,Colnum
  WIDTH Number
  Label
  [OK | CANCEL]
  [DEFAULT]
  VALUE Expression
  TAG Expression
  TO Buttonvar
```

Row and column positions are relative to the upper left corner of the dialog box, NOT the screen. You specify the button's WIDTH and the text Label to display on it.

> **Tip**
>
> Make the pushbutton's WIDTH equal to Label length plus 2. Paradox puts a space at each end of the Label automatically.

Tilde (~) characters around a letter in the Label text create a hot key. For example, "~C~ancel" highlights the letter C, so pressing Alt-C is equivalent to pressing the button. Do not count tildes when calculating button width or it may appear too wide.

OK and CANCEL tell Paradox what to do when a user presses the button. For example, it ends the dialog when a user presses a CANCEL button.

Paradox assigns the VALUE expression to the button variable when a user presses an OK button and ends the dialog.

The DEFAULT option selects a button automatically if the user presses Enter without pushing one.

The TAG expression is passed to the event procedure if an event in the list occurs.

Figure 5-3 shows a simple dialog box with a message and a single button.

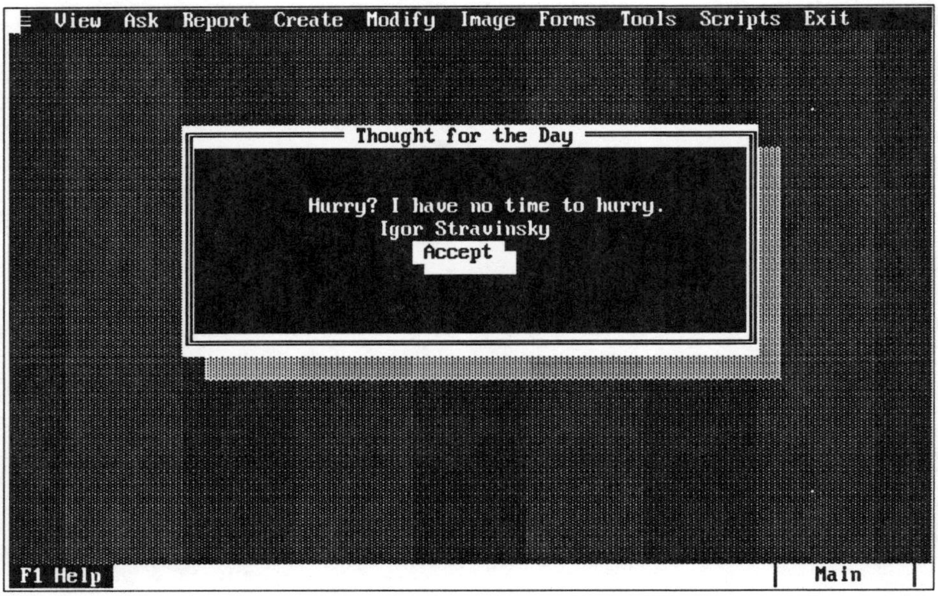

Figure 5-3. Dialog box displaying a message.

The following script processes the dialog box.

```
SHOWDIALOG "Thought for the Day"
  @ 5,15 HEIGHT 10 WIDTH 50
  @ 2,10 ?? "Hurry? I have no time to hurry."
  @ 3,10 ?? "      Igor Stravinsky"

PUSHBUTTON @ 4,18 WIDTH 10
  "~A~ccept"
  DEFAULT
  OK
  VALUE "OK"
  TAG "Yes"
  TO Button
ENDDIALOG
```

The script ends when the user presses Enter or selects and pushes the Accept button. *A* is its hot key.

Text Boxes

If you want more interaction, you can design text boxes to accept single values. The ACCEPT control element resembles the PAL ACCEPT command. Its general form is:

```
ACCEPT
  @ Rownum,Colnum
  WIDTH Number
  Datatype
  Optional Elements
  TAG Expression
  TO Acceptvar
```

The row and column position are relative to the box's upper left corner. WIDTH specifies the width of the highlighted area where the user types. You should make it at least 2 characters larger than the expected input. Paradox adds a space at both ends automatically.

Datatype tells Paradox what type of data to accept. It can be any standard type: A, D, M, N, S, or $.

Optional elements are the same as the choices for the PAL ACCEPT command, including MIN, MAX, and LOOKUP. HIDDEN is available only with dialog boxes. Paradox displays an asterisk for each character so unauthorized observers cannot read the entry.

The TAG expression identifies the control element for the dialog procedure. Paradox displays data stored in Acceptvar as the default and stores the new entry there.

Figure 5-4 shows a dialog box for entering a password. Program 5-5 accepts it and masks it with asterisks. The box includes both Accept and Cancel buttons, with hot keys *A* and *C*, respectively. The procedure returns the password or a null string (“”) if the user cancels the entry.

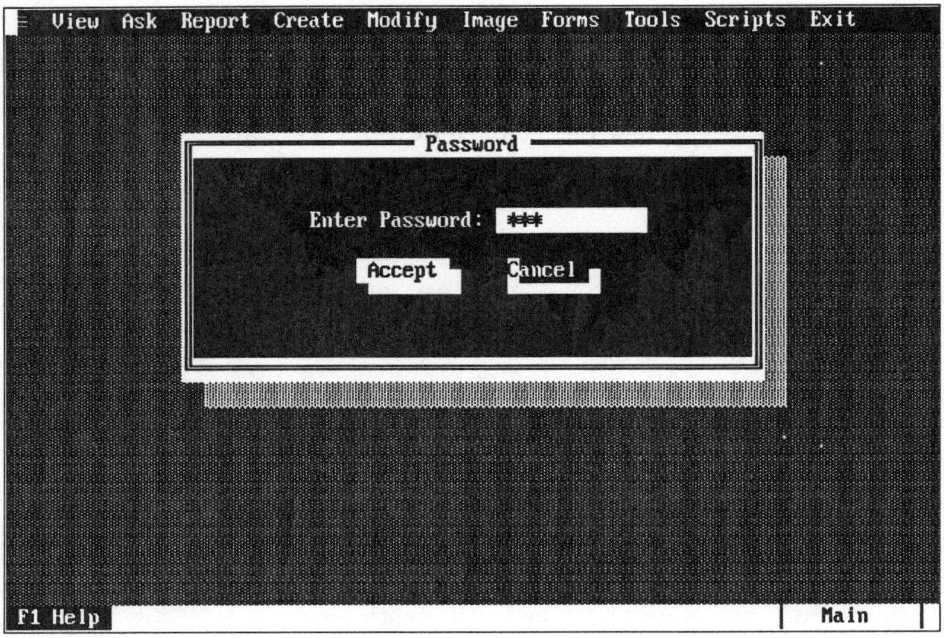

Figure 5-4. Dialog box for entering a masked password.

```
;Password.sc
;Dialog box to accept a password
;Typed characters are hidden
;Box includes Accept and Cancel buttons
;Use Alt-A and Alt-C as hot keys
;Procedure returns password or ""
;if Cancel button pressed
PROC Passmask()
PRIVATE
        Button,    ;Selected pushbutton
        Passwrd    ;Entered password

Passwrd = ""
Button = ""
SHOWDIALOG "Password"
  @ 5,15 HEIGHT 10 WIDTH 50
  @ 2,10 ?? "Enter Password:"

  ACCEPT @ 2,26
```

```
    WIDTH 13 "A10"
  REQUIRED
    HIDDEN
    TAG " "
    TO Passwrd


  PUSHBUTTON @ 4,13 WIDTH 10
    "~A~ccept"
    OK
    DEFAULT
    VALUE "OK"
    TAG "Yes"
    TO Button


  PUSHBUTTON @ 4,25 WIDTH 10
    "~C~ancel"
    CANCEL
    VALUE "CANCEL"
    TAG "No"
    TO Button
ENDDIALOG


IF NOT Retval THEN
  RETURN ""
ELSE
  RETURN Passwrd
ENDIF
ENDPROC
```

***Program 5-5.** Accept a Masked Password*

The following example calls Program 5-5. It displays the password or a message if the user canceled the entry.

```
  Mypass = Passbox()
  IF Mypass = "" THEN
    MESSAGE "No password entered"
  ELSE
    MESSAGE Mypass + " is the password"
  ENDIF
  SLEEP 2000
```

Radio Buttons

Radio buttons let a user make one choice from a list of options. The general form is:

```
RADIOBUTTONS
  @ Rownum,Colnum
  HEIGHT Number
  WIDTH Number
  Label1,Label2,...,LabelN
  TAG Expression
  TO Radiovar
```

Row and column are the top left coordinates relative to the dialog box. HEIGHT and WIDTH are the box's dimensions. Labels are text strings for the mutually exclusive choices. TAG identifies the control element to the dialog procedure. Radiovar contains the user's choice from the list.

Figure 5-5 shows a dialog box of color combinations. Radio (Program 5-6) lets a user choose his or her favorite and establishes the new colors with the STYLE command.

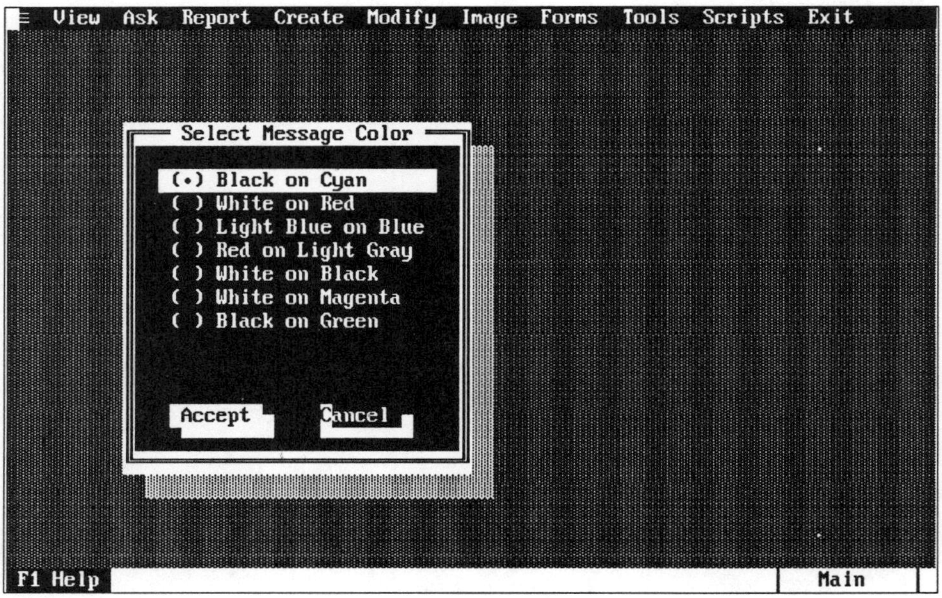

Figure 5-5. Selecting a color combination with a radio button.

```
;Radio.sc
;Select an item from a dialog box using a radio button.
;Box has Accept and Cancel buttons.
;Use Alt-A and Alt-C as hot keys
;Put choices into an array for easier selection

;Choices for radio buttons
ARRAY Colors[7] ;Text to display
ARRAY Values[7] ;Matching ASCII color codes
Colors[1] = "Black on Cyan"
Values[1] = 48
Colors[2] = "White on Red"
Values[2] = 79
Colors[3] = "Light Blue on Blue"
Values[3] = 25
Colors[4] = "Red on Light Gray"
Values[4] = 116
Colors[5] = "White on Black"
Values[5] = 15
Colors[6] = "White on Magenta"
Values[6] = 95
Colors[7] = "Black on Green"
Values[7] = 32

Button = ""
;Highlight first button
Character = 1

SHOWDIALOG "Select Message Color"
  @ 5,10 HEIGHT 15 WIDTH 30

  RADIOBUTTONS
    @ 1,2
    HEIGHT 8
    WIDTH 25
    Colors[1],
    Colors[2],
    Colors[3],
    Colors[4],
    Colors[5],
    Colors[6],
    Colors[7]
    TAG "Radiotag"
    TO ColorChoice
```

```
  PUSHBUTTON @ 11,2 WIDTH 10
    "~A~ccept"
    OK
    DEFAULT
    VALUE "OK"
    TAG "Yes"
    TO Button

  PUSHBUTTON @ 11,14 WIDTH 10
    "~C~ancel"
    CANCEL
    VALUE "CANCEL"
    TAG "No"
    TO Button
ENDDIALOG

IF NOT Retval THEN
  MESSAGE "No color combination selected"
ELSE
  STYLE ATTRIBUTE Values[ColorChoice]
ENDIF
```

Program 5-6. *Use Radio Buttons to Select Colors*

Check Boxes

Check boxes resemble radio buttons, but they allow the user to select more than one option. The general form is:

```
CHECKBOXES
  @ Rownum,Colnum
  HEIGHT Number
  WIDTH Number
  TAG Expression
  Label1 TO Variable1
  Label2 TO Variable2
  .
  .
  .
  LabelN TO VariableN
```

The row, column, height, width, and tag components work just as for radio buttons. Labels are text strings to display. Paradox initially sets all variables to False. If a user checks an option, it changes the corresponding one to True.

Figure 5-6 shows a check box to select states to include in a mailing. Checkbox (Program 5-7) uses two arrays to process the dialog. The first holds label text, and the second corresponding variables. It displays the user's choices or a message if he or she does not select anything.

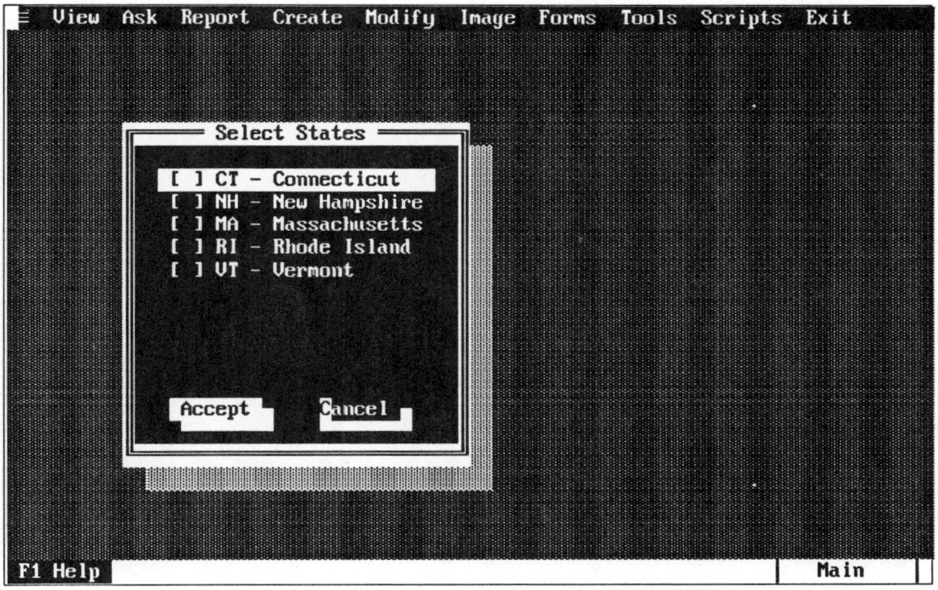

Figure 5-6. Select states using check boxes.

```
;Checkbox.sc
;Select items from a dialog box using check boxes
;Dialog box has Accept and Cancel buttons.
;Use Alt-A and Alt-C as hot keys.
;Put choices into array States.
;Corresponding array element in Checkbox is True
;if state checked, and False otherwise

;Choices for check boxes
ARRAY Checkbox[5]
ARRAY State[5]
State[1] = "CT - Connecticut"
State[2] = "NH - New Hampshire"
```

```
State[3] = "MA - Massachusetts"
State[4] = "RI - Rhode Island"
State[5] = "VT - Vermont"

SHOWDIALOG "Select States for Mailing"
  @ 5,10 HEIGHT 15 WIDTH 30

  CHECKBOXES
    @ 1,2
    HEIGHT 8
    WIDTH 25
    TAG "Checktag"
    State[1] TO Checkbox[1],
    State[2] TO Checkbox[2],
    State[3] TO Checkbox[3],
    State[4] TO Checkbox[4],
    State[5] TO Checkbox[5]

PUSHBUTTON @ 11,2 WIDTH 10
  "~A~ccept"
  OK
  DEFAULT
  VALUE "OK"
  TAG "Yes"
  TO Button

PUSHBUTTON @ 11,14 WIDTH 10
  "~C~ancel"
  CANCEL
  VALUE "CANCEL"
  TAG "No"
  TO Button
ENDDIALOG

IF NOT Retval THEN
  MESSAGE "No states selected"
  SLEEP 1000
ELSE
  FOR Choice FROM 1 TO 5
    IF Checkbox[Choice] = True THEN
      MESSAGE State[Choice] + " was picked"
    SLEEP 1000
    ENDIF
  ENDFOR
ENDIF
```

Program 5-7. *Select States with Check Boxes*

Pick Lists

PAL has PICK commands that resemble the SHOW commands, but provide more control over canvas elements. The commands are PICKTABLE, PICKFILE, PICKARRAY, and PICKDYNARRAY. The general form of PICKTABLE is:

```
PICKTABLE
  @ Rownum,Colnum
  HEIGHT Number
  WIDTH Number
  [COLUMNS Number]
  DOS Path
  TAG Expression
  TO Pickvar
```

The row and column numbers are relative to the upper left corner of the dialog box. HEIGHT and WIDTH are the box's dimensions. By default, data appears in a single column, but you may tell Paradox to use several with the COLUMN statement. DOS Path tells Paradox which directory to search for tables or files. The TAG expression is passed to the active dialog procedure. Paradox puts the user's choice in variable Pickvar.

Figure 5-7 shows a two column PICKTABLE dialog box. Picktbl (Program 5-8) lets the user select a table from the list and displays its name.

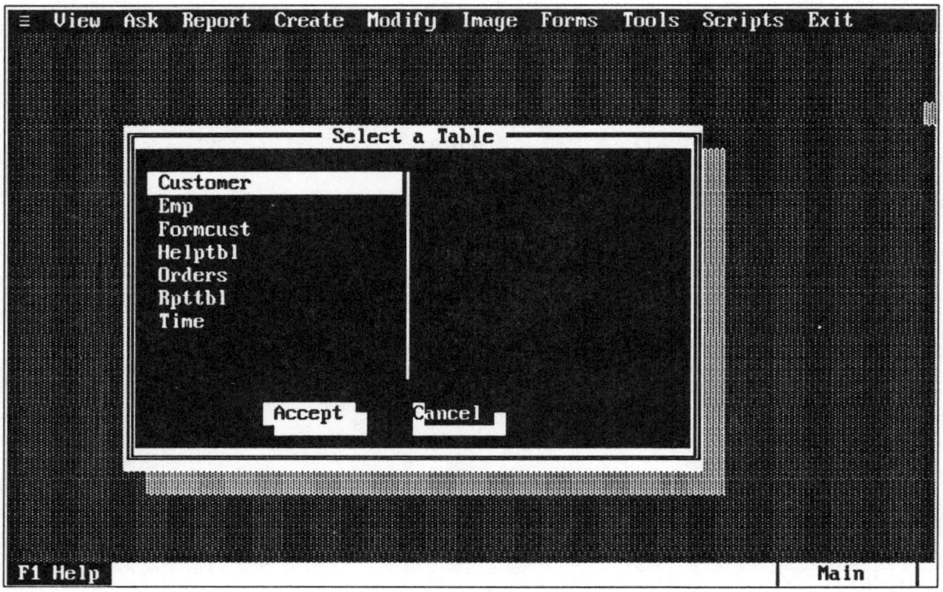

Figure 5-7. *Dialog box for picking a table from a list.*

```
;Picktbl.sc
;Display a dialog box of tables in the current
;directory. Procedure returns selected table
;or "" if no table selected

SHOWDIALOG "Select a Table"
  @ 5,10 HEIGHT 15 WIDTH 50

  ;Display choices from current directory
  ; using two columns
  PICKTABLE
    @ 1,1 HEIGHT 9 WIDTH 45
    COLUMNS 2
    ""
    TAG "Picktbl"
    TO Tbl

  PUSHBUTTON @ 11,10 WIDTH 10
    "~A~ccept"
    OK
```

```
    DEFAULT
    VALUE "OK"
    TAG "Yes"
    TO Button

  PUSHBUTTON @ 11,22 WIDTH 10
    "~C~ancel"
    CANCEL
    VALUE "CANCEL"
    TAG "No"
    TO Button
    ENDDIALOG

IF NOT Retval THEN
  MESSAGE "No table selected"
ELSE
  MESSAGE Tbl + " is picked"
ENDIF
SLEEP 1000
```

Program 5-8. *Pick List of Tables in Current Directory*

Controlling the Workspace

Most functions available in interactive Paradox have PAL equivalents. For example, the command to copy the Customer table and its family of forms, reports, etc. to Custbak is

```
COPY "Customer" "Custbak"
```

PAL has workspace commands (Table 5-6) that are not in interactive Paradox. They include ways to determine cursor position in a table, current menu choice, and workspace status.

Table 5-6. Workspace Command Summary

Command	Description
ATFIRST	Returns True if on first table record or first record in a restricted view, or if table is empty. Returns False otherwise.
ATLAST	Returns True if on last table record or last record in a restricted view. Returns False otherwise.
BOT	Returns True on attempt to move ahead of first table record. Returns False otherwise.
COLNO	Returns cursor position in record (1-255)
CURSORLINE	Returns text of line where cursor is
CURSORCHAR	Returns character under cursor
EOT	Returns True on attempt to move beyond last table record. Returns False otherwise.
FIELD	Returns current field name
FIELDINFO	Returns current field indicator. It may be a field name or a formula.
FIELDSTR	Returns current field contents as a string
FIELDTYPE	Returns field type (A,B,D,M,N,S,U, or $)
IMAGENO	Returns current image position or 0 if no images present
IMAGETYPE	Returns type of image: display, query, or none
ISFIELDVIEW	Returns True if current mode is Fieldview, False otherwise
ISFORMVIEW	Returns True if using a table with a form, False otherwise
MENUCHOICE	Returns current menu choice or Error if no menu displayed
NIMAGES	Returns number of images on the workspace
NIMAGERECORDS	Returns number of records in the current view
NRECORDS	Returns number of records in a table

RECNO	Returns current record number
ROWNO	Returns current row number in form or report editor (1-22)
TABLE	Returns current table name
WAIT	Lets user View or Edit current table
WINDOW	Contains current Paradox error message or null

Table Maintenance

The WAIT command used for table maintenance is the most important workspace action. The path Modify/Coedit puts a table on the workspace in interactive Paradox and lets the user do maintenance tasks such as inserting and deleting records. The equivalent PAL command, COEDIT, places the table on the workspace but hides it behind the canvas. "Who knows what evil lurks..." behind the canvas! The Shadow knows!

You must use a WAIT command to allow the user to interact with the table, with or without a form. WAIT has the following four scopes (from most to least restrictive): WAIT FIELD, WAIT RECORD, WAIT TABLE, and WAIT WORKSPACE.

WAIT FIELD holds the cursor in the current field until the user presses a key in the UNTIL list or a specified event occurs. WAIT RECORD allows cursor movement within a record. WAIT TABLE is the least restrictive within a table and duplicates cursor movement in interactive Paradox. WAIT WORKSPACE handles the F3 and F4 keys for moving between tables on the workspace without any explicit coding.

Paradox provides two variations on the WAIT command. The first is keypress-driven, that is, Paradox performs all actions based on keys the user presses. For example, you may end Coediting when he or she presses F2. The second version of WAIT is event-driven. Events include keypresses but may also include mouse actions such as clicking, and triggers such as departing a field (using keys or the mouse). You tell Paradox what events to WAIT for and how to respond to each one.

This section presents a single table maintenance procedure that is keypress-driven. It handles typical tasks such as inserting, deleting, and editing records. It checks for key conflicts during insert operations. It allows a user to navigate with arrow and page keys and also provides the Paradox Zoom and Zoomnext features for searching.

We also present an event-driven maintenance script for entering employee time card data. It checks for, and refuses, duplicate dates. It also disallows overtime if an employee works less than 8 hours in a particular day. (Slave driver that it is!)

Keypress-Driven WAIT

The general form of the keypress-driven WAIT command is:

```
WAIT {FIELD | RECORD | TABLE | WORKSPACE}
  PROMPT "Any text string"
  MESSAGE "Displays in bottom right corner"
UNTIL Keylist
```

The UNTIL keys can be names such as “F2” or ASCII values such as -20 (Alt-T). The keypress is available in Retval so you can decide what to do.

The PROMPT string appears on line 24. The MESSAGE is in the lower right corner; it disappears when the user presses a key. Table interaction ends when the user presses a key listed in UNTIL.

PAL enforces validity checks for all fields (including F1 for lookup tables). You need not include F1 in the UNTIL list.

The WINDOW function returns a string with the current contents of the message window. You see it automatically in interactive Paradox but not under program control. For example, if you enter a duplicate key in Coedit mode, WINDOW contains the Alt-L, Alt-K message for switching between the two records.

This section discusses how to enter, edit, and delete records using a WAIT statement and presents a single table maintenance procedure you can include in applications. It uses Coedit which allows multiuser table editing, so it is network-ready.

Entering New Records

You can open a new blank record using Ins or End Down. I prefer Ins on a network because another user may creep in (you cannot trust anyone these days!) to add a record between End and Down. As a result, the pointer is not where I expect.

You cannot lock the new record because it is in a buffer area, not in the table. After data entry, use LOCKRECORD to post it to the table and lock it. If the table is keyed, the cursor should follow the record to its new location in key sequence. If LOCKRECORD succeeds, the record was posted; if not, you probably have a key conflict.

Once you resolve the conflict and post the record, you should UNLOCKRECORD, or no other user can edit it until you end the maintenance session. You can do a few good deeds like this without ruining your reputation, as long as you do not make a regular habit of it.

Changing Records

To change a record, you must locate it and lock it to prevent others from trying to change it at the same time. If LOCKRECORD succeeds, I set IMAGERIGHTS to UPDATE so users cannot change keys in a keyed table. (I did a great deal of work to make sure the keys were unique, and I do not want to repeat it!)

When changes are complete, you must UNLOCKRECORD. The cursor remains on the record because the user did not change the keys. A nice feature is to save the original data in an array with COPYTOARRAY before editing. You can then let the user abandon editing and restore the original values with COPYFROMARRAY. This is a great relief if he or she has managed to get on a completely wrong track and has no hope of recovering.

Deleting Records

To delete a record, you must also first locate and lock it. If the lock succeeds, you can delete it. I always ask users to confirm deletions. They often confuse Del to delete a record with Backspace to delete a character (the poor dears). To paraphrase Solzhenitsyn (about animals), "if we stop loving [users], aren't we bound to stop loving humans too?" Just joking (and in private, please)—users ultimately pay my bills and presumably yours too.

You must decide which record to make current afterward. The default is the next one in sequence.

Single Table Maintenance

Program 5-9 is a single key table maintenance procedure. It accepts a table name, form number, and key name. You can pass -1 if there is no form. The form should not be multirecord or include embedded detail tables, but it may have multiple pages. The procedure contains routines to insert, edit, and delete records, and search on any field.

The UNTIL clause traps other keys: Dos (Alt-O), DosBig (Ctrl-O), and -18 (Alt-E). The Dos keys execute the PAL commands RUN and RUNBIG, respectively, accessing the DOS prompt without leaving Paradox. Alt-E starts the Paradox editor. Do not trap it if your table has a memo field, since the user may need it to edit the memo.

You cannot turn these keys off, so you must trap them in all WAIT commands. Note that there is no CASE to handle them. The procedure traps but ignores them.

The table starts in Coedit mode, picks the form (if there is one), and changes IMAGERIGHTS to READONLY. This limits the user to viewing data until he or she presses a key in the UNTIL list. Selecting a key changes the image rights. For example, when a user selects Ctrl-E (Edit), the procedure changes them to UPDATE to allow changes to all fields except the key. It returns to READONLY after the option is completed. It is easier to program starting from a predictable state rather than checking the cursor position and handling all possible situations.

The following is an example of a call to Tblmaint for a Customer table with form 1 and key field Cust Id.

```
Tblmaint("Customer",1,"Cust Id")
```

I use Tblmaint as the starting point for my maintenance applications and add features as needed. For example, you can add a choice to print a label for the current customer.

```
;Keywait.sc
;Maintain a single key table with or without a form
;using keypress-driven WAIT.
;Procedure accepts the table name (Tblname), table
;form (Frm) or -1 if no form, and table key (Tkey).
;It allows the following options:
```

```
; Ctrl-E - Edit current record  (5)
; Alt-Z  - ZoomNext
; Ctrl-Z - Zoom
; Del  - Delete current record
; Ins  - Insert record
;Turn off Alt-O (Dos), Ctrl-O (DosBig),
;and Alt-E (-18) so user cannot
;drop out of WAIT accidentally

PROC TblMaint(Tblname,Frm,Tkey)
PRIVATE
        Ans,        ;User choice for confirming record delete
        Keypic,     ;Field type of table key
        Nrecs,      ;Number of records currently in table
        Numpgs,     ;Number of pages in the form (if used)
        Prmpt,      ;Prompt line
        Procname,   ;Procedure name
        Savefld,    ;Save field location when switching records
        Savekey,    ;Save current record key to check for
                    ;duplicate
        Saverec     ;Save record values so user can cancel edit

Procname =  "TblMaint"

COEDIT Tblname
;Maximize window
WINMAX
Numpgs = 0
;If there is a form, switch to it
IF Frm > 0 THEN
  PICKFORM Frm
  WINMAX
  Numpgs = NPAGES()
ENDIF
;Clear top menu bar
SHOWPULLDOWN
ENDMENU

;Set up prompt line
;Zm is short for Zoom
;ZmNxt is short for ZoomNext
;Full prompts will not fit on one line
Prmpt =  "F2-Quit, Ins-Ins, Ctrl/E-Edit, Del-Del,"+
        " Ctrl/Z-Zm, Alt/Z-ZmNxt"

WHILE True
   ;Keep in view only mode until user selects function
   IF NOT ISEMPTY(Tblname) THEN
```

```
    IMAGERIGHTS READONLY
  ENDIF

  WAIT RECORD
    PROMPT Prmpt
  UNTIL  "F2","Ins",-18,"Del","Zoom","ZoomNext",
         "Up","Down","PgUp","PgDn","Dos","DosBig",5

  SWITCH
  CASE Retval = "F2":
    QUITLOOP

  ;Insert new record
  CASE Retval = "Ins":
    ;Allow user to enter new key
    IMAGERIGHTS
    INS
    MOVETO FIELD Tkey
    ;SaveKey used to recognize duplicate
    ; key entry
    SaveKey = ""
    WHILE True
      WAIT RECORD
        PROMPT "Press F2 to Save Record, Esc to Cancel"
      UNTIL "F2","Esc","Dos","DosBig",5
      SWITCH
        CASE Retval = "F2":
          MOVETO FIELD Tkey
          ;Try to post if key has changed
          IF SaveKey <> [] THEN
            LOCKRECORD
            ;If lock succeeds, record posted to table
            IF Retval THEN
              UNLOCKRECORD
              MOVETO FIELD Tkey
              QUITLOOP
            ELSE
              MESSAGE
              "Duplicate key - Press any key to correct"
              Ans = GETCHAR()
              MESSAGE ""
              ;Save current key in case user tries to
              ; save record again without changing it
              MOVETO FIELD Tkey
              SaveKey = []
              LOOP
            ENDIF
          ENDIF
```

```
        ;Abandon record
        CASE Retval = "Esc":
          DEL
          QUITLOOP
      ENDSWITCH
    ENDWHILE

  ;Change record values. 5 = Ctrl-E
  CASE Retval = 5:
    ;Do not let user change key value
    IMAGERIGHTS UPDATE
    LOCKRECORD
    IF Retval THEN
      ;Save original data
      COPYTOARRAY SaveRec
      WHILE True
        WAIT RECORD
          PROMPT "Press F2 to Save Record, Esc to Cancel"
        UNTIL "F2","Esc","Dos","DosBig",5
        SWITCH
          ;Keep changes
          CASE Retval = "F2":
            QUITLOOP

          ;Abandon changes
          CASE Retval = "Esc":
            IMAGERIGHTS
            COPYFROMARRAY SaveRec
            QUITLOOP
        ENDSWITCH
      ENDWHILE
      UNLOCKRECORD
    ELSE
      MESSAGE "Record unavailable for editing, press any key"
      Ans = GETCHAR()
      MESSAGE ""
    ENDIF

  ;Delete current record
  CASE Retval = "Del":
    MESSAGE "Confirm deletion (Y/N)?"
    Ans = GETCHAR()
    MESSAGE ""
    ;Test for Y and y
    IF Ans <> 89 AND Ans <> 121 THEN
      LOOP
    ENDIF
    ;Try to lock and delete record
```

```
      IMAGERIGHTS
      LOCKRECORD
      IF Retval THEN
        DEL
      ELSE
        MESSAGE "Cannot lock record, No Delete - Press any key"
        Ans = GETCHAR()
        MESSAGE ""
      ENDIF

    ;Search for value
    CASE Retval = "Zoom":
      ZOOM

    ;Search for next value
    CASE Retval = "ZoomNext":
      MESSAGE "Searching for duplicate..."
      ZOOMNEXT
      MESSAGE ""

    ;Allow cursor movement
    CASE  Retval = "Up" OR Retval = "Down"
          OR Retval = "PgUp" OR Retval = "PgDn":
      KEYPRESS Retval

ENDSWITCH
ENDWHILE
DO_IT!
CLEARALL
ENDPROC
```

Program 5-9. *Keypress-Driven WAIT Table Maintenance*

CheckPoint 5-3. Keypress-Driven WAIT

Objective: Modify the keypress-driven maintenance program (5-9) to let the user toggle between form and table view.

Hint: Add text to PROMPT "F7-Chg View," "F7" to UNTIL key list, and a CASE for Retval = "F7". Use FORMKEY to switch views.

Event-Driven WAIT

The general form of the event-driven WAIT is:

```
WAIT {FIELD | RECORD | TABLE | WORKSPACE}
  PROC Eventproc Eventlist
ENDWAIT
```

The event list contains events you want Paradox to trap. It can include mouse actions that move the cursor, keys such as "F2" that usually end WAIT interactions, messages such as CLOSE to close a window, and triggers such as DEPARTFIELD. Paradox transfers control to the procedure listed as the eventproc when something in the list occurs. There are no provisions for a prompt on line 24.

> **Tip**
>
> Use the PROMPT command to set a prompt before starting an event-driven WAIT.

Paradox sets ECHO to normal when the WAIT begins, regardless of its previous setting. It restores the original setting when the WAIT ends and when it calls the event procedure. Switching ECHO states can cause the application to run slowly as it refreshes the screen each time.

> **Tip**
>
> Set ECHO NORMAL before starting an event-driven WAIT and ECHO OFF afterward to increase execution speed.

Paradox passes the event procedure three arguments: a trigger type, an event record, and a cycle number. The trigger type is a string describing the event. For example, if the user presses the right arrow to leave a field, it would be DEPARTFIELD.

EventRecord is a dynamic array whose elements describe the event. For the DEPARTFIELD with right arrow example, two elements are:

```
EventRecord["TYPE"] = "KEY"
EventRecord["KEYCODE"] = -77 ;Right arrow
```

You can test elements to determine which event occurred if you trap several.

An event cycle may generate several triggers. For example, if a user presses the down arrow to leave a record in table view, Paradox creates the following four triggers:

```
DEPARTFIELD
DEPARTROW
ARRIVEROW
ARRIVEFIELD
```

Paradox assigns a unique number to each event cycle. If you include all four triggers in the event list, Paradox calls the event procedure four times when the user presses the down arrow to leave a record, but the cycle number remains the same. You can test it to determine if the event caused multiple calls.

> **Tip**
>
> Trap events with the broadest possible scope to avoid multiple calls to the event procedure. For example, use DEPARTROW and check several fields at the same time if required. This improves performance.

The event procedure must return 0, 1, or 2 to tell Paradox how to proceed.

- 0 executes the current action and proceeds to the next trigger in the cycle.
- 1 ignores the current action and all triggers left in the cycle.
- 2 ignores the current action and all triggers left in the cycle, and ends the WAIT.

The following employee time card application (Program 5-10) illustrates an event-driven WAIT. Employees fill out one line on the card per day, entering regular and overtime hours. Figure 5-8 shows the entry form. The Emp table is its master, and the Time table is embedded as a multi-record form linked on Clock Number.

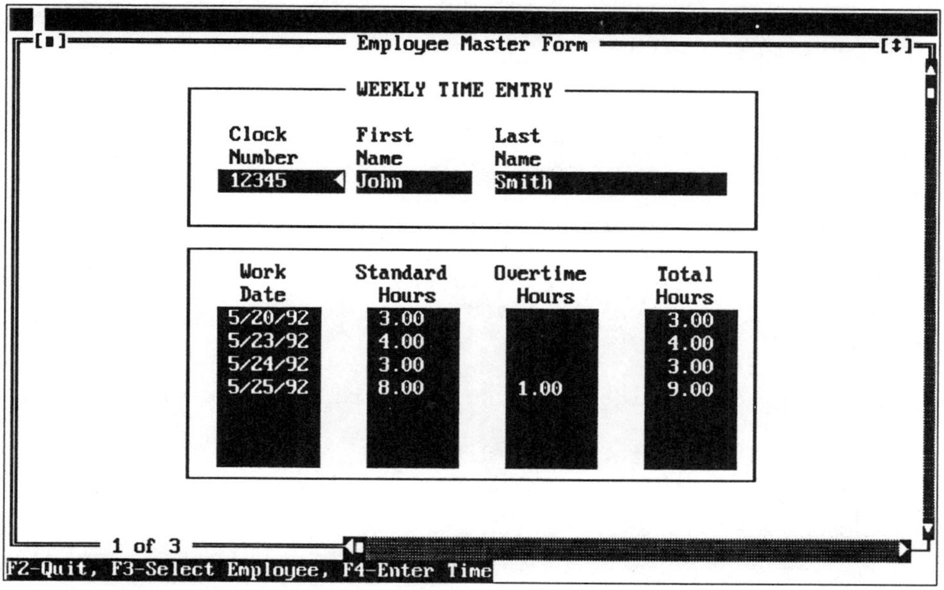

Figure 5-8. *Employee time card entry.*

Master fields Clock Number, First Name, and Last Name are display-only, so a clerk cannot accidentally change employee data while entering time cards. A ValCheck on Standard time limits it to 0 through 8 hours. Overtime is limited to 0 through 4 hours. Total time is calculated on the form by summing the two values.

The company has a business rule that an employee cannot work overtime unless he or she has worked 8 regular hours. Paradox cannot enforce this with a ValCheck (there is no way to compare field values), so we use a DEPARTROW trigger instead.

Date is the second part of the Time table key. A duplicate entry would cause Paradox to present the Alt-L/Alt-K duplicate key message to the user. We use a DEPARTFIELD trigger to check for it.

The scope is WAIT WORKSPACE. It lets the user press F3 and F4 to move between the employee and time tables without trapping the keys explicitly. We trap F2 to end data entry.

EventHandler is the event procedure. It tests for the two events DEPARTFIELD and DEPARTROW and the F2 key.

```
;Evenwait.sc
;Enter employee time cards. Employees are not
;allowed overtime unless regular time is 8 hours.
;Script uses event-driven WAIT to trap record
;depart for time check and field depart for
;duplicate date entry

PROC EventHandler(TriggerType,EventRecord,CycleNumber)

;Check for F2 (-60) to end Coedit
IF EventRecord["TYPE"] = "KEY" AND
  EventRecord["KEYCODE"] = -60 THEN
    RETURN 2
ENDIF

;Check for departing Date field in Time table. Duplicate
; dates are not allowed
IF UPPER(TABLE()) = "TIME" AND
   UPPER(FIELD()) = "DATE" AND
   TriggerType = "DEPARTFIELD" THEN
    ;Lock record to post it
    POSTRECORD
    IF NOT Retval THEN
      MESSAGE "Duplicate date not allowed"
      SLEEP 2000
      MESSAGE ""
      ;Deny event
      RETURN 1
    ELSE
      ;Event Ok, let it happen
      RETURN 0
    ENDIF
ENDIF

;Check for departing record in Time table.
;Overtime not allowed unless standard time = 8 hours
IF UPPER(TABLE()) = "TIME" AND
   TriggerType = "DEPARTROW" THEN
    IF [St Hours] < 8.00 AND
       [Ot Hours] > 0.00 THEN
        MESSAGE "No overtime allowed unless "+
          "standard hours = 8!"
```

```
          SLEEP 2000
          MESSAGE ""
          ;Deny event
          RETURN 1
     ELSE
          ;Event Ok, let it happen
          RETURN 0
     ENDIF
ENDIF

;Just a regular event, process it
RETURN 0
ENDPROC

;Coedit table, pick form, and maximize window
COEDIT "Emp"
PICKFORM 1
WINMAX

;Erase pulldown
SHOWPULLDOWN
ENDMENU

;Set prompt
PROMPT "F2-Quit, F3-Select Employee, F4-Enter Time"

;Allow Paradox to handle table navigation with F3/F4
;Make ECHO normal to speed WAIT procedure
ECHO NORMAL
WAIT WORKSPACE
  PROC "EventHandler"
  TRIGGER "DEPARTFIELD","DEPARTROW"
  KEY "F2"
ENDWAIT
;Turn off ECHO to restore environment
ECHO OFF
DO_IT!
CLEARALL
```

Program 5-10. *Event-Driven Wait for Time Card Entry*

CheckPoint 5-4. Event-Driven WAIT

Objective: Display the total hours worked when a user departs the Time table. Display message with hours until he or she presses a key.

Hint: Add a DEPARTTABLE trigger to the WAIT and an IF statement to the event procedure to test for it. SCAN the Time table and sum total hours. Display the total until the user presses a key.

Ad Hoc Queries

Users often need to query data after entering it. You can give them access to the Paradox Query-by-Example facility while controlling the keyboard. If they are unfamiliar with it (or do not like it), you can design a custom form instead with a technique called Query-by-Form. This section presents sample procedures for both approaches.

Query-by-Example

The Paradox query form is a table similar to ones you create. You can use the Ask option on the main Paradox menu with WAIT RECORD or WAIT TABLE to accept criteria.

Program 5-11 is a keypress-driven Query-by-Example procedure that allows multiple tables, example elements, and standard selection criteria such as check (F6) and checkplus (Alt-F6). It uses WAIT RECORD so you can define only one-line queries.

The program checks WINDOW when the user presses F2 to process the query. If it is formed incorrectly (for example, >4 and <6 instead of >4,<6), an error message appears and the user must edit the form. The program displays the Answer table if it finds matching records. Otherwise, it reports that the search failed.

You cannot use this method under Paradox Runtime, but you can use Query-by-Form instead.

Qbe has no arguments. It asks the user to select a table or press Esc when it starts.

```
;Qbe.sc
;Use Paradox Query-by-Example to let users
;make ad-hoc queries. Allows the following keys:
;Check, Checkplus, Examples, adding tables, and
;selection criteria. Queries limited to one line
;per table.
;This method does not work with Paradox Runtime.

PROC Qbe()
PRIVATE
        Ans,        ;User keypress for messages
        Ntbl,       ;Name of additional table
        Procname,   ;Procedure name
        Tblname     ;Name of first selected table

Procname = "Qbe"

CLEAR
;Select a table to query from working directory
SHOWTABLES
  ""
  "Highlight table to query and press Enter or Esc to quit"
TO Tblname
;Check for Esc, exit if pressed
IF NOT Retval THEN
  CLEARALL
  RETURN
ENDIF

;Clear pulldown menu
SHOWPULLDOWN
ENDMENU

;Load query form on workspace
Menu {Ask} SELECT Tblname

;Enter selection criteria
WHILE True
  ;Remove old messages
  MESSAGE ""
  WAIT RECORD
```

```
    PROMPT "F2-Query, Esc-quit, F6-_, Alt/F6-_+, "+
           "F3-Down, F4-Up, F5-Example, F10-Pick"
  UNTIL "F2","Esc","Check","CheckPlus","F10",
        "UpImage","DownImage","Example","Dos","DosBig"

SWITCH
  ;Process query
  CASE Retval = "F2" :
    DO_IT!
    ;Check window for Paradox error message if
    ; query misformed
    IF WINDOW() <> "" THEN
      MESSAGE WINDOW()," - Press any key"
      Ans = GETCHAR()
      MESSAGE ""
      LOOP
  ENDIF

    ;Check for empty Answer table
    IF ISEMPTY("Answer") THEN
      MESSAGE "No records fit your criteria.."
      SLEEP 1500
      MESSAGE ""
      MOVETO Tblname
      LOOP
    ENDIF

    ;View Answer table if matches found
    WHILE True
      WAIT TABLE
        PROMPT "F2 - Finish looking"
      UNTIL "F2","Dos","DosBig"
      IF Retval = "F2" THEN
        QUITLOOP
      ENDIF
    ENDWHILE
    ;Return to query form
    CLEARIMAGE
    MOVETO Tblname


    ;Done with queries
    CASE Retval = "Esc":
      QUITLOOP

    ;Pass special keys to Paradox
    CASE Retval = "Check" OR
         Retval = "CheckPlus" OR Retval = "Example" OR
```

```
          Retval = "UpImage" OR Retval = "DownImage":
        KEYPRESS Retval

      ;Add another table from working directory
      CASE Retval = "F10":
        SHOWTABLES
          ""
          "Highlight table to query and press Enter "+
            "or Esc to quit"
        TO Ntbl
        IF Retval THEN
          Menu {Ask} SELECT Ntbl
        ENDIF

  ENDSWITCH
ENDWHILE
CLEARALL
ENDPROC
```

Program 5-11. *Query-by-Example*

Query-by-Form

If you must use Paradox Runtime or if your users do not like Query-by-Example, you can design your own query form. It allows users to enter selection criteria for a single table on a form you design with the Paradox form editor.

You must create a dummy table for each table you want to query. It contains the same fields as the original, but all are alphanumeric with a length of 30 to 40 characters. The type change is necessary because selection criteria may include characters such as ">". Next you build a form for the dummy table using the Paradox form editor. You need not include all fields, only the ones users need to query.

Program 5-12 is a procedure that accepts the names of the real and dummy tables along with the query form number for the dummy. It loads the form, and the user enters selection criteria into a single record in the dummy table.

When the user presses F2 to process the query, the routine saves the selection criteria in an array. It loads the query form for the real table and copies the array to it. If there is a syntax error, it provides a message and redisplays the selection form for the user to correct. The Answer table includes all fields for matching records.

For example, the following call applies Program 5-12 (Formqry) to a Customer table. Formcust is the dummy table used with form 1.

```
Formqry("Customer","Formcust",1)
```

```
;Formqry.sc
;Create a query for a single table using a custom form.
;The real table is Tblname, dummy table is Tblform, and
;form number is Frm. The dummy table must have the same
;fields in the same order as the original table.

PROC FormQry(Tblname,Tblform,Frm)
PRIVATE
        Ans,          ;User keypress to end message
        Badselect,    ;Switch indicating whether
                      ; selection conditions are Ok
        Ctr,          ;Loop counter to transfer fields
        Procname,     ;Procedure name
        Pview         ;Array of selection criteria

PROCNAME = "FormQry"

;Clear pulldown menu
SHOWPULLDOWN
ENDMENU

;Start with empty query table
EMPTY TblForm
WHILE TRUE
  ;Assume user will enter selection correctly
  Badselect = False
  EDIT TblForm
  PICKFORM Frm
  ;Maximize window
  WINMAX
  WAIT RECORD
    PROMPT "F2 - Do Query,  Esc - Finished Queries"
  UNTIL "F2","Esc","Dos","DosBig"

SWITCH
  ;Process query
  CASE Retval = "F2":
    ;Save selection criteria in an array and
```

```
; clear dummy table
COPYTOARRAY Pview
DO_IT!
CLEARALL

;Load query form for real table
Menu {Ask} SELECT Tblname
CHECK

;Copy criteria from array to real query
; form for table. Check whether query
; is formed correctly by checking Paradox
; window for messages
FOR Ctr FROM 1 TO NFIELDS(Tblname)
  RIGHT
  IF WINDOW() <> "" THEN
    MESSAGE WINDOW()," - press any key to correct"
    Ans = GETCHAR()
    MESSAGE ""
    ;Clear query form for real table because
    ; there is a problem
    CLEARIMAGE
    Badselect = True
    QUITLOOP
  ENDIF

  ;Erase this column of query form
  ; and enter new condition
  CTRLBACKSPACE TYPEIN Pview[Ctr+1]
ENDFOR
IF Badselect THEN
  LOOP
ENDIF
MESSAGE "Processing Query..."
DO_IT!

;Check whether matching records found and
; display them
MESSAGE ""
IF ISEMPTY("Answer") THEN
  MESSAGE "No records fit your criteria..."
  SLEEP 1500
  MESSAGE ""
  LOOP
ELSE
  WAIT TABLE
    PROMPT "F2 - Finish Looking"
  UNTIL "F2","Dos","DosBig"
```

```
      LOOP
    ENDIF

  CASE Retval = "Esc":
    DO_IT!
    ;Do not leave an Answer table. System may
    ; check its status for other functions
    IF ISTABLE("Answer") THEN
      DELETE "Answer"
    ENDIF
    QUITLOOP
  ENDSWITCH
ENDWHILE
CLEARALL
ENDPROC
```

Program 5-12. *Query-by-Form*

Example Maintenance and Query System

A typical application includes table maintenance and query options. Program 5-13 controls a customer system with these choices. It assumes Tblmaint (Program 5-9), Qbe (Program 5-11), and Formqry (Program 5-12) are in a Utility library.

```
;Menu.sc
;Controlling menu for a Customer system with table
;maintenance and query options

;Clear workspace and canvas
RESET
CLEAR

;Declare autolib path Paradox will
; search for called procedure
Autolib = "Utility"

WHILE True
  CLEAR
  PAINTCANVAS ATTRIBUTE 31 0,0,24,79
```

```
  ;Display system menu
  SHOWPOPUP "Customer System" CENTERED
   "Maintenance"       : "Customer Maintenance" : "MaintTag",
   "Query-by-Example"  : "Query by Example"     : "QbeTag",
   "Query-by-Form"     : "Query by Form"        : "FormTag",
   "Return"            : "Return to DOS"        : "ReturnTag"

  ENDMENU
  TO Mchoice

  ;Process user request
  SWITCH
    CASE Mchoice = "MaintTag":
      Tblmaint("Customer",1,"Cust Id")
    CASE Mchoice = "QbeTag":
      Qbe()
    CASE Mchoice = "FormTag":
      Formqry("Customer","Formcust",1)
  OTHERWISE:
    QUIT
  ENDSWITCH
ENDWHILE
```

Program 5-13. *Controlling Menu for Customer System*

CheckPoint 5-5. Adding Menu Help

Objective: Revise Program 5-13 to add help using the F1 key. Display help text in a canvas window.

Hint: Use the KEYTO option of SHOWPOPUP to hide the F1 key. If the user presses it, create a canvas window and display help text. You might want to use GETCHAR to freeze the screen until the user presses any key to end help. Remember to close the window before looping back to redisplay the menu.

How to DO_IT!

Paradox calls the event procedure in a SHOWDIALOG command when something in the event list occurs. Events include keys such as "F2" and triggers such as departing or selecting a list member.

Paradox passes four arguments to the procedure: trigger type, tag value, event value, and element value. Trigger is the forcing action. For example, if a user clicks on an item in a pick list, the trigger is "UPDATE".

Tag value contains the expression TAG for the control element. Event value and element value are usually null. The major exception is that event value contains the index of the selected item if the control element is PICKARRAY.

Figure 5-9 shows a pick list of report names stored in an array. PAL executes the dialog procedure when a user selects a report and presses Info. The program then displays a popup box of additional report information. It remains until the user selects another report or accepts or cancels the dialog box. The Dialogproc procedure in Program 5-14 uses the index of the report name to locate corresponding text in another array, then displays it.

The program loads both arrays from a table to make the procedure more generic. You can add reports to the list simply by editing table Rpttbl without changing any code. This simplifies maintenance and reduces the likelihood of introducing errors.

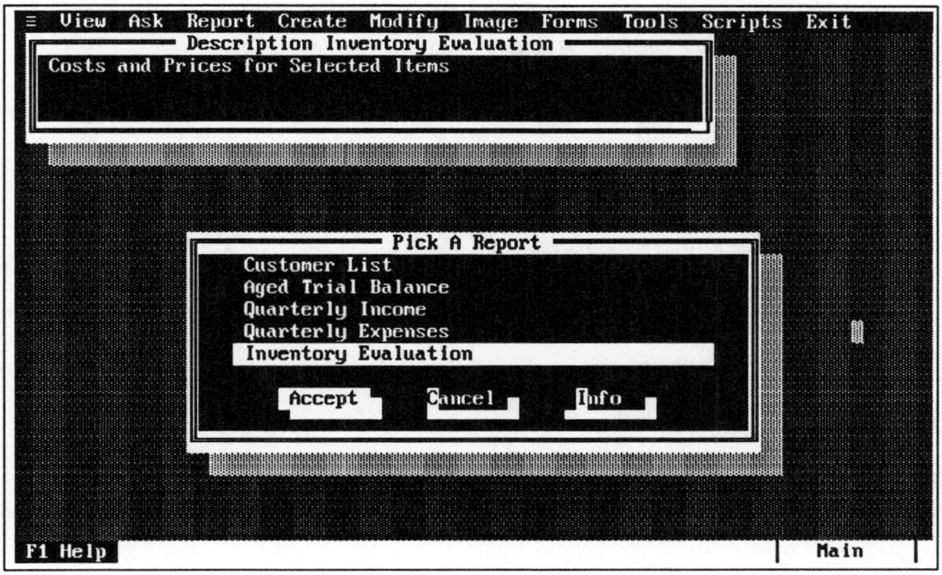

Figure 5-9. Pick list of report names with help text.

```
;Showar.sc
;Display a dialog box of array elements
;Return selected element or "" if no selection
;Display the corresponding text field if
;user clicks on Info box

PROC DialogProc(TriggerType,TagValue,EventValue,ElementValue)

;Close old description window, if open
IF ISASSIGNED(Textwindow) AND
    ISWINDOW(Textwindow) THEN
  WINDOW CLOSE
ENDIF

;If user moved highlight bar, get new array position
IF TriggerType = "UPDATE" THEN
  Choice = EventValue
  RETURN True
ENDIF
```

```
;If user picked Info button, display text
IF TriggerType = "DEPART" AND
   EventValue = "Info" THEN
     ;Create a canvas window to display text
     ;Float window to display above everything else
     DYNARRAY Atts[]
     Atts["TITLE"] = "Description " + Rptarray[Choice]
     Atts["FLOATING"] = True
     Atts["CANCLOSE"] = False
     Atts["CANMAXIMIZE"] = False
     WINDOW CREATE ATTRIBUTES Atts
       @ 1,1 HEIGHT 5 WIDTH 60 TO Textwindow
     @ 0,1 ?? Rpttext[Choice]
     RETURN False
ENDIF

RETURN True
ENDPROC

;Load report and description arrays
; from a table
Nrecs = NRECORDS("Rpttbl")
ARRAY Rptarray[Nrecs]
ARRAY Rpttext[Nrecs]
VIEW "Rpttbl"
Ctr = 0
SCAN
  Ctr = Ctr + 1
  Rptarray[Ctr] = [Rptname]
  Rpttext[Ctr]  = [Rpttext]
ENDSCAN
CLEARIMAGE

;Assume highlight is on first array element
Choice = 1
Rept = ""
SHOWDIALOG "Pick a Report"
  PROC "DialogProc"
  ;UPDATE trigger occurs when user moves highlight
  ;DEPART trigger occurs when user picks Info button
  TRIGGER "UPDATE","DEPART"
  @ 10,15 HEIGHT 10 WIDTH 50

  ;Show report array in dialog box with Accept,
  ; Cancel and Info buttons. Pressing Info
  ; displays help popup.
  PICKARRAY
    @ 0,3
```

```
      HEIGHT 5
      WIDTH 42
      Rptarray
      TAG "Pickar"
      TO Rept

   PUSHBUTTON @ 6,6 WIDTH 10
      "~A~ccept"
      OK
      DEFAULT
      VALUE "OK"
      TAG "Yes"
      TO Button

   PUSHBUTTON @ 6,18 WIDTH 10
      "~C~ancel"
      CANCEL
      VALUE "CANCEL"
      TAG "No"
      TO Button

   PUSHBUTTON @ 6,30 WIDTH 10
      "~I~nfo"
      OK
      VALUE "INFO"
      TAG "Info"
      TO Button
ENDDIALOG

IF Retval THEN
   MESSAGE "Print "+ Rptarray[Rept]
ELSE
   MESSAGE "No report selected!"
ENDIF
SLEEP 1500
MESSAGE ""
```

Program 5-14. *Display Help Text for Info Pushbutton*

The dialog procedure tests the handle to determine if the window exists and is open. If so, Paradox closes it.

If the user moves the highlight bar, the procedure stores the new array position in variable Choice.

If the user selects the Info pushbutton, the procedure creates a dynamic array and changes the title to match the report name. It also sets the window attribute "FLOATING" to True to display the help text on top of all other windows. Think of this as floating the new window to the top of the heap. The procedure displays help text in the floating window.

Dialog procedures must return True or False. True tells Paradox to process the event normally, False denies it and control returns to the original element. Dialogproc returns False when the user selects the Info button. In practice, this means the user sees the same dialog box at the end of the procedure as before. The process resembles returning the cursor to a field after the user presses F1 for help.

Summary

As application director, you control what appears on the Paradox stage. Remember—the director takes the blame, but the performers get the credit. This chapter presented a summary of commands to control canvas and workspace windows, along with examples of common techniques such as providing access to the Paradox report and Query-by-Example facilities. If users prefer, you can create custom forms and provide query features with Query-by-Form instead.

We presented two variations on the WAIT command to let users perform table maintenance. The single table maintenance procedure is keypress-driven and includes the ability to add, edit, delete, and search for records. You can use it as a starting point for applications. The program is network ready and performs locking as required to change and delete records.

We also showed an event-driven WAIT program to enter daily time cards. It trapped events DEPARTFIELD to test for duplicate date entries, and DEPARTROW to stop entry of unauthorized overtime hours.

The How to DO_IT! section showed how to add popup help for dialog box choices using the dialog procedure. Choices and help text are stored in a table to simplify maintenance.

Remember that the scenery and costumes (your interface) can be as important as the play itself! Nowadays, users have high expectations, and you must try to meet them with limited time and resources.

6

Error Proofing

The true test of maturity is not how old a person is but how he reacts to awakening in the mid-town area in his shorts.

—Woody Allen

Introduction

Shakespeare's melancholy Dane says, "Readiness is all". Today he might explain (with Polonius' help!) that error proofing consists of activities designed to protect users from themselves (or revengeful ghosts). You preserve system integrity by assuring that users enter correct data into appropriate tables to solve the current problem.

This chapter discusses four integrity issues: the limits of Paradox ValChecks (a fine name indeed, I must say!), assuring unique key values, preserving master and detail table relationships, and processing transactions.

It also describes such potential trouble spots in applications as system startup parameters, special key handling in menus and WAIT interactions, resource management, and queries.

Remember—users will make any error you can imagine, as well as others beyond the comprehension of any living being. As Mrs. Patrick Campbell said, "My dear, I don't care what they do, so long as they don't do it in the street and frighten the horses."

How to DO_IT!

This section presents a data dictionary procedure you can call during a WAIT interaction in table view to ensure referential integrity. Paradox checks master/detail table relationships on forms but not in table view.

System Integrity

A popular restaurant once advertised, "A roast beef sandwich with integrity." Most people thought it was a low-calorie substitute for mayonnaise. A system with integrity accepts only correct data and processes it according to rules defined by the user. It handles the four issues listed in Table 6-1.

Table 6-1. Integrity Issues

Issue	Definition
Concurrency	Assure correct transaction processing
Domain	Assure correct field type and values
Referential	Preserve master/detail table relationships
Table	Assure unique key values for records

Table Integrity

Paradox enforces table integrity by rejecting entries with duplicate key values. When a user enters a new key or changes one, you must check whether it is unique before posting the record.

If you post a duplicate key in Coedit mode, Paradox displays the Alt-L/Alt-K message on the workspace. You will get a script error or an unexpected result unless you test for the error message and force the user to confirm the new key or fix the problem.

Program 6-1 lets a user insert a new customer record. It posts the record to the table by trying to lock it. If this works, the new key is unique; if not, it is probably a duplicate. The user must change the value or delete the record.

```
;Insert.sc
;Insert new Customer record and check for duplicate key

;Remove pulldown
SHOWPULLDOWN
ENDMENU

COEDIT "Customer"
PICKFORM 1
;Maximize window to fill screen
WINMAX
WHILE True
  WAIT RECORD
    PROMPT "F2-Finish, Ins-Insert new record"
  UNTIL "F2","Ins","Dos","DosBig"
  SWITCH
    CASE Retval = "F2":
      QUITLOOP
    CASE Retval = "Ins":
      INS
      ;Use Savekey to test whether user has
      ; changed key value
      Savekey = ""
      WHILE True
        WAIT RECORD
          PROMPT "F2-Save record, Esc-Cancel"
        UNTIL "F2","Esc","Dos","DosBig"
        SWITCH
          CASE Retval = "F2":
            ;Try to post record if key changed
            IF Savekey <> [Cust Id] THEN
              LOCKRECORD
              ;If lock succeeds, record posted
              IF Retval THEN
                 UNLOCKRECORD
                 QUITLOOP
              ELSE
                 MESSAGE "Duplicate key"
                 SLEEP 2000
                 MESSAGE ""
                 ;Save value for testing
                 Savekey = [Cust Id]
                 LOOP
              ENDIF
            ENDIF
```

```
          ;Abandon record
          CASE Retval = "Esc":
            DEL
            QUITLOOP
        ENDSWITCH
      ENDWHILE
  ENDSWITCH
ENDWHILE
DO_IT!
CLEARALL
```

Program 6-1. *Check for Duplicate Key*

If the user enters a duplicate key in Edit mode, Paradox replaces the old record with the new one *with no warning* when he or she presses F2 to finish.

In DataEntry mode, Paradox puts records with duplicate keys in a KeyViol table. You must test for it and let the user edit its records before adding them to the main table explicitly.

Tip

Use Coedit mode instead of Edit or DataEntry even on single-user systems. In it, Paradox catches key violations when they occur, so they are easier to fix. Do not use Edit mode in which Paradox simply replaces old records with new ones when duplicate keys occur.

Referential Integrity

Paradox enforces referential integrity with multi-table forms. For example, suppose you have a form that shows a master customer record and includes an embedded form for orders. If you try to delete the customer record, Paradox stops you with a message about linked details.

You must delete all associated orders before you can delete the master record. However, because Paradox enforces integrity only through forms, you can delete the same Customer record in table view. Think of the problems this can create if you lose a customer because of competition, merger, bankruptcy, divestiture, shutdown, loss of credit, disagreement over terms, or other issues.

The How to DO_IT! section presents a data dictionary solution that preserves referential integrity during WAIT interactions in table view.

Concurrency Integrity

You assure concurrency by completing all parts of a transaction. For example, say I transfer money by telephone between bank accounts. If I ask the bank to move $100 from savings to checking, I assume they withdraw it from one account and deposit it in the other.

What happens if the bank is currently printing statements and the program locks my checking account records? The $100 is removed from my savings but never put in my checking account. Who knows, maybe it will allow my bank to stay solvent for another day!

You must lock all tables and records involved in a transaction. If all locks succeed, the transaction (barring natural disaster) will complete. In the bank example, you place prevent write locks on the checking and savings account tables to ensure that you can Coedit them. You lock the specific records so you can change their contents.

Program 6-2 shows the locking sequence for the bank transfer transaction. It assumes that you have the requested amount in your savings account—or a forgiving bank. Of course, a bank is unlikely to be forgiving about $100, but if you are overdrawn by $100 million, they will probably look the other way!

```
;Concurr.sc
;Transfers money from customer's savings to checking
;account if all locks succeed.

;Remove pulldown
SHOWPULLDOWN
ENDMENU

;Get account number and amount to transfer
@ 2,1 ?? "Enter Account Number ==>"
ACCEPT "A6" TO Account_Num
@ 3,1 ?? "Enter Amount ==>"
ACCEPT "$" TO Transfer_Amount
```

```
;Put prevent write lock on savings and checking tables
LOCK "Checking" PWL, "Savings" PWL
;If table locks succeed, lock records in both tables
IF Retval THEN
  VIEW "Savings"
  COEDIT "Checking"
  MOVETO [Account]
  LOCATE Account_Num
  LOCKRECORD
  ;If checking locked, try to lock savings
  IF Retval THEN
    MOVETO "Savings"
    MOVETO [Account]
    LOCATE Account_Num
    LOCKRECORD
    ;Transfer if both records locked
    IF Retval THEN
      [S_Balance] = [S_Balance] - Transfer_Amount
      MOVETO "Checking"
      [C_Balance] = [C_Balance] + Transfer_Amount
      UNLOCKRECORD
      MOVETO "Savings"
      UNLOCKRECORD
    ELSE
      ;Unlock checking record
      MOVETO "Checking"
      UNLOCKRECORD
      MESSAGE "Could not lock savings record"
      SLEEP 2000
      MESSAGE ""
    ENDIF
  ELSE
    MESSAGE "Could not lock checking record"
    SLEEP 2000
    MESSAGE ""
  ENDIF
  ;Unlock tables
  UNLOCK "Checking" PWL, "Savings" PWL
  DO_IT!
  CLEARALL
ELSE
  MESSAGE "Could not lock savings and checking tables"
  SLEEP 2000
ENDIF
```

***Program 6-2.** Concurrent Checking and Savings Transaction*

Domain Integrity

You select a Paradox data type for each field when creating a table. Paradox enforces type checking during all table operations. You cannot, for example, enter a date in a numeric field. Each field may also have a domain or set of legal values for entries. It may be discrete (countable) such as the months of the year, or continuous such as a credit limit range of $0.00 to $9999.99. You establish the legal domains for all fields and use Paradox ValChecks to define them.

Paradox must be in Edit mode for you to define ValChecks (or DataEntry with exclusive use). It puts a full lock on tables in Edit mode so users cannot enter values while you are changing domains!

The ValCheck choices are LowValue, HighValue, Default, TableLookup, Picture, Required, and Auto.

> **Warning**
>
> Paradox uses ValChecks to verify new data, but what is already in the table may not conform. If you never reedit the fields, tables may contain invalid entries.

> **Warning**
>
> Write PAL scripts to check tables for valid data before using Insert queries or Adding tables. Paradox does not enforce ValChecks during these operations.

ValChecks are part of a table family; they cannot stand alone. Paradox synchronizes family members with a date/time stamp in their header records that must match the one in the table header. If Paradox detects that a family member is out of synchronization, it labels the table as corrupt or obsolete and cannot read it. You can corrupt ValChecks and other family members by doing an incremental backup or by making changes from DOS rather than in Paradox. It is so incredibly easy to break up a family these days!

> **Tip**
>
> Use the Paradox COPY command for a single table or a backup program for an entire directory to avoid corrupting tables. To avoid corrupting ValChecks, do not change tables from DOS or make partial backups.

ValChecks are useful, but they have the following limitations.

The LowValue, HighValue, and Default options are independent. For example, you can accidentally enter a LowValue of 100, a HighValue of 10, and a Default of 500. You will then never be able to enter anything into the field until you change the ValChecks. It is like a special fare available only to those who are both under 12 and over 65 years old.

If the ValChecks are obsolete, any lookup tables you defined will not be available for help. Even locking them before Coediting the main table does not assure that they are good. Paradox lets you lock nonexistent and damaged tables!

Paradox enforces lookup integrity in only one direction. It forces users to enter values in the table, but does not stop you from deleting or restructuring the table itself.

You can put a password on a lookup table (Paradox encrypts it). Then, unless you include the PASSWORD command in your procedures, you cannot use it. It is protected completely, like a safe with the combination locked inside.

You cannot use lookup tables with multiple fields. Strangely, you can define the connection and use it during the current Edit session. The next time you use the table, however, the lookup is invalid. The rules apply only after the fact!

You can use Picture ValChecks to define how the data should appear in the main table. For example, Paradox converts a last name to all uppercase if its picture is *!. However, the ACCEPT command does not enforce ValCheck pictures. For example,

```
ACCEPT "A20" TO [Lname]
```

accepts whatever the user enters, regardless of any pictures defined. You must add a matching picture clause as in

```
ACCEPT "A20" PICTURE "*!" TO [Lname]
```

You can also override the picture by specifying a lookup table, as lookup values supersede pictures. Paradox lets you define a picture longer than the field width and then stops you from entering data.

Even with all these strange limitations, ValChecks are still helpful. But you must use them carefully.

Anticipating Problems

In programming, the best offense is a good defense. There are always precautions you can take to handle unpredictable conditions such as off-line printers and open disk drive doors. Trouble spots include the application startup environment, the Escape key, WAIT interactions, unavailable or inadequate resources, and query problems.

Startup Environment

Since users may have a variety of machines, memory resident programs, and network software, you should always check whether there is enough memory for your application. The following example uses the MEMLEFT function in the startup script to test whether 100K of RAM is available.

```
IF MEMLEFT() < 100000 THEN
  MESSAGE "You must have at least 100K to start"
  SLEEP 3000
  EXIT
ENDIF
```

You can use the Paradox custom script to set system defaults. However, they may not be what you expect when your application begins. The two configuration options that cause the most trouble are QueryOrder and Blank=Zero.

You can set QueryOrder to Table or Image Order. In Table Order, Paradox keeps Answer table fields in the same order as the table structure even if the user rotated them before pressing F2 to perform a query.

Paradox produces a rotated Answer table if the configuration is set to Image Order and the user presses Ctrl-R before DO_IT! If you count on copying a master table report to the Answer table, you may get incompatible structures with an Image Order setting.

Programs can check the setting and change it, but they should restore the original value afterward. The following example changes the environment to Table Order for processing, then sets it back.

```
;Save original order
Save_Order = QUERYORDER()

;Make sure query order is Table Order
SETQUERYORDER TABLEORDER

** Program **

;Restore original order
IF Save_Order = "ImageOrder" THEN
  SETQUERYORDER IMAGEORDER
ELSE
  SETQUERYORDER TABLEORDER
ENDIF
```

Blank=Zero is the other configuration option that can affect how your application operates. By default, Paradox considers a blank numeric field as valid. In the following example, the result is zero if either field is blank. If the custom configuration does not treat blanks as zeros, it causes a script error.

```
Extension = [Price] * [Qty]
```

You cannot change the setting from your program, but you can test it at system startup as follows:

```
IF NOT ISBLANKZERO() THEN
  MESSAGE "Paradox must be configured for Blank=Zero"
  SLEEP 3000
  EXIT
ENDIF
```

Checking for Escape

The user can escape from any SHOW or ACCEPT command rather than selecting or entering a value. The next example repeatedly ACCEPTs a record key and calls a lookup procedure until the user presses Esc to quit. ACCEPT sets Retval to True if the user enters a value and False if he or she presses Esc.

```
WHILE True
  @ 1,0 CLEAR EOL
  @ 1,0 ?? "Enter search key ==>"
```

```
  ACCEPT "A6" TO Custid
  IF NOT Retval
    QUITLOOP
  ELSE
    Lookup_Cust(Custid)
  ENDIF
ENDWHILE
```

If the user presses Esc during a SHOW command, the option is "Esc" and Retval is False. In the following example, Paradox returns control to DOS if the user presses Esc to leave a menu.

```
WHILE True
  SHOWMENU
        "Maint"    : "Customer Maintenance",
        "Reports"  : "Print Reports"
  TO Moption
  SWITCH
    CASE Moption = "Maint":
      Maint()
    CASE Moption = "Reports":
      Reports()
    CASE Moption = "Esc":
      EXIT
  ENDSWITCH
ENDWHILE
```

WAITing for Trouble

WAIT commands allow the user full access to all Paradox table editing keys. Usually you must control which ones are active. In a keypress WAIT, you disable keys by including them in the UNTIL clause and not processing them. For example, Ctrl-O (Dos) and Alt-O (DosBig) transfer control to a DOS shell. There is no configuration setting to turn them off, so you must always trap them. In the following example, the user views a Customer table until he or she presses F2. Pressing Ctrl-O or Alt-O causes a loop so the user keeps viewing the table.

```
VIEW "Customer"
WHILE True
  WAIT TABLE
    PROMPT "Press F2 to finish viewing"
  UNTIL "F2","Dos","DosBig"
  IF Retval = "F2" THEN
    QUITLOOP
```

```
    ENDIF
  ENDWHILE
  CLEARALL
```

When Coediting a keyed table with WAIT, you should disable LockKey (Ctrl-L). Otherwise, if the user causes a violation by adding a new record with a duplicate key or changing a key to match an existing one, pressing Ctrl-L replaces the old record with the new one. The old one is lost forever.

When viewing a table with WAIT, if query order is ImageOrder, you should trap Ctrl-R. If the user rotates columns and later performs a query, the Answer table will have its columns in unpredictable order. If you try to copy a master table report to it, the structures will be incompatible.

The last problem key in a WAIT is Zoom. Suppose a user presses Ctrl-Z, starts entering a search value, and then accidentally presses a key in the UNTIL clause. The result is to drop out of the WAIT immediately. The user is no longer zooming; Paradox begins executing the logic for the new key!

To allow searching, trap the key and use LOCATE instead. In Program 6-3, the user views a table until he or she presses F2 to finish or Ctrl-Z to search for a table value. It uses LOCATE to search so the program cannot drop out of the WAIT unexpectedly. A further benefit is that LOCATE sets Retval to True if it finds the record and False otherwise. Zoom does not set Retval.

```
;Waitsrch.sc
;Trap Ctrl-Z in a keypress WAIT to search for a value.
;Accept value to search for and use LOCATE to find it.

;Remove pulldown
SHOWPULLDOWN
ENDMENU

VIEW "Customer"
WHILE True
  WAIT TABLE
    PROMPT "F2-finish viewing, Ctrl-Z to search"
  UNTIL "F2","Zoom","Dos","DosBig"
  SWITCH
```

```
    CASE Retval = "F2":
      QUITLOOP
    CASE Retval = "Zoom":
      ;Get search value from user
      @ 23,0 CLEAR EOL
      @ 23,0 ?? "Value: "
      ;Find data type of current field
      Fldtype = FIELDTYPE()
      ACCEPT Fldtype TO Searchkey
      ;Stop searching if user pressed Esc
      IF NOT Retval THEN
        LOOP
      ENDIF
      ;Look for matching record
      LOCATE Searchkey
      ;If found, cursor on new record and
      ; Retval is True
      IF NOT Retval THEN
        MESSAGE "No matching record"
        SLEEP 2000
        MESSAGE ""
      ENDIF
  ENDSWITCH
ENDWHILE
CLEARALL
```

Program 6-3. *Trap Zoom Key and Search for Value*

It's Eight O'clock. Do You Know Where Your Resources Are?

My grandfather always wore both a belt and suspenders because he never trusted either alone to hold his pants up. (He was a substantial gentleman). I never trust that the objects I need are available, and I always suspect there are ones around that I do not want. The following program ensures that an Answer table has records before displaying it to the user.

```
IF ISEMPTY("Answer") THEN
  MESSAGE "There are no records to view"
  SLEEP 2000
  MESSAGE ""
ELSE
  WHILE True
    WAIT TABLE
```

```
        PROMPT "Press F2 to finish viewing"
      UNTIL "F2","Dos","DosBig"
      IF Retval = "F2" THEN
        QUITLOOP
      ENDIF
    ENDWHILE
  ENDIF
```

If you use Paradox keypress commands to copy objects, you may generate an additional Cancel/Replace menu. You must select Replace to continue the copy or Cancel to stop it. The following example copies report 1 from the Customer table to the Answer table. If Answer already has a report 1, Paradox displays the confirmation menu.

```
{Tools} {Copy} {Report} {DifferentTable} {Customer}
  {1} {Answer} {1}
;If Answer has report 1, ask for confirmation
IF MENUCHOICE() = "Cancel" THEN
  MESSAGE "Report exists - overwrite it? (Y/N)"
  Ans = GETCHAR()
  ;Check for y (ASCII 89) and Y (ASCII 121)
  IF Ans = 89 OR Ans = 121 THEN
    {Replace}
  ELSE
    {Cancel}
  ENDIF
ENDIF
CLEARALL
```

Abbreviated menu commands are a powerful Paradox shortcut. The following command copies report 1 from Customer to Answer without asking for confirmation.

```
COPYREPORT "Customer" "1" "Answer" "1"
```

Paradox will present conditional menus during Import/Export operations if tables or files already exist. It also presents them when you Create or Restructure if problems or KeyViol tables exist.

Trapping Query Errors

You cannot live with users and you cannot live without them. We could create great systems if users were either not involved or behaved properly. But people are constantly finding new and inventive ways to put a wrench (or spanner) in the works and you must watch them vigilantly.

I like to let users build queries on-the-fly with either Query-by-Example (if they have a full Paradox system) or Query-by-Form (if they have only a Runtime version). In either case, they can build queries that do not work. For example, a common problem is using AND in a single query field instead of a comma (>65 AND <99 should be >65,<99). No wonder this confuses users! Because Paradox displays error messages on the workspace, not on the canvas, they do not see the problem.

Programs 5-11 (Query-by-Example) and Program 5-12 (Query-by-Form) both check WINDOW when the user presses F2 to perform a query. If there is a problem, they display the Paradox error message and force the user to correct the query.

How to DO_IT!

This section shows how to create a data dictionary you can use to enforce referential integrity without Paradox forms.

Using a Data Dictionary

Paradox enforces referential integrity only through forms. That is, you cannot delete a master record with logically linked details in form view, but you can in table view.

A data dictionary is a good solution to this problem because it works in both views. It is a table of table names, the tables they logically link to, and the linking key field for each relationship. Think of it as the database equivalent of some years ago's bestseller, *The Book of Lists*, a list of all the major lists in existence. When the user presses Del in a WAIT interaction, you use the dictionary to check for linked detail records.

For example, assume the following structure for a Customer table in an order entry system:

```
Customer ┬─Field Name ─┬─ Field Type
         │ Cust Id     │  N*
         │ Name        │  A30
         │ Address     │  A30
```

A customer may have open orders for unshipped items and open invoices for ones shipped but unpaid. Both detail tables are linked logically to the

Customer table by the customer id. Here are the structures of the Order and Invoice tables.

Order	Field Name	Field Type
	C_Id	N*
	Order No	N*
	Date	D
	Amount	$

Invoice	Field Name	Field Type
	Cust	N*
	Invoice No	N*
	Date	D
	Total	$

The C_Id field in Order and the Cust field in Invoice match Cust Id in the Customer table. The data dictionary will contain two records, one for each relation. Here is its structure and entries for the tables.

Datadict	Field Name	Field Type
	Master	A8*
	Linked	A8*
	Keyname	A10

Datadict	Master	Linked	Keyname
	Customer	Order	C_Id
	Customer	Invoic	Cust

Master is the master table, Linked is the logically linked one, and Keyname is the linking key field. Program 6-4 coedits the Customer table in table view and traps the Del key. It passes the table name and key field to a data dictionary procedure (Program 6-5). Check_Del returns True if the record can be deleted, False if it cannot because of linked records.

```
;Delcust.sc
;Coedit customer table and trap Del key.
;Check data dictionary for logically linked
;tables with detail records.
;If there are any, do not allow deletion.

;Remove pulldown menu
SHOWPULLDOWN
ENDMENU

;Data dictionary table must be on workspace
VIEW "Datadict"

COEDIT "Customer"
WHILE True
  WAIT TABLE
    PROMPT "F2 - Finish, Del - Delete"
  UNTIL "F2","Del","Dos","DosBig"

  SWITCH
    CASE Retval = "F2" :
      QUITLOOP

    CASE Retval = "Del" :
      ;Save current table name, field, and value
      Save_tbl = TABLE()
      Save_fld = FIELD()
      Keyfld = [Cust Id]
      Key_Name = "Cust Id"

      ;Close table and use dictionary to
      ; check if delete is allowed
      DO_IT!
      Ok = Check_Del(Save_tbl,Keyfld)

      ;Restore cursor to original table and record.
      ;The record may no longer exist so check
      ; if still available
      MOVETO Save_tbl
      COEDITKEY
      MOVETO FIELD Key_Name
      LOCATE Keyfld
      IF NOT Retval THEN
        MESSAGE "Record no longer in table!"
        SLEEP 1500
        MESSAGE ""
```

```
        LOOP
      ELSE
        MOVETO FIELD Save_fld
      ENDIF

      ;If delete allowed, lock record and proceed
      IF Ok THEN
        LOCKRECORD
        IF Retval THEN
          DEL
        ENDIF
      ENDIF
  ENDSWITCH
ENDWHILE
DO_IT!
CLEARALL
```

***Program 6-4.** Coedit Customer Table with Data Dictionary*

```
;CheckDel.sc
;Accepts a table name and table key value. Looks up table
;in data dictionary and checks for linked records.
;Returns True if master record has no linked records
;and False otherwise.
;Data dictionary table must already be on workspace

PROC Check_Del(Tbl,Tblval)
PRIVATE
        Ctlinked,     ;Count number of linked tables
                      ; with records
        Ctr,          ;Count number of linked tables
        Keys,         ;Array of linked key names
        Lnk,          ;Array of linked table names
        Procname,     ;Procedure name
        Tblct         ;Loop control to check for linked tables

Procname = "Check_Del"

;Allow up to 50 linked tables
ARRAY Lnk[50]
ARRAY Keys[50]
Ctr = 0
Ctlinked = 0
```

```
;Create list of linked tables and keys
; using Data Dictionary table
MOVETO "Datadict"
MOVETO FIELD "Master"
LOCATE Tbl                   ;Locate table
WHILE Retval                 ;It may appear more than once
  Ctr = Ctr + 1
  Lnk[Ctr] = [Linked]        ;Save linked table name
  Keys[Ctr] = [Keyname]      ;Save linked key name
  IF ATLAST() THEN
    Quitloop
  ENDIF
  DOWN
  LOCATE NEXT Tbl
ENDWHILE

;If no linked table, Ok to delete record
IF Ctr = 0 THEN
  RETURN True
ENDIF

;Count number of linked tables with detail records
FOR Tblct FROM 1 TO Ctr
  VIEW Lnk[Tblct]
  MOVETO FIELD Keys[Tblct]
  LOCATE Tblval
  IF Retval THEN
    Ctlinked = Ctlinked + 1
  ENDIF
  CLEARIMAGE
ENDFOR

;If there are linked tables with details,
; display a message and do not allow deletion
IF Ctlinked > 0 THEN
  MESSAGE "Linked records in " + STRVAL(Ctlinked) +
    " tables - No delete allowed"
  SLEEP 1500
  MESSAGE ""
  RETURN False
ELSE
  RETURN True
ENDIF
ENDPROC
```

Program 6-5. *Data Dictionary Procedure for Del Key*

CheckPoint 6-1. Data Dictionary

Objective: Revise Program 6-4 (Delcust.sc) to use an event-driven WAIT command to trap the F2 and Del keys. Write an event handling procedure to process them. Refer to Program 5-10 for an example of event-driven WAIT interaction.

Summary

Arthur Bloch said that the first rule of acting is, "Whatever happens, look as if it were intended." I spend about half my programming time anticipating trouble. Most problems involve integrity issues, such as checking for unique key values, maintaining referential integrity, assuring correct transaction processing, and monitoring user entered data. The Paradox equivalent of conducting fire drills, checking smoke alarms, and performing fire inspections!

I must watch Paradox almost as much as I watch my users! It will not work as expected if the startup environment does not match program requirements. Paradox also processes the Esc key in SHOW and ACCEPT even though they do not include it. Other keys such as Alt-O, Ctrl-O, and Zoom can cause surprising results during WAIT interactions, so you must trap them in the UNTIL clause. You may have more tables than you expect (Problems and KeyViol) or conditional menus (Cancel/Replace) you did not anticipate. Lastly, users may rotate columns in queries, so COPY commands will not work.

Finally, this chapter presented a data dictionary procedure your programs can call during a WAIT interaction to enforce referential integrity.

If it's working, keep doing it.
If it's not working, stop doing it.
If you don't know what to do, don't do anything.

—Medical School Advice given to Dr. Melvin Konner

7

Multiuser Applications

A team effort is a lot of people doing what I say.

—Michael Winner, British Film Director

Introduction

A multiuser application allows several people to use Paradox objects such as tables and forms simultaneously. For example, in an order entry system, two clerks can be entering orders while another prints packing slips. The application must assure that everyone can do his or her job without interfering with others. It must also assure that the system accepts only valid data. For example, it cannot allow duplicate order numbers.

Multiuser systems are much more difficult to design than single user ones. You must keep your eyes, figuratively speaking, on everyone at once. If two customers could order the same item simultaneously, you must lock the inventory record for the first one, wait until the order is completed, and unlock it for the second one. How do you keep the second operator busy while he or she waits for the record to become available? You should at least display a message (and play some awful recorded music) so he or she will not press keys or turn the terminal off out of frustration!

A transaction can update several tables. You must lock all of them to assure completion. In the order entry system, a new order leads to an order header record in one table and multiple product records in another. The system also must update available inventory and customer year-to-date sales.

The accounting system would contain errors if an operator could create the order but then abandon the transaction before updating inventory and customer balances. You must design the system either to complete the entire transaction or to delete it all. The system must be decisive, not political!

This chapter explains the three types of Paradox directories and how to lay them out on network and local drives for a multiuser system. It also describes control files Paradox creates to manage concurrent use of objects in shared and private directories.

Paradox locks records and files automatically during some commands, but it does not provide enough security for transaction processing. We describe commands that invoke automatic locks and show how to program defensively to account for them. Explicit locks can assure maximum concurrent use and data integrity when automatic locking is insufficient.

This chapter also discusses testing methods and explains how to develop a test plan for special multiuser problems such as query restarts.

How to DO_IT!

Paradox puts group and write record locks on master and detail tables when a user coedits them on a multi-table form. In practice, thus, Paradox locks a master record and its associated detail records when a user starts to edit it.

This section presents the Tombstone Police Department's crime tracking system. It is a networked application that uses a multi-table form to coedit suspect and arrest information. It shows how to lock tables and records for maximum concurrent use. Of course, the criminals will surely counter with even faster and more sophisticated systems!

Setting Up Directories

Paradox allows three types of directories in a multiuser application: system, shared, and private. System files must be in a shared network directory, and all users must have read access to them.

Tip

If you cannot create a read-only directory on your network, use the DOS ATTRIB command to make Paradox system files read-only and thus avoid sharing violations as follows:

ATTRIB +R Paradox.*

You must place shared tables and their families in a shared network directory with read/write/create/delete access. Users need write/create privileges even if they cannot change objects; the reason is that Paradox creates and deletes files in the directory to control multiuser access. Users must also have at least read access to shared directories containing application scripts and libraries.

Each user must have a private directory located either on a network drive or on his or her local hard disk. (It cannot be on a floppy). Paradox stores temporary objects such as Answer tables there and needs space to sort and restructure tables. Other users cannot access objects in that directory. A side benefit is that you need not worry about locking them since Paradox hides them automatically. Outside Paradox, however, anyone with sufficient network privileges may access files in a private directory.

Do not build the private directory's name explicitly into applications, as it makes them too specific. Instead, always access it indirectly via the PRIVDIR function. For example, the following code displays a menu of the private directory's files.

```
SHOWFILES
  PRIVDIR()
  "Select a file or press Esc to exit"
TO Mytable
```

I use the private directory as a scratchpad where users can run a report with different sets of data. I attach the report specification to the master table in a shared directory. Users can run their own queries as long as they keep all table fields in the Answer table. I use tilde variables to substitute for selection criteria and copy the master report to the Answer table.

For example, Program 7-1 asks the user to enter a Zip Code and Paradox substitutes it for tilde variable Zipcode before running the query. If the Answer table is not empty, the program copies the master report to it and prints the result.

```
;Zipcopy.sc
;Ask user to enter a single Zip Code, then
;replace it in the query and get an Answer table.
;If there are selected records, copy Customer
;report to Answer table and print.


WHILE True
   ;Ask user to enter Zip Code
   CLEAR
   @ 1,0 ?? "Enter Zip Code or Esc to quit==>"
   ACCEPT "A5" PICTURE "#####" TO Zipcode
   ;If user presses Esc, leave program
   IF NOT Retval THEN
     QUITLOOP
   ENDIF


   ;Substitute value for tilde variable in
   ;query and execute
   Query

   Customer    | Cust Id     | Name    | Zip              |
               | Check       | Check   | Check ~Zipcode   |

   Endquery
   DO_IT!

   ;If Answer table has records, copy and print
   ;report
   IF ISEMPTY("Answer") THEN
     MESSAGE "No records for Zip Code " + Zipcode
     SLEEP 1500
     MESSAGE ""
     LOOP
   ENDIF

   COPYREPORT "Customer" "1" "Answer" "1"
   {Report} {Output} {Answer} {1} {Printer}
ENDWHILE
CLEARALL
```

Program 7-1. *Copy Shared Report to Answer Table*

Special Multiuser Control Files

Paradox uses three types of special files to control multiuser access to shared and private directories. They are configuration files, network control files, and object lock files.

Configuration Files

Paradox creates a custom configuration file, Paradox.CFG, when you run the Custom Configuration script. It contains default settings for each user, including the location of his or her private directory. You can store one copy of the configuration on the network or individual copies in the private directories of each user.

The advantage of having a network version is that all users will default to the same settings. This is especially important for ones such as TableOrder and Blank=Zero. For example, if the application totals entries in a quantity column and some are blank, Paradox creates a script error for the following SCAN command. It cannot add a blank value to a numeric unless Blank=Zero is Yes in the configuration.

```
Total = 0
SCAN
  Total = Total + [Quantity]
ENDSCAN
```

The network configuration file also has several disadvantages. First, all private directories must have the same name, at least to start the application. But how do you know where a particular user wants the directory or has room for it? Second, what happens if a user accidentally (surely not deliberately!) deletes the private directory from the hard drive, or is already using it for another program?

One solution is to specify the default private directory on the network and store Paradox.CFG there along with an Init script. Paradox executes that script, if it exists, before any other on the command line. Program 7-2 uses it to specify a private directory on the local drive (C or D) with the most space. If the directory does not exist, the program creates it.

```
;Init.sc
;Assign private directory to drive C or D, whichever
;has more space available. Set Autolib path and
;execute top level menu procedure

;Determine whether drive C or D has more space

Cbytes = 0
Dbytes = 0

IF DRIVESTATUS("C") THEN
  Cbytes = DRIVESPACE("C")
ENDIF

IF DRIVESTATUS("D") THEN
  Dbytes = DRIVESPACE("D")
ENDIF

;Assign private directory to C or D, whichever
;has more space. Create directory if it does
;not exist

;Leave Paradox if hard disk is full
IF Cbytes = 0 AND Dbytes = 0 THEN
  MESSAGE "Cannot establish private directory"
  SLEEP 2000
  EXIT
ENDIF

IF Cbytes > Dbytes THEN
  Dir = "C:\\Paradata"
ELSE
  Dir = "D:\\Paradata"
ENDIF

;Create directory if necessary
Havedir = DIREXISTS(Dir)
IF Havedir = 0 THEN
  RUN "MKDIR " + Dir
ENDIF
SETPRIVDIR(Dir)

;Change working directory for application
SETDIR("L:\\Acctsrec")
```

```
;Set Autolib path and call first menu
AUTOLIB = "L:\\Acctsrec\\Library"
Mainmenu()
```

Program 7-2. *Assign Private Directory with Init Script*

Network Control Files

Besides configuration files, Paradox uses special control files to track network users. Pdoxusrs.NET is a list of current users, containing their login names and network counts. Paradox assigns a sequential number to each person when he or she starts the program. You tell it where to create Pdoxusrs.NET during network installation.

> **Tip**
>
> Paradox uses a number rather than the Username to track users on the network. In practice, you can thus log in from different terminals at the same time. This is helpful when testing or debugging an application.

You can display a list of active users with Tools/Info/Who. When a user starts Paradox, the software tries to find Pdoxusrs.NET in the location designated by Paradox.SOM. Paradox creates Paradox.SOM during installation. Besides containing the network path, it also stores serial numbers. If Pdoxusrs.NET is not in the specified directory, Paradox creates it and adds entries for users as they log in. When they leave, Paradox removes their entries. The file is empty when the last user logs out, much like a house after the last child leaves home and the dog dies.

If the system fails while users are active, their entries stay in the NET file, reducing the number of available slots for others. The network administrator can restart Paradox and delete the NET file to clear it before allowing users to log back in. The number of available slots is based on the serial numbers entered during installation.

Other typical difficulties with NET files are:

- Paradox.SOM points to a nonexistent logical drive or directory. Paradox does not check if specified drives and directories exist during installation. Administrators should assign drives and create directories beforehand.
- Paradox.SOM points to an existing drive and directory, but the user lacks read/write access to it. Administrators must assign the correct access rights to Paradox users. Remember that they need write access to directories even if they do not change objects, as Paradox creates and deletes lock files there.
- A user cannot access network data from a locally installed copy of Paradox. The problem is that the user told Paradox during installation that he or she did not need to access shared data. The only solution is to either log on to a network copy of Paradox or reinstall the local copy to allow the option.
- A user cannot use shared tables to which he or she previously had access. Someone has made the working directory his or her private directory. That person will have to change private directories or log off. This can happen if you allow users into interactive Paradox as well as applications.

Tip

Avoid problems with private directories by forcing all users to start at an application menu that has an option for exiting to Paradox. They can enter interactive Paradox only if they have the password.

Lock Files

Paradox creates a Paradox.LCK file in each user's private directory at login. It blocks others from accessing objects there. Paradox also maintains another copy in the working directory to prevent users from making it private. The LCK file contains an entry for each user who has locked an object with the following information:

- User name
- User count
- Lock type (FL, WL, RL, PFL, etc.)

Each time a user locks an object, Paradox examines the NET file to get his or her name and the count for the entry. You can display lock information with Tools/Info/Lock/Tablename.

You cannot change information in LCK files directly. Activities in either interactive Paradox or PAL trigger actions there. Paradox knows a shared from a non-shared directory through Paradox.SOM and does not write LCK files to non-shared ones.

Paradox creates Pdoxusrs.LCK in each private and working directory to track individual users. It creates lock files to track users' table and record locks in those directories.

Paradox also creates a $PALMEM$ file in each private and working directory. It uses the file to store information about PAL variables and alphanumeric expressions longer than 255 characters.

Locking Tables and Records

You should follow two rules when writing multiuser systems. The first is to program defensively. Make sure all the tables and records you need to complete a transaction are available when you need them, not locked by other users. The second rule is to program inoffensively. Put as few restrictions on others as possible.

For example, if I need to Coedit a table, I can place a full lock on it to guarantee my right to insert records or change fields, but I also lock all other users out completely! They cannot even select the table from a menu. If I place a prevent write lock, I guarantee that I can Coedit but I allow others to Coedit too. Fortunately, being nice to others has its redeeming features. As Michael Frayn wrote, "[otherwise] you'd never know what a relief it was to stop being good."

Implicit Table Locking

Paradox locks tables implicitly for the commands shown in Table 7-1.

Table 7-1. Paradox Commands That Lock Tables

Command	Implicit Lock Applied
ADD	Write on source, prevent write on target
CAVERAGE	Write
CCOUNT	Write
CMAX	Write
CMIN	Write
CNPV	Write
COEDIT	Group and Write Record (in multi-table forms)
COPY	Write and family on source, full on target
CREATE	Prevent write on source, full on target
CSTD	Write
CSUM	Write
CVAR	Write
DELETE	Full on table and family
EMPTY	Full on table and family
IMAGECAVERAGE	Write
IMAGECCOUNT	Write
IMAGECMAX	Write
IMAGECMIN	Write
IMAGECSUM	Write
INDEX	Full
RENAME	Full on table and family
SORT	Full on table if replacing original, write otherwise
SUBTRACT	Full on source and target

RETRYPERIOD returns how long (in seconds) Paradox will retry operations continuously. The default is 0. You can set it in the custom configuration or during an application with SETRETRYPERIOD N where N is an integer between 0 and 30,000. If Paradox cannot place locks during this time, it creates a script error.

To avoid such errors, you should lock tables explicitly to match the implicit locks before trying the operations. Here is an example that tries to place a full lock on the Neworder table before emptying it.

```
LOCK "Neworder" FL
IF Retval THEN
  EMPTY "Neworder"
ELSE
  MESSAGE "Could not empty New Order table"
  SLEEP 1500
  MESSAGE ""
ENDIF
```

Explicit Table Locking

You place explicit locks to guarantee access to a Paradox object. They restrict what others can do.

You can request four types of table locks: full lock (FL), write lock (WL), prevent write lock (PWL), and prevent full lock (PFL). Others can lock the same objects, either explicitly or implicitly, as long as all locks can coexist (see Table 7-2). The lock types are as follows in order of increasing concurrency.

- Full lock prevents others from accessing the table at all. They cannot even choose it from a menu, so the lock also limits access to family members such as reports and forms.
- Write lock prevents others from changing a table's contents. They can still view it, and they can use forms and reports.
- Prevent write lock prevents others from placing a write lock or full lock on a table. You guarantee your ability to make table changes, and others can still lock and change individual records.
- Prevent full lock prevents others from putting a full lock on a table. You guarantee your ability to at least read the table.

Table 7-2. Table Lock Coexistence Matrix

	Full Lock	Write Lock	Prevent Write Lock	Prevent Full Lock
Full Lock	No	No	No	No
Write Lock	No	Yes	No	Yes
Prevent Write Lock	No	No	Yes	Yes
Prevent Full Lock	No	Yes	Yes	Yes

Using Table Locks Defensively

Lock every table (sung to the tune of "Climb Every Mountain") and record you need for a transaction, thus guaranteeing that you can complete it. For example, adding a sales order creates a record in the Orders table, updates inventory records, and includes a customer lookup. Here is an example of guaranteeing access to all tables.

```
LOCK "Orders" PWL, "Invent" PWL, "Customer" PFL
IF NOT Retval THEN
  MESSAGE "Could not add an order"
  SLEEP 2000
  MESSAGE ""
ENDIF
```

Paradox sets Retval to True if it can lock all tables, and to False otherwise. A prevent write lock lets the application insert records and change fields in the Orders and Invent tables. A prevent full lock assures that the user can look up customers in the Customer table.

Rather than just display a message and stop processing when table locks fail, you can keep retrying them for a while, hoping that whoever is blocking you will eventually yield control. He or she has to go home, out to lunch, or to the bathroom eventually! There is nothing like a good network tug-of-war to raise the competitive spirit. What if a poisonous snake were to appear in the other person's office or a particularly repulsive piece of week-old Limburger cheese? And there is always Thumbscrew Eddie's Reminder Service!

Getflocks (Program 7-3) accepts a string of files to lock and the number of seconds to retry. It returns True if Paradox gets the locks and False otherwise. You must use a backslash before each quotation mark in the string so Paradox will interpret it literally, not as a control character. The following example shows the lock string for the order entry example.

```
Lockstring = "LOCK \"Orders\" PWL, \"Invent\" PWL, "+
            "\"Customer\" PFL"
```

The next sequence calls Getflocks with the lock string and a retry period of five seconds.

```
Locked = Getflocks(Lockstring,5)
IF NOT Locked THEN
  MESSAGE "Could not add an order"
  SLEEP 2000
  MESSAGE ""
ELSE
  *** order processing ***
ENDIF
```

Getflocks uses the EXECUTE statement that interprets the contents of Lockstring as a command and runs it.

```
;Filelock.sc
;Accepts lock series as a string, for example:
;    "LOCK \"Client\" PFL \"Orders\" PFL"
;and tries to place the locks for the specified
;number of seconds. limit is an Integer such as 5.
;Note that a backslash must precede the quotation
;marks around the table names so Paradox will interpret
;them literally.

;Procedure returns True if locks obtained
;and False otherwise
PROC Getflocks(locks,limit)
PRIVATE
        Ctr,      ;Count of retry attempts so far
        Procname, ;Procedure name
        Success   ;True if locks succeed

Procname = "Getflocks"
Success = False
Ctr = 0
```

```
WHILE Ctr < limit
  EXECUTE Locks
  IF Retval THEN
    Success = True
    QUITLOOP
  ENDIF
  ;Wait a second
  MESSAGE "Please wait..."+STRVAL(ctr)
  SLEEP 1000
  Ctr = Ctr + 1
ENDWHILE
IF NOT Success THEN
  BEEP
  MESSAGE "Could not obtain access to required tables..."
  SLEEP 2000
ENDIF
RETURN Success
ENDPROC
```

Program 7-3. *Get a Series of File Locks*

Locking Records for a Transaction

A transaction is a set of actions your program must perform to complete a specific task. To start an order in the order entry example, a customer record must be on file and available exclusively. The program must also be able to obtain the next sequential order number. Otherwise, the transaction cannot continue.

You can guarantee a unique order number by creating a separate table to hold the next sequential value. Design a form for it and embed it as an unlinked table on the multi-table order form. Make it invisible by styling the foreground and background the same color to avoid distracting the user.

Program 7-4 asks the user to select a customer for the next order. If the customer is on file, it calls Getorder (Program 7-5) to obtain the next sequential order number. If both operations succeed, order entry continues.

```
;Startord
;Get customer and order numbers for next order. If
;both actions succeed, begin order entry.

;Lock all tables for order entry
LOCK "Orders" PWL, "Customer" PWL, "Nextord" PWL
IF NOT Retval THEN
  MESSAGE "Could not lock tables"
  SLEEP 2000
  MESSAGE ""
  RETURN
ENDIF

COEDIT "Orders"
;Customer table is embedded on order form
;along with Nextord table for sequential
;order numbers

PICKFORM 1
WINMAX

;Remove pulldown menu
SHOWPULLDOWN
ENDMENU

WHILE True
  CLEAR
  @ 1,0 ?? "Enter Customer number==>"
  ACCEPT "N" TO Cid
  ;Stop order entry if user pressed Esc
  IF NOT Retval THEN
    QUITLOOP
  ENDIF

  ;Search for customer
  MOVETO "Customer"
  MOVETO [Cust Id]
  LOCATE Cid
  ;Stop order entry if customer not on file
  IF NOT Retval THEN
    MESSAGE "Customer not on file"
    SLEEP 2000
    MESSAGE ""
    LOOP
  ENDIF
```

```
  ;Lock customer record for duration of order
  LOCKRECORD
  ;Stop order entry if lock fails
  IF NOT Retval THEN
  MESSAGE "Someone is entering orders for "+
    "customer " + STRVAL(Cid)
  SLEEP 2000
  MESSAGE ""
  LOOP
ENDIF

  ;Get next order number
  Order = Getorder()
  ;Stop order entry if could not get an order number
  IF Order = -1 THEN
    MESSAGE "Could not get an order number"
    SLEEP 2000
    MESSAGE ""
    ;Unlock customer record
    MOVETO "Customer"
    UNLOCKRECORD
    RETURN
  ENDIF

  ;Have customer and order, begin entry
  OrdEntry()
ENDWHILE
DO_IT!
;Release locks and clear desktop
RESET
```

***Program 7-4.** Get Customer and Order Number for Order Entry*

```
;Getorder.sc
;Get next sequential order number from embedded
;Nextord table. Return order number or -1 if
;not obtainable.

PROC Getorder()
PRIVATE
        Ctr,       ;Retry counter
        Nextkey    ;Next sequential key value
```

```
MOVETO "Nextord"
Ctr = 0
Nextkey = ""
;Try to get order number 100 times if necessary
WHILE Ctr < 100
  LOCKRECORD
  IF Retval THEN
    ;Store next sequential number
    Nextkey = [Order Number]
    [Order Number] = [Order Number] + 1
    UNLOCKRECORD
    QUITLOOP
  ENDIF
ENDWHILE
;Test Nextkey to see if got an order
IF Nextkey <> "" THEN
  RETURN Nextkey
ELSE
  RETURN -1
ENDIF
ENDPROC
```

***Program 7-5.** Get Next Order Number*

CheckPoint 7-1. File Locks

Objective: Change the order processing program (7-4) to be more persistent about locking tables at the beginning of the transaction. Substitute a call to the procedure Getflocks rather than using the LOCK command directly.

Getflocks (Program 7-3) is persistent about file locking. We can handle a record lock the same way. Getrlock (Program 7-6) tries to lock the current record for the specified number of seconds. It returns True if Paradox can get the lock and False otherwise.

```
;Reclock.sc
;Tries to lock the current record for the specified
;number of seconds. Limit is an Integer value such as 5.
;USE IT ONLY TO LOCK EXISTING RECORDS!
;TRYING TO LOCK A NEW RECORD WITH A DUPLICATE KEY
;WILL THROW AWAY THE OLD ONE AND KEEP THE NEW ONE!

;Procedure returns True if locks obtained
;and False otherwise
PROC Getrlock(limit)
PRIVATE
        Ctr,       ;Count of retry attempts so far
        Procname,  ;Procedure name
        Success    ;Whether locks succeeded

Procname = "Getrlock"
Success = False
Ctr = 0
WHILE Ctr < limit
  LOCKRECORD
  IF Retval THEN
    Success = True
    QUITLOOP
  ENDIF
  ;Wait a second
  MESSAGE "Please wait..."+strval(Ctr)
  SLEEP 1000
  Ctr = Ctr + 1
ENDWHILE
IF NOT Success THEN
  BEEP
  MESSAGE "Could not obtain access to required record..."
  SLEEP 2000
ENDIF
RETURN Success
ENDPROC
```

Program 7-6. *Lock Current Record*

Warning

Use Getrlock only to lock existing records in keyed tables. If you use it to post a new record with a duplicate key, the first LOCKRECORD fails and the second keeps the new record and discards the old one with no warning.

CheckPoint 7-2. Record Locks

Objective: Write a procedure to accept two table names necessary for a transaction, Customer and Invoice, for example. Assume Paradox has located the correct record in each one. Use Getrlock to lock both records. Return True if the records are locked and False otherwise. Remember to unlock the first record if the second lock fails.

Group and Write Record Locks

Paradox uses a *group lock* to maintain referential integrity between linked master and detail tables on a form. This means you cannot delete a master record until you delete all linked details. On the other hand, Paradox will let you delete the same master record in table view! What you do behind closed doors is your own business, as long as you maintain the proper public appearance. Paradox is a great database for gangsters, politicians, and other scoundrels!

When you Coedit (or Edit) with a multi-table form and begin changing a master record, Paradox places a group lock on all linked detail records. Others cannot change them (or the master) in either form or table view until you release the master. However, they can still edit other master or detail records.

A *write record lock* is the reverse of a group lock. If you lock a detail record, Paradox automatically tries to lock the corresponding master. It succeeds only if it can lock them both.

The How to DO_IT! section presents a multiuser maintenance system that takes advantage of group and write record locks to preserve referential integrity.

Testing Multiuser Applications

You cannot test multiuser applications by yourself (even if you have a split personality). A lock you place on an object (usually a table) applies to others, but not to you. You cannot lock yourself out. I wish my house and car worked that way!

Concurrency testing assures that several users can access Paradox objects in your application without contention. For example, if two users try to edit a master record, the application must allow the first one to proceed and notify the second that the record is unavailable. You may optionally retry the editing until the first user finishes or the application times out in a loop.

Paradox automatically retries queries and reports based on RESTART-COUNT. You can set it and test whether the operation succeeded. You can also set an option telling Paradox to continue with a query even if another user changes table data. This choice means you run the risk that your Answer table will not have the most current data, but Paradox will work faster.

Concurrency Testing

Once you design the logic for a task such as editing a customer record, you can develop a concurrency test plan for it. The plan lists actions such as locating the customer, all possible outcomes (customer in table or not), and a response for each. The following example shows a code segment to locate and edit a customer record. The actions include locating the customer and locking the record for maintenance.

```
MOVETO [Cust Id]
LOCATE Custkey
;Retval is True if record is in table
IF Retval THEN
  LOCKRECORD
  ;If lock succeeds, user can edit record
  IF Retval THEN
    ** record level processing **
    UNLOCKRECORD
```

```
    ELSE
      QUIT "Could not lock record"
    ENDIF
  ELSE
    QUIT "Could not find record"
  ENDIF
```

Table 7-3 shows the test plan. It includes two actions, locating and locking a customer record. Each has two possible outcomes, success or failure, and each outcome produces a response.

Table 7-3. Customer Processing Test Plan

Action	Result Success	Result Failure	Response
Locate Customer	X		Try to Lock
		X	Quit
Lock Record	X		Edit Record
		X	Quit

If a test fails and you change the program, rerun all tests in the same order with the same data to be sure you have solved the problem.

> **Tip**
>
> Keep test data in a special table so you can copy it to rerun tests.

Testing for Paradox Restarts

By default, Paradox bases reports, queries, and crosstabs on a snapshot of the data in shared tables. If a user changes a table while Paradox is taking the snapshot, Paradox restarts it. The number of restarts is limited by RESTARTCOUNT which has a default value of 0. That is, Paradox will keep restarting until it succeeds. If the table is large (several thousand records) or maintenance activity is heavy, it may keep restarting indefinitely! It is like a modern Sisyphus, doomed to try starting his car battery forever and always hearing a few encouraging noises.

You can limit the restart count, but you must then test whether the operation (query, report, or crosstab) succeeded. In a query, Paradox sets Errorcode to 27 if it cannot get a snapshot in the allotted number of retries. Because Crosstab is a temporary table, you can test whether it exists. if not, the operation timed out. If a report is based on an Answer table, you can test for it also.

It is difficult to determine whether reports on regular tables failed because a snapshot failed. There are two reasonable approaches. You can send the report to a disk file and test for its existence, or you can place write locks on tables before starting the report (so users cannot update them) and release them when the report finishes.

If accuracy does not concern you (perhaps an estimate is all you need), you can tell Paradox to ignore table changes and continue to create the snapshot regardless. The following series of keypress commands turns the restart option off.

```
Tools/Net/Changes/Continue
```

> **Warning**
>
> If you use the Continue option, there is no way to test if Paradox took a full snapshot or continued with a partial one. You should assume the Answer is incomplete.

You cannot use the Continue option with Delete, Insert, or ChangeTo queries as they require a full lock on all tables.

How to DO_IT!

Paradox applies a group lock to records on a multi-table form to preserve referential integrity. In practice, this means that if a master record lock succeeds, all linked detail records are also locked. Paradox uses the write record lock to preserve integrity in the other direction. That is, if you lock a detail record, it locks the corresponding master one.

Figure 7-1 shows a multi-table form for the Tombstone police department crime tracking system. It includes a master Suspect table and an embedded multi-record Arrest table.

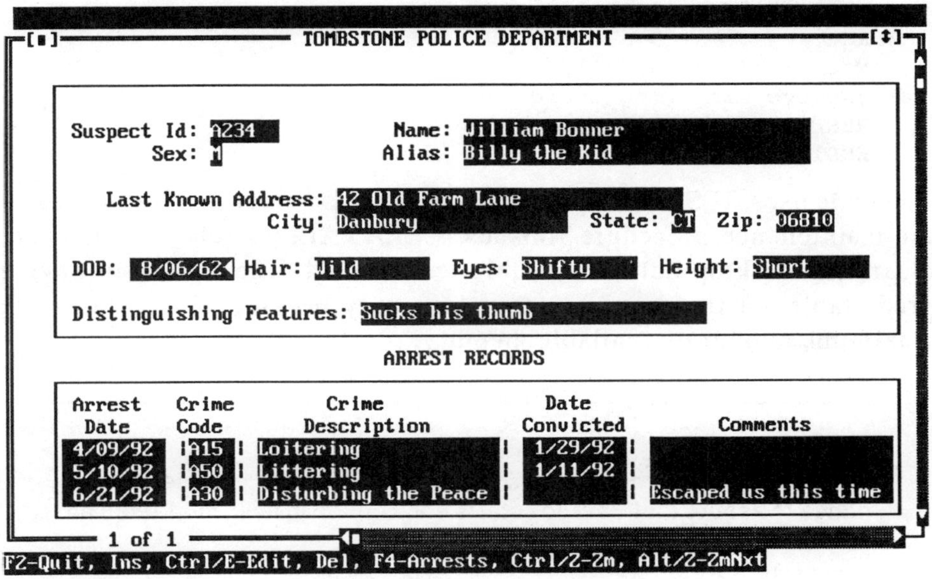

Figure 7-1. Tombstone police arrest record screen.

Locking Tables

The police department has other forms to access Suspect and Arrest tables, so the system uses Paradox's group and write record locks to maintain data integrity. Surely the suspects have no integrity of their own!

The system must lock both tables before calling a maintenance procedure to assure that the user may coedit information. The Arrest table has a lookup table (Crimes) for crime codes, so the application must lock it too.

The system uses prevent write locks (PWL) on all tables. They guarantee that a user may coedit, but allow others to coedit also in table or form view. The following code locks the tables and calls the maintenance procedure if it succeeds.

```
LOCK "Suspect" PWL, "Arrest" PWL, "Crimes" PWL
IF NOT Retval THEN
  MESSAGE "Could not lock tables!"
  SLEEP 2000
```

```
    MESSAGE ""
  ELSE
    Netmaint("Suspect",1,"Suspect Id")
    ;Remove lingering table locks
    RESET
    ENDIF
```

The code uses RESET to remove table locks and clear the desktop when the maintenance procedure finishes. CLEARALL, a related command, clears the desktop but leaves table locks intact. The idea is to have a predictable starting environment. An empty desktop also assures the maximum amount of available memory.

> **Tip**
>
> Use RESET after completing a major function such as table maintenance to assure that Paradox starts each option in main mode with an empty desktop.

You can unlock a table explicitly by including its name and the lock in an UNLOCK command. The following statement removes the locks set for Tombstone maintenance and clears the desktop. Meanwhile, Marshal Earp can check if there are any devious suspects loitering around the OK Corral.

```
UNLOCK "Suspect" PWL, "Arrest" PWL, "Crimes" PWL
CLEARALL
```

Editing Suspects

NetMaint (Program 7-7) is the Suspect maintenance procedure. It accepts a table name (Suspect), form number (1), and table key name (Suspect Id). It assumes the table is a master with one key field.

The procedure coedits the table, picks the form, and maximizes the window. It uses a keypress-driven WAIT command that includes Insert, Edit, and Delete options along with cursor movement keys such as PgUp, searching using Zoom and ZoomNext, and switching control to the embedded Arrest table with the F4 key.

The WAIT command traps and ignores Ctrl-O (Dos), Alt-O (DosBig), and Alt-E (ASCII -18). The first two leave Paradox temporarily and give control to DOS; the last one invokes the editor. A user generally finds the sudden appearance of the DOS prompt to be disturbing and confusing. He or she may turn off the machine, causing Paradox to corrupt open tables. Since neither the Suspect nor the Arrest table has memo fields, the WAIT also turns off access to the editor. You are not going to trap the insidious Dr. Fu Manchu with a balky system.

If the Suspect table is not empty, Netmaint changes IMAGERIGHTS to READONLY. Now the user may view data only until he or she requests an action such as Insert or Delete. It is easier to program if you know the application always starts a function from a predictable state. If the table is empty, IMAGERIGHTS READONLY causes a script error.

When a user presses Ins to insert a record, the program changes to IMAGERIGHTS to let him or her enter data for all fields, including the key. It checks for a duplicate key after he or she presses F2 to accept the new record. If it finds one, the user may change the value or press Esc to delete the record. The procedure reverts to READONLY image rights when it loops to the WAIT RECORD command.

NetMaint changes IMAGERIGHTS to UPDATE when the user presses Ctrl-E to edit the current record. UPDATE stops a user from changing key values. Without it, you must check for duplicate key entry during edit operations as well as inserts. If Paradox can lock the master Suspect record, all linked Arrest records are also locked with a group lock. Others may view them, but not edit or delete them. The program saves original Suspect data in an array. If the user presses Esc to abandon changes, it restores original record values from there.

If a user chooses to delete the current Suspect, the program confirms the action and then tries to place a record lock (or "handcuffs" in this application!). If it succeeds, it deletes the record. The program checks the window after pressing the Del key. Paradox displays status messages there that are visible during interactive operation, but hidden by the canvas during script play. The WINDOW function returns the text of the current message. The program assumes that if anything appears in the window, the delete failed. Paradox cannot delete a master record with linked details.

Pressing F4 moves the cursor from the Suspect table to the Arrest table. Case closed, but the details linger in endless data files to be used later on television shows!

```
;Netwait.sc
;Maintain a single key table with a form
;using keypress-driven WAIT. Table has embedded
;detail table (two keys).
;Procedure accepts the table name (Tblname), table
;form (Frm), and table key (Tkey)
;It allows the following options:
; Ctrl-E - Edit current record (5)
; Alt-Z  - ZoomNext
; Ctrl-Z - Zoom
; Del    - Delete current record
; Ins    - Insert record
;Turn off Alt-O (Dos), Ctrl-O (DosBig),
;and Alt-E (-18) so user cannot
;drop out of WAIT accidentally

PROC NetMaint(Tblname,Frm,Tkey)
PRIVATE
        Ans,        ;User choice for confirming record delete
        Nrecs,      ;Number of records currently in table
        Prmpt,      ;Prompt line
        Procname,   ;Procedure name
        Savekey,    ;Save current record key to check for
                    ;duplicate
        Saverec     ;Save record values so user can cancel edit

Procname = "NetMaint"

COEDIT Tblname
PICKFORM Frm
;Maximize window
WINMAX

;Clear top menu bar
SHOWPULLDOWN
ENDMENU

;Set up prompt line
Prmpt = "F2-Quit, Ins, Ctrl/E-Edit, Del, F4-Arrests,"+
       " Ctrl/Z-Zm, Alt/Z-ZmNxt"

WHILE True
  ;Keep in view only mode until select function
  IF NRECORDS(Tblname) > 0 THEN
    IMAGERIGHTS READONLY
  ENDIF
```

```
WAIT RECORD
  PROMPT Prmpt
UNTIL "F2","Ins",5,"Del","F4","Zoom","ZoomNext",
      "Up","Down","PgUp","PgDn","Dos","DosBig",-18

SWITCH
CASE Retval = "F2":
  QUITLOOP

;Insert new record
CASE Retval = "Ins":
  ;Let user enter new key
  IMAGERIGHTS
  INS
  MOVETO FIELD Tkey
  ;SaveKey used to determine duplicate
  ; key entry
  SaveKey = ""
  WHILE True
    WAIT RECORD
      PROMPT "Press F2 to Save Record, Esc to Cancel"
    UNTIL "F2","Esc","Dos","DosBig",-18
    SWITCH
      CASE Retval = "F2":
        MOVETO FIELD Tkey
        ;Try to post if key has been changed
        IF SaveKey <> [] THEN
          LOCKRECORD
          ;If lock succeeds, record posted to table
          IF Retval THEN
            UNLOCKRECORD
            MOVETO FIELD Tkey
            QUITLOOP
          ELSE
            MESSAGE "Duplicate - Press any key to correct"
            Ans = GETCHAR()
            MESSAGE ""
            ;Save current key value in case user tries
            ; to save record again without changing it
            MOVETO FIELD Tkey
            SaveKey = []
            LOOP
          ENDIF
        ENDIF

      ;Abandon record
      CASE Retval = "Esc":
        DEL
```

```
        QUITLOOP
      ENDSWITCH
    ENDWHILE

  ;Change record values
  CASE Retval = 5:
    ;Do not let user change key value
    IMAGERIGHTS UPDATE
    LOCKRECORD
    IF Retval THEN
      ;Save original data
      COPYTOARRAY SaveRec
      WHILE True
        WAIT RECORD
          PROMPT "Press F2 to Save Record, Esc to Cancel"
        UNTIL "F2","Esc","Dos","DosBig",-18
        SWITCH
          ;Keep changes
          CASE Retval = "F2":
            QUITLOOP

          ;Abandon changes
          CASE Retval = "Esc":
            IMAGERIGHTS
            COPYFROMARRAY SaveRec
            QUITLOOP
        ENDSWITCH
      ENDWHILE
      UNLOCKRECORD
    ELSE
      MESSAGE "Record unavailable for editing - Press any key"
      Ans = GETCHAR()
      MESSAGE ""
    ENDIF

  ;Delete current record
  CASE Retval = "Del":
    MESSAGE "Are you sure you want to delete? (Y/N)"
    Ans = GETCHAR()
    MESSAGE ""
    ;Do not delete unless response is Y or y
    IF Ans <> 89 AND Ans <> 121 THEN
      LOOP
    ENDIF
    ;Try to lock and delete record
    IMAGERIGHTS
    LOCKRECORD
    IF Retval THEN
```

```
    DEL
    ;Del fails if linked detail records exist
    IF WINDOW() <> "" THEN
      MESSAGE WINDOW()
      SLEEP 2000
      MESSAGE ""
      UNLOCKRECORD
      LOOP
    ENDIF
  ELSE
    MESSAGE "Cannot lock record, No Delete - Press any key"
    Ans = GETCHAR()
    MESSAGE ""
  ENDIF

;Move to Arrest table
CASE Retval = "F4":
  PLAY "Arrest"
  MOVETO Tblname
  MOVETO FIELD Tkey

;Start search
CASE Retval = "Zoom":
  ZOOM


;Search for next value
CASE Retval = "ZoomNext":
  MESSAGE "Searching for duplicate..."
  ZOOMNEXT
  MESSAGE ""

;Allow cursor movement
CASE Retval = "Up" OR
     Retval = "Down" OR Retval = "PgUp" OR Retval = "PgDn":
  KEYPRESS Retval

ENDSWITCH
ENDWHILE
DO_IT!
CLEARALL
ENDPROC
```

Program 7-7. Edit Master Suspect Records

Editing Arrests

In Program 7-8, the user may edit arrest records or suspects with the same keys. F3 replaces F4 to let the user switch tables.

When a user presses Ctrl-E to edit or Del to delete the current Arrest record, Paradox tries to lock it as well as the corresponding master Suspect record with a write record lock. It sets Retval to True if it can lock both records and False otherwise.

```
;Arrest.sc
;Maintain Arrest table embedded in Tombstone Police
;suspect form. Allow insert, edit, delete, and zoom

Dettable = "Arrest"
MOVETO Dettable

WHILE True
  ;Create string with current record number and
  ; total number of table records
  Nrecs = STRVAL(NRECORDS(Dettable))
  IF NRECORDS(Dettable) > 0 THEN
    IMAGERIGHTS READONLY
  ENDIF

  WAIT RECORD
    PROMPT "F2-Quit, Ins, Ctrl/E-Edit, Del, F3-Suspects, " +
           "Ctrl/Z-Zm, Alt/Z-Zmnxt"
  UNTIL "F2","Ins",5,"Del","F3","Zoom","ZoomNext",
        "Up","Down","PgUp","PgDn","Dos","DosBig",-18


  SWITCH
    ;End editing session
    CASE Retval = "F2":
      DO_IT!
      CLEARALL
      QUIT

    ;Insert new record
    CASE Retval = "Ins":
      IMAGERIGHTS
      INS
      MOVETO [Date of Arrest]
      ;Save key value for duplicate record test
```

```
      Savekey = BLANKDATE()
      WHILE True
        WAIT RECORD
          PROMPT "Press F2 to Save Arrest, Esc to Abandon, "+
                 "F1-Crime Code Help"
        UNTIL "F2","Esc","Dos","DosBig",-18
        SWITCH
          CASE Retval = "F2":
           ;Check for blank fields
            IF ISBLANK([Date of Arrest]) OR
               ISBLANK([Crime Code]) THEN
                 MESSAGE "Must fill in date and crime code"
                 SLEEP 2000
                 MESSAGE ""
                 LOOP
            ENDIF
            ;Check for duplicate date by posting
            IF [Date of Arrest] <> Savekey THEN
              LOCKRECORD
              IF NOT Retval THEN
                MESSAGE "Duplicate date - please correct"
                SLEEP 2000
                MESSAGE ""
                Savekey = [Date of Arrest]
                LOOP
              ELSE
                UNLOCKRECORD
                QUITLOOP
              ENDIF
            ELSE
              MESSAGE "Duplicate or blank date"
              SLEEP 2000
              MESSAGE ""
              Savekey = [Date of Arrest]
              LOOP
            ENDIF

          ;Abandon record
          CASE Retval = "Esc":
            DEL
            QUITLOOP
          ENDSWITCH
        ENDWHILE

;Lock current record for changes
      CASE Retval = 5:
```

```
    ;Check for record data
    IF ISBLANK([Date of Arrest]) THEN
      MESSAGE "Must edit existing arrest"
      SLEEP 2000
      MESSAGE ""
      LOOP
    ENDIF
    LOCKRECORD
    IF Retval THEN
      ;Do not allow key updating
      IMAGERIGHTS
      ;Save original data
      COPYTOARRAY SaveRec
      WHILE True
        WAIT RECORD
          PROMPT  "Press F2 to Save Arrest, Esc to "+
                  "Abandon F1-Crime Code Help"
        UNTIL "F2","Esc","Dos","DosBig",-18
        SWITCH
          ;Keep changes
          CASE Retval = "F2":
            IMAGERIGHTS
            QUITLOOP

          ;Abandon changes
          CASE Retval = "Esc":
            IMAGERIGHTS
            COPYFROMARRAY SaveRec
            QUITLOOP
        ENDSWITCH
      ENDWHILE
      UNLOCKRECORD
    ELSE
      MESSAGE "Cannot lock arrest record - Press any key"
      Ans = GETCHAR()
      MESSAGE ""
    ENDIF

  ;Delete current record
  CASE Retval = "Del":
    ;Check for blank record
    IF ISBLANK([Date of Arrest]) THEN
      MESSAGE "Must delete existing arrest"
      SLEEP 2000
      MESSAGE ""
      LOOP
    ENDIF
    MESSAGE "Are you sure you want to delete? (Y/N)"
```

```
        Ans = GETCHAR()
        MESSAGE ""
        ;Test for Y and y
        IF Ans <> 89 AND Ans <> 121 THEN
          LOOP
        ENDIF
        ;Try to lock and delete record
        LOCKRECORD
        IF Retval THEN
          IMAGERIGHTS
          DEL
        ELSE
          MESSAGE "Cannot lock arrest record - Press any key"
          Ans = GETCHAR()
          MESSAGE ""
        ENDIF

      ;Zoom
      CASE Retval = "Zoom":
        ZOOM

      ;Zoom Next
      CASE Retval = "ZoomNext":
        MESSAGE "Searching..."
        ZOOMNEXT
        MESSAGE ""

      CASE Retval = "F3":
        QUITLOOP

      ;Allow cursor movement
      CASE Retval = "Up" OR Retval = "PgUp"
        OR Retval = "PgDn":
          KEYPRESS Retval


      ;Down is a special case because it can
      ; add a record at the bottom of the table
      CASE Retval = "Down":
        IF RECNO() <> NRECORDS(Dettable) THEN
          DOWN
        ENDIF
    ENDSWITCH
ENDWHILE
```

Program 7-8. *Edit Detail Arrest Records*

Group and Write Record Lock Effects

By using the two lock types on a multi-table form, Paradox ensures referential integrity without placing unreasonable restrictions on what a user can do. For example, if one user is editing suspects and arrests via this form, another could be editing either the Suspect or Arrest table on the same form, on another one, or in table view.

Because Paradox enforces referential integrity only on the form, a user could delete a suspect in table view even if he or she had arrest records. The records then become orphans. Sounds lonely, and they occupy a lot of disk space. Imagine poor arrest records simply waiting on a dingy corner of a disk, hoping for a suspect to appear.

> **Tip**
>
> Place related tables on multi-table forms and link them to have Paradox enforce referential integrity. If you do not want a user to see them, color them to be invisible. The user will not even know they are there.

Summary

A multiuser application lets several people use Paradox objects simultaneously. It handles contention problems such as two of them trying to change the same record.

This chapter explained the three types of Paradox directories: system, shared, and private. It also described the files Paradox uses to control concurrent object use. It presented a list of commands during which Paradox sets implicit table locks and suggested that you lock resources explicitly to avoid contention problems.

Paradox provides four types of explicit table locks besides individual record locking. You should lock tables and records required for a transaction such as adding a customer order to assure completion. You should also allow users to abandon a transaction when necessary and roll back the partial update.

Besides file and record locking, Paradox uses group and write record locks on multi-table forms to preserve data integrity. The How to DO_IT! section presented the example of the Tombstone police crime tracking system. The suspects may be devious, but the system has integrity.

8

Combining Paradox with Other Programs

Never send a man to do a horse's job.

—Mr. Ed, "*Mr. Ed*"

Introduction

Like any product, Paradox has strengths and weaknesses. Rather than make it do things for which it is ill-suited, we can combine it with other programs. For example, you can create form letters with WordPerfect, then send them to a client list kept in Paradox. You can use Paradox to search, sort, and format addresses for a secondary merge file.

This chapter first describes typical ways to combine Paradox and WordPerfect. They apply to other word processors with only minor modifications. The examples produce a mail merge file of client names and addresses, attach WordPerfect documents such as memos and contracts to Paradox records, and transfer a single name and address from Paradox to WordPerfect to type a memo or letter.

You may also want to use a spreadsheet such as Quattro Pro to perform statistical analysis and create what-if scenarios. Quattro has a feature called Paradox Access that lets you transfer data easily. You can also combine Paradox with other spreadsheets such as Lotus 1-2-3 by exporting an ASCII file of cross-tabulated data.

This chapter explains how to set up your working environment to use Paradox Access. It shows an expense reporting example using Paradox to enter and summarize data and Quattro to format and print it.

Using WordPerfect with Paradox

You can use WordPerfect with Paradox to handle jobs involving both database and word processing functions and thus get all the advantages of both packages. This section first describes the PAL RUN command used to execute WordPerfect within Paradox. It then shows three typical examples: a mail merge, note maintenance, and address transfer. It assumes you know how to create a WordPerfect mail merge letter and a simple macro.

PAL RUN Command

The PAL RUN command suspends Paradox and executes another program such as WordPerfect. It remembers Paradox's current state, including open tables and record pointers. When you leave the external program, Paradox restores the original environment exactly. Table 8-1 summarizes RUN's options.

Table 8-1. RUN Command Options

Option	Description
Big	Frees 500K to run large external programs
Norefresh	Leaves PAL canvas on screen while Paradox is suspended. If an external program writes to the screen, it overwrites the canvas.
Noshell	Prevents Paradox from loading a new copy of COMMAND.COM
Sleep	Waits up to 30 seconds so a user can see the result of an external program such as the DOS DIR command

RUN frees about 200K of memory and does not require Paradox to store information in extended memory or on disk. You must use the Big option with WordPerfect because it requires more space. Does anything run in a mere 200K these days? Big frees approximately 500K and swaps Paradox into temporary storage in extended memory or on disk if there is not enough room.

You start WordPerfect within Paradox via the following command. WordPerfect must be in the PATH statement of your AUTOEXEC.BAT file (otherwise, you must include its full path).

```
RUN BIG NOSHELL "WP"
```

You can define a SETKEY macro to activate WordPerfect with a hot key. For example, to attach Alt-W (-17), enter

```
SETKEY -17 RUN BIG NOSHELL "WP"
```

WordPerfect Mail Merge

You can send form letters to a client list stored in your Paradox database. Why shouldn't you add to the junk cluttering people's mailboxes? You must run the Paradox custom configuration program and the WordPerfect setup program to define field delimiters before creating the merge file. You need specify them only once.

Paradox Setup

Play the Custom script (usually in the Paradox system file directory) and select ASCII. Leave a quotation mark as the string delimiter and a comma as the field separator, but change Delimit to All Fields.

By default, Paradox places quotation marks only around text fields. This option forces it to place them around all fields so WordPerfect will recognize them.

WordPerfect Setup

Follow these steps to set up WordPerfect for a mail merge:

- Press Shift-F1 to select the setup menu
- Select 4 - Initial settings
- Select 1 - Merge for the merge menu
- Select 1 - Field Delimiters and enter " for Begin and ", for End

- Select 2 - Record Delimiters, leave Begin blank, and enter "Ctrl-M for End
- After you press F7 to exit the function, you should see "[CR] for End

Formatting a Merge File

A typical client database contains first and last names, company name, multiple address lines, and city/state/Zip code information. Address lines may be blank if fields are empty. You could use WordPerfect macros to remove them, but it is difficult because you cannot predict their positions. Addresses with blank lines look strange and may confuse the easily bewildered postal authorities.

It is simpler to use Paradox to format the address lines before creating the merge file. Figure 8-1 shows a query to extract client information for a mailing. It combines the first and last names into a field called Name. Paradox removes all extra spaces in-between, so you must insert one as a separator.

The query selects the company and both address lines. Finally, it combines the city, state, and Zip Code into a field called Ctyst.

```
Query

Client | First |              Last                  | Company |
       | _f    | _l,calc _f + " " + _l as Name      | Check   |

Client | Address1  | Address2 | City | State |
       | Check     | Check    | _c   | _s    |

Client |                    Zip                       |
       |_z,calc _c + ", " + _s + "  " + _z as Ctyst   |

Endquery
```

Figure 8-1. Query to extract mail merge records.

Figure 8-2 shows the Answer table structure. Some records may have blank company or address lines. The fields are in the same order as the check marks in the query form; Paradox places calculated fields such as Name and Ctyst last in the structure.

Answer	Field Name	Field Type
	Company	A30
	Address1	A30
	Address2	A30
	Name	A31
	Ctyst	A31

Figure 8-2. Table structure for merge file.

You can use PAL to compress lines as in the Paradox report generator before exporting the table. All addresses will have five lines, but blank ones will be at the bottom rather than in the middle.

You should set up your merge letter using all five lines without a macro to test for blanks. Program 8-1 (MailFmt) accepts a table name and moves filled address lines to the top of the structure by swapping them with blank ones.

```
;Mailfmt.sc
;Format addresses for WordPerfect mail merge
;Move blank lines to end of address
PROC MailFmt(Tbl)
PRIVATE Switched,  ;True if line moved, false otherwise
        Ctr        ;Counter for switches
COEDIT Tbl
SCAN
  ;Keep checking address lines as long as one has been
  ; switched. There are at most 4 switches if
  ; all address lines are blank. The counter keeps the
  ; loop from executing forever in that case.
  Switched = True
  Ctr = 0
  WHILE Switched AND Ctr < 5
    ;Assume no address lines will be
    ; switched
    Switched = False
    ;Check company and both address lines for
    ; blanks. If a field is blank, move it up
    ; a line in address.
    IF LEN([Company]) = 0 THEN
      [Company] = [Address1]
      [Address1] = ""
```

```
      Switched = True
    ENDIF
    IF LEN([Address1]) = 0 THEN
      [Address1] = [Address2]
      [Address2] = ""
      Switched = True
    ENDIF
    IF LEN([Address2]) = 0 THEN
      [Address2] = [Ctyst]
      [Ctyst] = ""
      Switched = True
    ENDIF
    Ctr = Ctr + 1
  ENDWHILE
ENDSCAN
DO_IT!
ENDPROC
```

Program 8-1. *Swap Blank Address Lines to Bottom*

After reformatting the address table, you can export it to an ASCII file for the WordPerfect merge. In Paradox, select the following path and enter the table name:

```
Tools/ExportImport/Export/Ascii/Delimited
```

The fields in the ASCII file are delimited by quotation marks and separated by commas. Empty fields are at the end of the record and appear as null strings. For instance, the following example has no company name:

```
"24 Westfield Ave","Apt 5","Danbury, CT 06810","Sam Spade",""
```

Performing the Mail Merge

Prepare the merge letter in WordPerfect using all five fields. Blank ones print at the end of the address. Figure 8-3 shows a sample letter.

```
{DATE}

{FIELD}4~
{FIELD}1~
{FIELD}2~
{FIELD}3~
{FIELD}5~

Dear {FIELD} 4~,

We are pleased to offer you the opportunity
to buy preview samples of our newest
product, the Supreme Widget Wonder. It
slices potatoes, mashes tomatoes, shreds
coaxial cable, and makes beautiful floral
designs out of old floppy disks. Please
contact me at your earliest convenience to
arrange delivery and payment terms.

Best regards,


J. Danforth Schlemiehl
Vice-President, Sales and Marketing
```

Figure 8-3. *WordPerfect form letter.*

Proceed as follows to perform the merge:

- Press Ctrl-F9 (Merge/Sort)
- Select 1 - Merge and enter the name of your primary letter file.
- Press Ctrl-F5 (Text In/Out). When prompted for the secondary file, enter the ASCII file name exported from Paradox.

Attaching WordPerfect Documents to Paradox

Paradox has a text field type with a maximum length of 255 characters, and a memo type with a maximum length of 64 megabytes. You can use them to attach notes to database records. However, they are quite restricted in practice as there is no spell checking, line and page formatting, or any other typical word processing functions for them.

You can access these facilities plus all the power of a full-featured word processor by writing the documents in WordPerfect and associating them with clients in a Paradox database. Besides the main Client table, you must create a Notes table keyed with a matching client number plus a document name.

You must design a multi-record embedded form for the Notes table and include it on the master form for your client database. The user selects a client and a note and presses a hot key to switch to WordPerfect with the document. He or she may create the document if it does not exist.

Designing Tables and Forms

Figure 8-4 shows the structure for a typical client database with name and address information. Its key is an identification number.

Client	Field Name	Field Type
	Id	N*
	First	A10
	Last	A20
	Company	A30
	Address1	A30
	Address2	A30
	City	A15
	State	A2
	Zip	A10

Figure 8-4. *Client database structure.*

A separate Notes table has client identification number plus document name as its key. Figure 8-5 shows its structure. It contains the date the document was created or revised and a short description of it.

Notes	Field Name	Field Type
	Id	N*
	Document	A25*
	Date	D
	Desc	A30

Figure 8-5. *Notes database structure.*

Figure 8-6 shows a sample form for the Client table with the embedded multi-record Notes form.

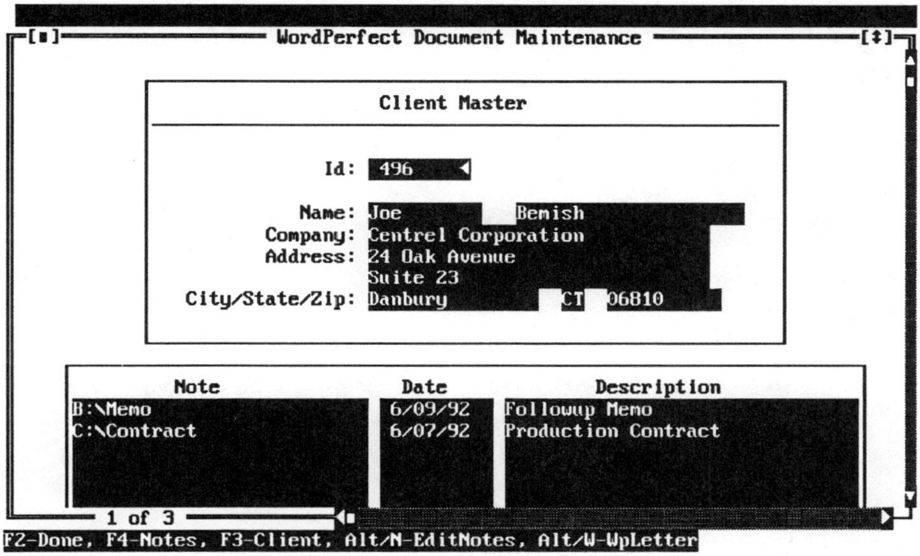

Figure 8-6. Client maintenance form.

Note Maintenance Procedures

Program 8-2 is the PAL code to Coedit the client table with this form. It lets the user move between the client and notes tables to select a note for editing with WordPerfect.

It uses the WAIT TABLE command and does not trap the Del key or handle duplicate record keys. You will probably want to embed it in a complete table maintenance procedure. It passes the document name to the NoteMaint procedure for processing.

```
;Editnote.sc
;Edit client table. User presses Alt/N (-49) to
;edit client notes. Program transfers control
;to NoteMaint procedure with document name.
;Remove pulldown menu
SHOWPULLDOWN
ENDMENU
COEDIT "Client"
PICKFORM 1
WINMAX
WHILE True
  WAIT TABLE
    PROMPT "F2-Done, F4-Notes, F3-Client, Alt/N-EditNotes"
  UNTIL "F2","F3","F4",-49,"Dos","DosBig"
  SWITCH
    CASE Retval = "F2":
      QUITLOOP

    CASE Retval = "F3":
      MOVETO "Client"

    CASE Retval = "F4":
      MOVETO "Notes"

    ;Alt/N for note maintenance
    CASE Retval = -49:
      IF UPPER(TABLE()) = "NOTES" THEN
        NoteMaint([Document])
      ELSE
        MESSAGE "You must select a note first..."
        SLEEP 1500
        MESSAGE ""
      ENDIF
  ENDSWITCH
ENDWHILE
DO_IT!
CLEARALL
```

Program 8-2. *Coedit Client Table with Notes*

NoteMaint (Program 8-3) accepts a document name that may contain backslashes in its path, for example, C:\Contract. Paradox interprets them as control characters, so NoteMaint replaces them with their character equivalents to form a true path statement. It calls WordPerfect with the converted name.

If the document does not exist, the procedure asks the user whether to create it. He or she can do so on the fly by entering the name on the master Paradox form. Program 8-2 does not delete the document if a user deletes the Notes record.

```
;Notes.sc
; Edit notes attached to current record on workspace.
; Notes is the field in the table that contains the path
; to the document.
;
; You create documents with your own word processor.
; This example uses WordPerfect to edit the attached note.
; The word processor's name is in variable Wordproc.

PROC NoteMaint(Notes)
PRIVATE
        Ans,         ;User choice to create a new note file
        Ch,          ;Single character from notes string
        Ctr,         ;Loop controller
        Length,      ;Length of notes field
        Oldnotes,    ;String with backslashes removed
        Wordproc     ;Word processor

;Create word processor name. Leave one
; space at the end.
Wordproc = "WP "
IF ISBLANK(Notes) THEN
  MESSAGE "You must enter a path first!"
  SLEEP 2000
  RETURN
ENDIF
IF NOT ISFILE(Notes) THEN
  MESSAGE "No word processing file " +
    Notes + " create it? (Y/N)"
  Ans = GETCHAR()
  MESSAGE ""
  ;89 = y  121 = Y
  IF Ans <> 89 AND Ans <> 121 THEN
    RETURN
  ENDIF
```

```
  RUN BIG NOSHELL Wordproc + Notes
ELSE
  ;Paradox treats the \ as a control
  ; code. You must parse the string
  ; and replace it with the character
  ; equivalent.
  Length = LEN(Notes)
  Oldnotes = ""
  FOR Ctr FROM 1 TO Length
    Ch = SUBSTR(Notes,Ctr,1)
    Oldnotes = Oldnotes + Ch
  ENDFOR
  RUN BIG NOSHELL Wordproc + Oldnotes
ENDIF
ENDPROC
```

Program 8-3. *Edit WordPerfect Notes*

CheckPoint 8-1. Delete WordPerfect Documents

Objective: Change Program 8-2 (Editnote) to delete the corresponding document when a user deletes a record in the Notes table.

Hint: Add a key such as Alt-D (ASCII -32) to the PROMPT and the UNTIL list for the WAIT on the Client table. Add a CASE to handle the new key. Test for the file using the ISFILE function. If it exists, use the RUN command to leave Paradox and erase it; otherwise, display an error message. Remember to delete the Notes record also.

Transferring Names and Addresses to WordPerfect

You can use your client database as a source and transfer a name and address to WordPerfect for a letter or memo. Figure 8-7 shows a business letter heading that includes the current date.

```
June 1, 1992
Mr. Rock Maninoff
Rumplestiltskin's
Sewing School
24 Rapunzel Avenue
Danbury, CT 06810
```

Figure 8-7. Business letter heading.

The user selects a client record and presses a hot key to transfer the name and address to WordPerfect. The program creates a letter header, then includes the current date and the name and address without blank lines. It lets the user specify the top and left margins.

It writes the information to an intermediate ASCII file and loads it into WordPerfect. You can create a simple WordPerfect macro to move the cursor below the last address line, ready to type. Figure 8-6 shows the Client form using Alt-W as a hot key for the transfer.

Program 8-4 is the script to coedit the Client table. It passes the name and address data to the transfer procedure, along with the left and top margins.

```
;Addrtran.sc
;Edit client table. Move current name and
;address to WordPerfect to type memo or
;letter when user presses Alt/W.

COEDIT "Client"
PICKFORM 1
WINMAX
WHILE True
```

```
  WAIT TABLE
    PROMPT "F2-Done, F4-Notes, F3-Client, "+
           "Alt/W-WpLetter"
  UNTIL "F2","F3","F4",-17,"Dos","DosBig"
  SWITCH
    CASE Retval = "F2":
      QUITLOOP

    CASE Retval = "F3":
      MOVETO "Client"

    CASE Retval = "F4":
      MOVETO "Notes"

    ;Alt/W (ASCII -17) to move address to WordPerfect
    CASE Retval = -17:
      IF UPPER(TABLE()) = "CLIENT" THEN
        ;Send name and address information, left margin
        ; in spaces, and top margin in lines
        Transfer([First],[Last],[Company],[Address1],
                 [Address2],[City],[State],[Zip],0,10)
      ELSE
        MESSAGE "You must select a client first..."
        SLEEP 1500
        MESSAGE ""
      ENDIF
  ENDSWITCH
ENDWHILE
DO_IT!
CLEARALL
```

***Program 8-4.** Coedit Client Table with Address Transfer*

The transfer procedure (Program 8-5) deletes the old address file. It skips the specified number of blank lines from the top of the page and formats the date. It combines the first and last names on the first address line and tests for blank company and address lines before writing them. Finally, it loads WordPerfect with the ASCII file.

```
;Transfer.sc
; Transfer the current date, name, and address to your word
; processor and start a letter.
;
; Creates an ASCII file called Letter.sc with the
; proper spacing.
;
; First,Last,Company,Address1,Address2,City,State, and Zip
; are the address information for the current record on the
; workspace. Lindent is left margin in spaces, Skipit is top
; margin in lines.
;
; Note: Some word processors require Lindent, and others
; handle it through the format settings. For example,
; WordPerfect does not need it.

PROC Transfer(First,Last,Company,Address1,Address2,City,
              State,Zip,Lindent,Skipit)
PRIVATE
        Ctr,        ;Loop control variable
        Cty,        ;Combined City,State,Zip line
        Dte,        ;Current Date
        Indent,     ;Number of spaces to indent
        Letter,     ;Script ASCII text file
        Wordproc    ;Word processor

;Could select any script name for temporary file
Letter = "Letter.sc"
;Delete old file if any
IF ISFILE(Letter) THEN
  RUN "Erase Letter.sc"
ENDIF

;Include current date
Dte = FORMAT("D2",TODAY())
Wordproc = "WP "
Ctyst = City + ", " + State + " " + Zip
Indent = SPACES(Lindent)

;Skip lines from top of page
FOR Ctr FROM 1 TO Skipit
  PRINT FILE Letter "\n"
ENDFOR

;Put address lines in file. Do not include blank ones.
PRINT FILE Letter Indent,Dte,"\n","\n"
```

```
PRINT FILE Letter Indent,First," ",Last,"\n"
IF LEN(Company) > 0 THEN
  PRINT FILE Letter Indent,Company,"\n"
ENDIF
IF LEN(Address1) > 0 THEN
  PRINT FILE Letter Indent,Address1,"\n"
ENDIF
IF LEN(Address2) > 0 THEN
  PRINT FILE Letter Indent,Address2,"\n"
ENDIF
PRINT FILE Letter Indent,Ctyst,"\n"

;Run word processor
RUN BIG NOSHELL Wordproc + Letter
ENDPROC
```

Program 8-5. *Transfer Name and Address to WordPerfect*

WordPerfect Summary

This section showed three common ways to integrate WordPerfect with Paradox. You can take your client information from Paradox and then perform a WordPerfect mail merge after initial setup and removing blank address lines with a simple PAL procedure.

You can attach WordPerfect documents to client records with a Paradox Notes table, linking by client number and document name. This gives you the advantage of access to both WordPerfect features such as spell checking, formatting, and fonts and Paradox features such as Query-by-Example. The embedded form shows the user all attached notes, and the PAL program lets him or her choose one and switch into WordPerfect with it. If it does not exist, the user can create it on the fly.

Lastly, you can use your client database as a source and move an individual name and address into WordPerfect to type a letter.

Using Paradox with WordPerfect provides all the advantages of both a relational database and a full-featured word processor.

Using Quattro Pro with Paradox

Paradox Access is a Quattro Pro feature that lets you run it within Paradox. You can load a Paradox table into a spreadsheet, process it in Quattro, and return to Paradox with one keystroke. The biggest advantage of this approach is that you can use Paradox's Query-by-Example to join tables and import the Answer table into Quattro for analysis, graphing, and publication.

Expense reporting is a good example of combining Quattro and Paradox. Figure 8-8 shows an expense report for the User-Hostile Software Company. Each service representative must complete a weekly one including categories such as food, lodging, and transportation.

Representatives can use Paradox to enter charges for hotels, meals, and parking and toll receipts. Paradox can summarize the amounts by week and by category. The report generator does not support line drawing and fonts directly so producing the report in Paradox would be difficult.

What is the solution? After doing the summary, the representative simply moves the data into Quattro for publication. It supports line drawing, shading, and fonts so User-Hostile Software can have beautiful reports unobtainable from its own products.

Note: You cannot connect Paradox to other spreadsheets such as Lotus 1-2-3 directly. You can combine them indirectly by exporting the summarized expense data to an ASCII file and importing it into the spreadsheet.

This section shows how to set up Quattro and Paradox to use Paradox Access. It then explains how to produce the User-Hostile Software expense report using Paradox for data entry and summarization and Quattro for publication.

System Requirements

You must have Quattro Pro Version 2.0 or later because Paradox Access uses Borland's VROOMM memory management. Workstations must be 80286/AT class or faster with at least 2 MB of RAM. How could you have less and still show your face in polite society?

USER HOSTILE SOFTWARE, INC.
Expense Report

WEEK ENDING: June 6, 1992 NAME: Bill Gates
Please print or type

DAY	SUN	MON	TUE	WED	THU	FRI	SAT	TOTALS
DATE	5/31/92	6/1/92	6/2/92	6/3/92	6/4/92	6/5/92	6/6/92	
CITY VISITED	NY	NY	NY	NY	NY	NY	NY	
BREAKFAST	$0.00	$0.00	$5.00	$4.00	$0.00	$0.00	$0.00	$9.00
LUNCH	$0.00	$10.00	$3.00	$7.00	$0.00	$0.00	$0.00	$20.00
DINNER	$0.00	$30.00	$15.00	$25.00	$0.00	$0.00	$0.00	$70.00
TOTAL MEALS	$0.00	$40.00	$23.00	$36.00	$0.00	$0.00	$0.00	$99.00
LODGING	$0.00	$75.00	$75.00	$75.00	$0.00	$0.00	$0.00	$225.00
TELEPHONE	$0.00	$5.00	$7.00	$2.00	$0.00	$0.00	$0.00	$14.00
MILEAGE-PERSONAL	$0.00	$0.00	$0.00	$0.00	$0.00	$0.00	$0.00	$0.00
* AIR/RAIL	$0.00	$250.00	$0.00	$0.00	$0.00	$0.00	$0.00	$250.00
* LIMO/TAXI/PARKING/TOLLS	$0.00	$5.00	$0.00	$0.00	$0.00	$0.00	$0.00	$5.00
* ENTERTAINMENT	$0.00	$0.00	$100.00	$0.00	$0.00	$0.00	$0.00	$100.00
OTHER	$0.00	$0.00	$0.00	$0.00	$0.00	$0.00	$0.00	$0.00
TOTAL FOR THE DAY	$0.00	$375.00	$205.00	$113.00	$0.00	$0.00	$0.00	$693.00
EXPLANATION: Precise Optical Scanners for Beta Test					TOTAL REIMBURSEMENT			$693.00
of new equipment					LESS PREPAID ITEMS			
					LESS TRAVEL ADVANCE			$500.00
					BALANCE DUE			$193.00

* Attach Ticket Stubs/Receipts

ALL EXPENSES WERE INCURRED IN THE PERFORMANCE OF COMPANY BUSINESS

SIGNED: ______________________ DATE: ____________

APPROVED: ______________________ DATE: ____________

Figure 8-8. Example expense report.

If you are accessing data on a network server running SQL (Structured Query Language), you must also have Paradox SQL Link (a separate product) and a database server such as Borland's InterBase or Microsoft's SQL Server that supports it.

Setting up Paradox Access

You must configure the environment to share resources between Paradox and Quattro as follows.

Do not install both in the same directory. Put Quattro in the PATH statement of your AUTOEXEC.BAT file.

Be sure the FILES setting in CONFIG.SYS, located in the boot directory on your hard drive, is at least 40. Quattro will report an error (not enough file handles) if it is too low.

Run the DOS SHARE command which loads a terminate and stay resident (TSR) module enabling file and record locking. You can add it to your AUTOEXEC.BAT file, so you need not run it each time you start Paradox Access.

The PXACCESS.BAT file on the Quattro distribution diskettes runs SHARE and loads Paradox with default command line switches suitable for most configurations.

The Paradox working and private directories must differ. If you are on a network, this is handled already, but it applies even on a stand-alone system. You can use the Paradox custom script to set a default private directory, or you can change it during the current session with Tools/Net/Setprivate.

Quattro must point to the directory containing the PDOXUSRS.NET file. It controls the number of concurrent network users. In Quattro, choose Options/Other/Paradox/Directory to set the path to it.

If you are not on a network, specify the root directory of your hard drive (C:\) and set Options/Other/Paradox/Network Type to Other.

You can now run Quattro within Paradox by pressing Ctrl-F10. Paradox opens Quattro and passes control to it. By default, Quattro looks in the private directory for an Answer table and loads it automatically. You can also load it from a script with the PAL command TOQPRO.

Warning

Once Paradox Access is enabled, you should trap Ctrl-F10 in WAIT commands to avoid calling Quattro inadvertently.

Creating the Expense Reports

Service representatives enter individual expense receipts on the Paradox form shown in Figure 8-9. After they complete the entries for a particular week, they run a PAL script to summarize them and cross-tabulate them into spreadsheet format. The script calls Quattro which is set up to load the Crosstab table automatically.

The user opens a second Quattro window with the expense report template and runs a macro to copy the data into it. He or she may also fill in other information on the report, including explanations and mileage amounts. The user can save the report and print it on a laser printer. When he or she leaves Quattro, control returns to Paradox at the point where it left off.

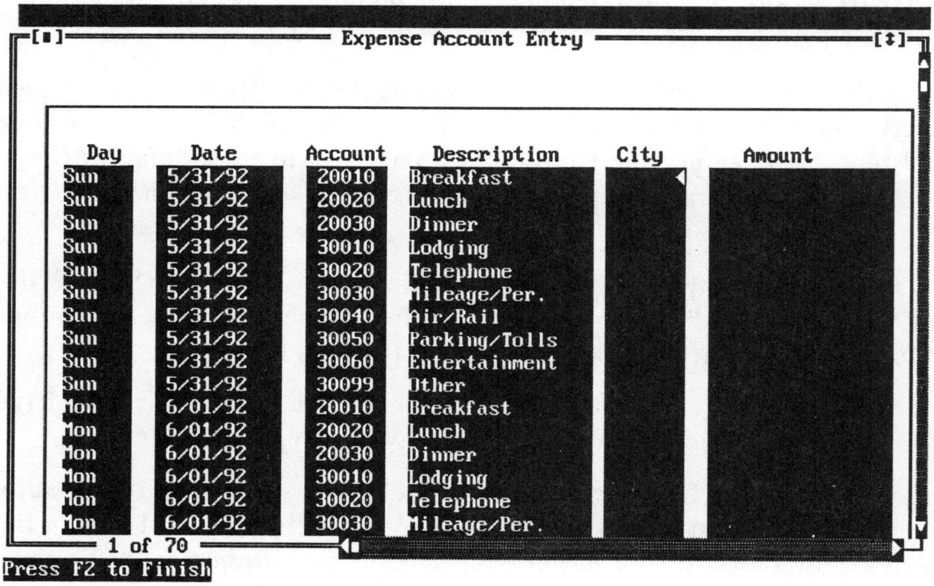

Expense Account Entry

Day	Date	Account	Description	City	Amount
Sun	5/31/92	20010	Breakfast		
Sun	5/31/92	20020	Lunch		
Sun	5/31/92	20030	Dinner		
Sun	5/31/92	30010	Lodging		
Sun	5/31/92	30020	Telephone		
Sun	5/31/92	30030	Mileage/Per.		
Sun	5/31/92	30040	Air/Rail		
Sun	5/31/92	30050	Parking/Tolls		
Sun	5/31/92	30060	Entertainment		
Sun	5/31/92	30099	Other		
Mon	6/01/92	20010	Breakfast		
Mon	6/01/92	20020	Lunch		
Mon	6/01/92	20030	Dinner		
Mon	6/01/92	30010	Lodging		
Mon	6/01/92	30020	Telephone		
Mon	6/01/92	30030	Mileage/Per.		

1 of 70

Press F2 to Finish

Figure 8-9. Expense report data entry.

Entering Expenses into Paradox

Figure 8-10 shows the structures of the Paradox Expense and Account tables. The Account table is a master table of expense categories such as food and lodging. The Expense table contains one record for each receipt by date and account. The account description is copied from the Account table. The user enters the city and amount.

Expense	Field Name	Field Type
	Date	D*
	Account	S*
	Desc	A15
	City	A6
	Amount	$

Account	Field Name	Field Type
	Account	S*
	Desc	A15

Figure 8-10. Expense account table structure.

The user runs a script to create an Expense table for a new week. He or she enters the beginning date (Sunday), and the script generates table entries for each category on each day.

Representatives will typically not use all the slots, but data entry and summarization is easier if they need not worry about inserting records and looking up expense codes. Program 8-6 is the Newexp script that creates a weekly Expense table.

```
;Newexp.sc
; Create an Expense table with a record for each
; weekday in each category. User enters the Sunday
; date. Form comes up for data entry when the table
; is completed.

WHILE True
  CLEAR
```

```
   ? "Enter Sunday's Date (MM/DD/YY) or Esc to quit ==>"
   ACCEPT "D" TO Start
   ;Stop if user presses Esc
   IF NOT Retval THEN
     RETURN
   ENDIF

   ;Check if date is a Sunday
   DayOfWeek = DOW(Start)
   IF UPPER(DayOfWeek) <> "SUN" THEN
     MESSAGE STRVAL(Start) + " is not a Sunday!"
     SLEEP 2000
     MESSAGE ""
     LOOP
   ENDIF
   QUITLOOP
ENDWHILE

;Create expense table entries
Start = Start - 1
MESSAGE "Creating new expense sheet..."
EMPTY "Expenses"
MESSAGE ""
VIEW "Accounts"
COEDIT "Expenses"
MOVETO "Accounts"
SCAN
  MOVETO "Expenses"
  FOR Days FROM 1 TO 7
    INS
    [Date] = Start + Days
    [Account] = [Accounts->Account]
    [Desc] = [Accounts->Desc]
  ENDFOR
  MOVETO "Accounts"
ENDSCAN
DO_IT!
CLEARALL

;Coedit expenses with form
COEDIT "Expenses"
;Do not let user edit keys to avoid duplicate
; key problems
IMAGERIGHTS UPDATE
PICKFORM 1
MOVETO [City]
;Trap for F30-TOQPRO and ignore it.
```

```
;This stops user from inadvertently switching
; to Quattro
WHILE True
  WAIT TABLE
    PROMPT "Press F2 to Finish"
  UNTIL "F2","Dos","DosBig","F30"
  SWITCH
    CASE Retval = "F2":
      QUITLOOP
  ENDSWITCH
ENDWHILE
DO_IT!
CLEARALL
```

***Program 8-6.** Create a New Expense Table*

After finishing the expense report entries, the user plays the script shown in Program 8-7. It extracts the date, account numbers, and amounts from the Expense table and cross-tabulates them into spreadsheet format. It calls Quattro which is set to look for the Crosstab table in the user's private directory.

```
;Expense.sc
; Summarize Expense table by category.
; It crosstabulates the Answer table to
; create rows for each one and calls Quattro Pro

;Extract Expenses fields and crosstab sums
MESSAGE "Summing expenses..."
Query

  Expenses | Date  | Account   | Amount |
           | Check | Check     | Check  |

Endquery
DO_IT!
;Insert zeros for blank amounts so Paradox does
; not delete them during crosstab
Query
```

```
 Answer  | Amount              |
         | blank,changeto 0    |

Endquery
DO_IT!
CLEARALL
VIEW "Answer"
Right Rotate Right Rotate Left Menu {Image}
  {Graph} {CrossTab}
{1) Sum} Enter Right Enter Right Enter
CLEARALL
;Switch to Quattro
TOQPRO
```

***Program 8-7.** Expense Table Crosstabulation*

Formatting the Quattro Pro Report

Quattro automatically loads the Crosstab table into window 1. The user must open a second window with the Expense Report template using the path File/Open/Exprpt.wq1. You could write a Quattro macro and store it in a library to automate this process; otherwise, you must document the procedure.

The template has a macro to copy data from window 1. Play it with Alt-F2/Execute/F3 and choose COPY. It is located at G44 in the template.

The user fills in other information, including name, trip explanation, and mileage, and prints the spreadsheet. Figure 8-11 shows the Quattro COPY macro.

Quattro Pro Summary

You can use the Paradox Access feature of Quattro Pro to link the two products. It lets you use the data entry and query facilities of Paradox to collect and summarize data and the advanced publication features of Quattro to print the results.

```
{GOTO}e9~
{NEXTWIN}
{/ Block;CopyContents}b2..h4
{NEXTWIN}~
{NEXTWIN}
{GOTO}
e13~
{NEXTWIN}
{/ Block;CopyContents}b5..h11
{NEXTWIN}~
{NEXTWIN}
{GOTO}a1~
```

Figure 8-11. *Quattro macro to copy expense data to template.*

This section explained how to configure the environment to share resources between Paradox and Quattro Pro. It then presented an expense report example to demonstrate the connection.

Although other spreadsheets such as Lotus 1-2-3 do not link seamlessly with Paradox, you can still use them together by tranferring ASCII files.

Summary

Hybrid applications combine the best features of several products. This chapter described how to use WordPerfect with Paradox to perform a mail merge, attach documents to records, and transfer a single name and address for typing a memo or letter.

It also explained how to set up your system software to use Paradox Access from Quattro Pro. The expense report example used Paradox for data entry and summarization and Quattro for publication with multiple fonts.

We can generalize the techniques to work with other word processors and spreadsheets. With some imagination, you can also extend them to use Paradox with entirely different products, such as desktop publishers and project managers. This saves you, the developer, time and effort, and lets users work with familiar programs.

9

Table Driven Applications

No man . . . who has wrestled with a self-adjusting card table can ever quite be the man he once was.

—James Thurber

Introduction

You can modify a table driven application by changing information in Paradox tables. You need not revise the program. This saves time, makes an application more flexible, and gives users some latitude. And an alternative to calling the developer (you) at undesirable hours! In an inventory system, for example, a user can change the cost evaluation method from Last In/First Out (LIFO) to First In/First Out (FIFO) and thus change calculations on screens and reports automatically. All without knowing anything about PAL programming or software development!

Interactive Paradox uses this technique when it lets you define lookup tables. Changing values in them alters the validity checks for associated fields elsewhere.

This chapter discusses table driven applications using an inventory system example. It describes three types of tables: data tables that store information such as inventory items, application tables that hold reports and forms but do not contain records, and system tables that contain data such as menu choices.

Utility procedures are the key to using system tables effectively. You write one to accept variable information such as a table name; the program action, such as table maintenance, stays the same. This chapter contains procedures to accept and validate sign-on ids, display and execute menu options, and provide context-sensitive help. It also shows how to use system tables to store company information and printer setup strings.

The chapter also presents dialog box procedures to display messages and accept dates and part number ranges. You can use them in your own table driven applications.

Table Types

You are probably most familiar with Paradox data tables that contain information about entities such as inventory items, customers, and vendors. But you can use tables to do much more than just hold data.

Sometimes the table you need does not exist; you create it through queries that combine fields from other tables or include calculated ones. You can use an application table with the Answer table structure to hold a report specification. After executing the query, you can copy the report to the Answer table and print it.

System tables are even more flexible. For example, if you store menu choices in tables along with corresponding procedure names, you need just one procedure to process all system menus. The application loads menu text from a table into an array and displays array elements. After a user selects an option such a printing a report, the application finds and executes the corresponding procedure.

All you must do to add a report to the system is record a script selecting the table, report number, and print destination. You then edit the menu table and add the text and recorded script name. The next time the application displays the menu, it includes the new report. You changed the system with little or no programming. This is a feat worthy of the magician David Copperfield on a good day. In fact, you probably should not tell users how easy it was or they will ask for more. Close your office door, then moan a bit and gnash your teeth while reading a magazine. You deserve a rest. If you feel particularly lazy, you can make a recording of some plaintive groaning and other sympathy-inducing sounds.

If you want to let the secret out, you can probably train a user to add options such as new reports to system menus. He or she can change the application without you, leaving you free to work on difficult problems or go home early (even on time would be nice).

Example Table Driven Application

We use the inventory system developed for Gulag Products to show how to design a table driven application. The company sells torture devices that have been converted to unique interior decorating pieces. Their two biggest sellers, for example, are a six foot rack made into a coffee table and an iron maiden floor clock. They also offer a fine selection of tiger cages, whips, chains, stakes, and thumbscrews. What customers (such as "social clubs" and friendly foreign governments) do with them is obviously their own business.

The application is general enough to handle most business inventories (even those with less exotic products). It uses the six system tables described in Table 9-1.

Table 9-1. Gulag System Tables

Table	Description
Company	Company name, inventory method (LIFO or FIFO), and printer choice
Helptbl	Data table names, field names, and help text
Mainmenu	Menu text, procedure names and parameters, and access level codes
Printers	Printer names, descriptions, ports, and setup strings
Rptmenu	Menu text, procedure names and parameters, and access level codes
Signon	Sign-on ids and menu procedures

The following sections show how the Gulag inventory system stores sign-on ids in a table to control access to menus. After the user enters a valid sign-on, the program loads company and printer information from other tables into arrays used by application procedures. It also displays and processes menu choices stored in tables along with corresponding procedure names. Finally, the application stores context-sensitive field help in tables and displays information during maintenance activities using embedded forms.

Storing sign-on ids in a system table means an authorized user can change them without changing source code. Most companies have employee turnover. Gulag employees who leave are never seen again, except when consorting with Jimmy Hoffa or Elvis Presley. If a developer must change the system every time an employee leaves, he or she would have time for little else and the company would soon run out of money. Particularly since Gulag employees tend to depart abruptly without giving two weeks notice!

Storing help text in tables also makes the system more adaptable. If a developer adds new fields or changes the way a field works, he or she can edit help text stored in tables rather than change source code.

System Security via Tables

Most systems have functions such as month end closing and the office football pool that must be protected from unauthorized users. The Gulag inventory system uses a sign-on id to display the appropriate menu for each user. If someone is promoted, demoted, reeducated, or screams too much over football losses, you can change his or her sign-on id, thus changing the displayed menu.

A user must enter a sign-on id to start the system as shown in Figure 9-1.

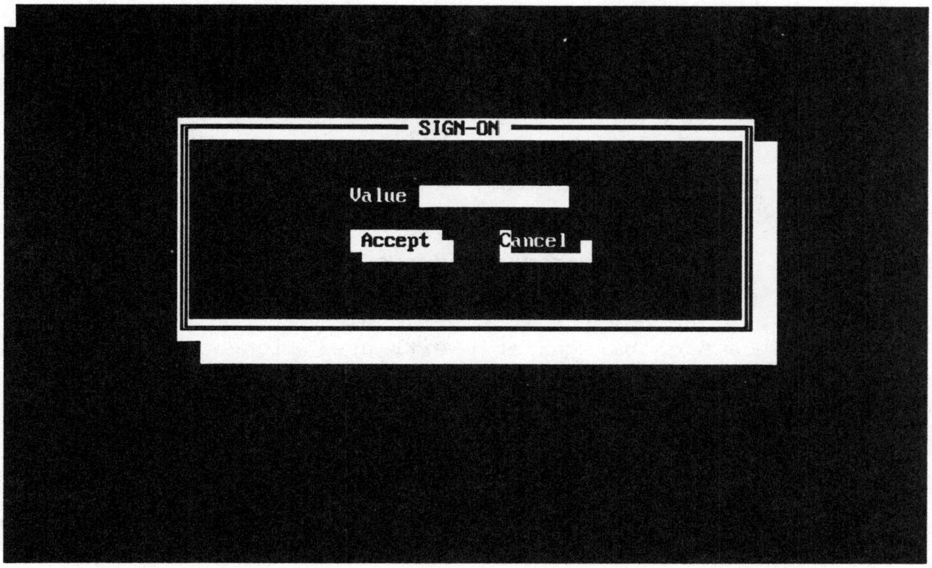

Figure 9-1. Gulag sign-on dialog box.

The application locates the value in the Signon table and assigns the associated menu procedure name to the global variable Yourmenu. We can thus place functions such as item maintenance and report printing on different menus and direct a user to one based on the sign-on id. A user need not look at a menu with options that are irrelevant to his or her job. Figure 9-2 shows the Signon table structure and sample data. The system displays the main menu when Bill signs on.

Field Name	Type	Sample Data
Signon	A10*	BILL
Menuproc	A15	MAINMENU

Figure 9-2. Sign-on table structure.

The Getsignon procedure (Program 9-1) gives a user three chances to enter a valid sign-on id. Otherwise, it returns control to the operating system.

```
;Getsign.sc
;Get a sign-on (directs program to a menu procedure)
;User gets three tries and then system exits
;Procedure returns name of menu procedure
;YourSignon is a global variable with user sign-on
;YourMenu is a global variable with first menu
PROC Getsignon()
PRIVATE
        Ctr,          ;Number of tries
        FirstMenu,    ;First user menu
        Procname,     ;Procedure name
        Sign          ;Sign-on returned from PassBox

Procname = "Getsignon"

Ctr = 0
VIEW "Signon"
WHILE Ctr < 3
  CLEAR
  Sign = PassBox("SIGN-ON")
  ;Check if user pressed Esc
  IF Sign = "" THEN
    RESET
    EXIT
  ENDIF
  MOVETO [Signon]
  LOCATE Sign
  IF NOT Retval THEN
    BEEP
    Ctr = Ctr + 1
    MESSAGE "Sign-on not on file! - Try "+STRVAL(Ctr)+ " of 3"
    SLEEP 1500
    LOOP
  ELSE
    FirstMenu = [Menuproc]
    QUITLOOP
  ENDIF
ENDWHILE
IF Ctr > 2 THEN
  BEEP
```

```
  MESSAGE "A C C E S S  D E N I E D - B A D  S I G N-O N"
  SLEEP 2000
  RESET
  EXIT
ENDIF
RESET
RETURN FirstMenu
ENDPROC
```

Program 9-1. *Accept User Sign-on Allowing Three Tries*

A utility procedure is the key to using a system table. You write one to perform a single job, such as validate a sign-on id, and send variable information, such as the sign-on table name, to change the data it works on.

Getsignon calls another utility procedure PassBox (Program 9-2) to accept a user's sign-on id. It uses the HIDDEN option of the ACCEPT control element to mask typed characters so international spies cannot copy them down (who knows why they would want to?). The procedure returns the entered value or a null string ("") if a user presses Esc or selects the Cancel button.

```
;PassBox.sc
;Dialog box to accept a sign-on
;Typed characters are hidden
;Box includes Accept and Cancel buttons
;Use Alt-A and Alt-C as hot keys
;Procedure returns password or "" if
; Cancel button pressed
PROC PassBox(Title)
PRIVATE Button,    ;Selected pushbutton
        Passwrd,   ;Entered password
        Procname   ;Procedure name

Procname = "PassBox"

Passwrd = ""
Button = ""
SHOWDIALOG Title
```

```
  @ 5,15 HEIGHT 10 WIDTH 50
  @ 2,14 ?? "Value"

  ACCEPT @ 2,20
    WIDTH 13 "A10"
    HIDDEN
    TAG " "
    TO Passwrd

  PUSHBUTTON @ 4,13 WIDTH 10
    "~A~ccept"
    OK
    DEFAULT
    VALUE "OK"
    TAG "Yes"
    TO Button

  PUSHBUTTON @ 4,25 WIDTH 10
    "~C~ancel"
    CANCEL
    VALUE "CANCEL"
    TAG "No"
    TO Button
ENDDIALOG

IF NOT Retval THEN
  RETURN ""
ELSE
  RETURN Passwrd
ENDIF
ENDPROC
```

Program 9-2. *Dialog Box to Accept and Mask Password*

Background Information via Tables

The Inventory system stores information related to a particular installation in two tables: Company and Printers. The Company table (Figure 9-3) contains one record with fields for the company name to display on screens and reports, inventory method (LIFO or FIFO), and printer type (Hewlett-Packard LaserJet or dot-matrix).

Field Name	Type	Sample Data
Name	A30*	GULAG, INC.
Inventory Method	A4	LIFO
Printer	A15	DOT MATRIX

Figure 9-3. *Company table structure.*

Storing company specific information in a table lets the user change names, inventory methods, and printers without requiring a program change. In practice, you can install the same inventory program for different clients, and by revising the table, change the entire costing scheme and titles on screens and reports. The result is a custom program in minutes! Charge the client a large fee for tailoring the application to his or her precise needs, then spend the rest of your day on the golf course!

The program stores company information in a global array G_Company to avoid passing it as an argument to every procedure. You must include global variables and arrays in the USEVARS statement of a closed procedure, or it and others it calls will not know about them.

The printer name in the Company table corresponds to a record in the Printers table (Figure 9-4) that contains required setup strings for reports.

Field Name	Type	Sample Data
Name	A15*	DOT MATRIX
Desc	A30	All Epson Compatibles
Portrait Letter Compress	A40	\015
Portrait Letter Normal	A40	\018
Reset	A40	\018
Port	A4	LPT1

Figure 9-4. *Printers table structure.*

Each printer record contains the port (such as LPT1) and the setup strings for compressed and normal print. Changing the printer in the Company table changes the port destination and setup strings to match. In practice, you can run the application on a local machine and switch printers mechanically. You can also install it on a network and direct printing to a local printer or a network printer.

The Gulag system stores printer information in a global array G_Printer passed to closed procedures via the USEVARS statement so it is available to all print procedures.

Controlling Menus

After the application loads global company and printer information, it runs the menu stored in variable Yourmenu by the sign-on procedure. A table controls each menu. It has one record for each choice containing text to display, the corresponding procedure to execute, and the argument list (if any). Figure 9-5 shows the main menu for Gulag's inventory system.

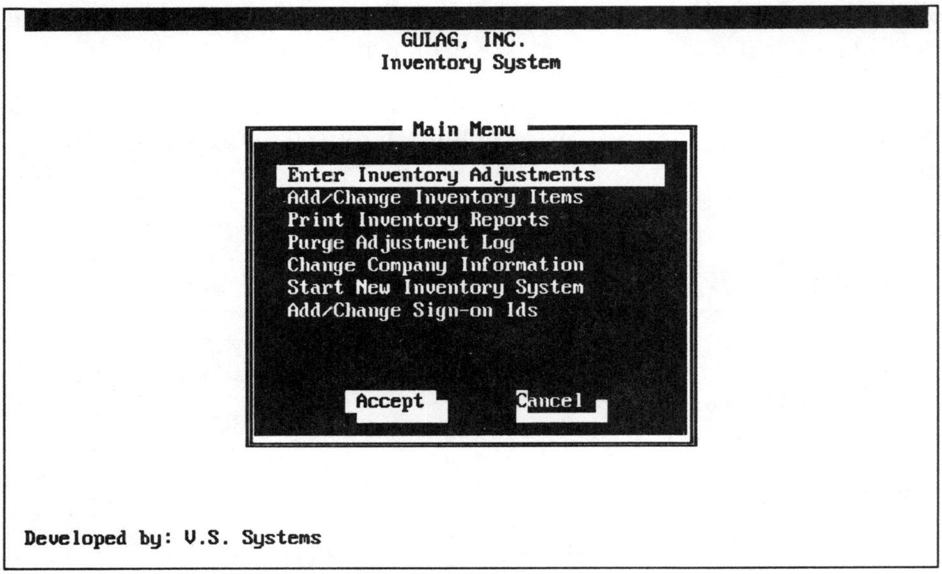

Figure 9-5. Gulag inventory system's main menu.

Storing menu information in tables has two advantages. First, the application displays the appropriate menu for each user based on his or her sign-on id by loading options from different tables. A manager sees only the reports menu, whereas a data entry clerk can choose to enter orders.

Second, you can add or change menu options by editing a menu table rather than changing source code. This saves time and reduces the possibility of introducing new bugs into a system simply by editing its scripts. I delete or change the wrong lines occasionally while making changes. Maybe this never happens to you!

Figure 9-6 shows the menu table structure. It contains the text to display for inventory adjustment maintenance, the procedure to execute (Logmaint), and an optional argument list. The Logmaint procedure requires a table name and form number as arguments.

Field Name	Type	Sample Data
Item	A30	Enter Inventory Adjustments
Procnm	A30	Logmaint
Parmlist	A70	"Tranlog",1

Figure 9-6. Menu table structure.

Get_Choice (Program 9-3) is the utility procedure that processes menus. It accepts the table name, two titles to display at the top of the screen, a dialog box title, the box's top left coordinates, its height and width, and the number of display columns. It also accepts a developer's logo to display in the bottom left screen corner.

It loads arrays from the table before displaying the menu so it can clear the image from the workspace. This leaves the maximum amount of memory available to execute the selected option. When a user makes a choice, Get_Choice calls the procedure with the argument list.

The procedure arbitrarily displays the menu using white text on a blue background. You could pass additional arguments to select colors.

```
;GetCh.sc
;Display a dialog box with a list of menu choices
;loaded from a table. Tbl is the table.
;Title1 and Title2 are centered at top of screen.
;BoxTitle is centered at top of box.
;Tlr and Tlc are top left box coordinates.
;Hgt and Wid are height and width of dialog box.
;Colm is the number of columns.
;Logo is the developer's logo.
;Box has Accept and Cancel buttons.
;Use Alt+First letter for hot key.
;Procedure executes menu choice.

PROC Get_Choice(Tbl,Title1,Title2,BoxTitle,
Tlr,Tlc,Hgt,Wid,Colm,Logo)
PRIVATE   Button,         ;Selected pushbutton
          ButtonIndent,   ;Spaces to indent button display
          Ctr,            ;Loop counter
          Item,           ;Selected item
          Itemar,         ;Array of items to display
          Nrecs,          ;Number of records in table
          Parmlist,       ;Array of parameters
          Procnm,         ;Array of procedure names
          Procname        ;Procedure name

Procname = "Get_Choice"

;Load arrays from table
Nrecs = NRECORDS(Tbl)
ARRAY Itemar[Nrecs]
ARRAY Procnm[Nrecs]
ARRAY Parmlist[Nrecs]
VIEW Tbl
Ctr = 1
SCAN
  Itemar[Ctr]   = [Item]
  Procnm[Ctr]   = [Procnm]
  Parmlist[Ctr] = [Parmlist]
  Ctr = Ctr + 1
ENDSCAN
CLEARIMAGE

Item = ""
Button = ""
```

```
;Prepare screen
;Erase pulldown menu
SHOWPULLDOWN
ENDMENU
CANVAS OFF
CLEAR
;Display logo
@ 23,1 ?? Logo
;Paint screen with white foreground/blue background
PAINTCANVAS ATTRIBUTE 31 0,0,24,79
;Display screen titles in white on cyan
STYLE ATTRIBUTE 63
@ 1,0 ?? SPACES(80)
@ 2,0 ?? SPACES(80)
@ 1,0 ?? SPACES(INT((80-LEN(Title1))/2)) + Title1
@ 2,0 ?? SPACES(INT((80-LEN(Title2))/2)) + Title2
;Reset default style
STYLE
CANVAS ON

;Calculate number of spaces to indent first button
ButtonIndent = INT((Wid - 25)/2)

;Display dialog box of choices
SHOWDIALOG BoxTitle
  @ Tlr,Tlc HEIGHT Hgt WIDTH Wid

  PICKARRAY
    @ 1,2
    HEIGHT Hgt-6
    WIDTH Wid-6
    COLUMNS Colm
    Itemar
    TAG "Picktag"
    TO Item

  PUSHBUTTON @ Hgt-4,ButtonIndent WIDTH 10
    "~A~ccept"
    OK
    DEFAULT
    VALUE "OK"
    TAG "Yes"
    TO Button

  PUSHBUTTON @ Hgt-4,ButtonIndent+14 WIDTH 10
    "~C~ancel"
    CANCEL
    VALUE "CANCEL"
```

```
    Tag "No"
    TO Button
ENDDIALOG

IF Retval THEN
  EXECUTE Procnm[Item] + "(" + Parmlist[Item] + ")"
  RETURN Itemar[Item]
ELSE
  RETURN " "
ENDIF
ENDPROC
```

Program 9-3. *Display Menu Stored in a Table*

CheckPoint 9-1. Menu Display

Objective: Revise the Get_Choice procedure to accept and use a color attribute for screen display. It is currently 31 (white on blue).

Mainmenu (Program 9-4) puts the call to Get_Choice in a loop until the user presses Esc to exit the menu. It is a closed procedure and includes the variables Autolib, Errorproc, and Ulib so Paradox will know what libraries to search for called procedures. The statement also includes global arrays G_Company and G_Printer.

Mainmenu passes Get_Choice the table name ("Mainmenu"). It also passes the company name from the Name element of the global array G_company and a text string as menu titles. "Main Menu" is the dialog box title. The menu displays at row 5 column 20 and is 15 rows high by 40 characters wide. Items appear in a single column.

```
;Mainmenu.sc
;Main menu for inventory system
;Yourlevel is global access level
PROC CLOSED Mainmenu()
USEVARS AUTOLIB,ERRORPROC,Ulib,G_Company,G_Printer
PRIVATE
        Key,      ;Extra buffered keys
        Mchoice,  ;User's menu selection
        Procname  ;Procedure name

Procname = "Mainmenu"
READLIB Ulib ErrorHandler

WHILE True
  ;Throw away buffered keypresses-otherwise,
  ; Paradox processes them all
  WHILE CHARWAITING()
    Key = GETCHAR()
  ENDWHILE
  Mchoice = Get_Choice( "Mainmenu",G_Company["Name"],
                        "Inventory System",
                        "Main Menu",5,20,15,40,1,
                        "Developed by: V.S. Systems")
  IF Mchoice = " " THEN
    QUITLOOP
  ENDIF
ENDWHILE
ENDPROC
```

Program 9-4. *Display Gulag Main Menu*

CheckPoint 9-2. Add Printer Maintenance

Objective: Add an option to the main menu to let a user change the Printers table.

Hint: Use the Tblmaint procedure that the application uses for sign-on maintenance. It accepts a table name, a form number or -1 for no form, and the table key.

Help during WAIT Interactions

Most applications include maintenance options available from menus. You can provide context sensitive help during a WAIT interaction by storing help text in a system table.

You can get field-level help by adding a key to the UNTIL clause of a keypress-driven WAIT command. You need not include F1 to access lookup tables defined as ValChecks. Paradox recognizes them in both table and form view without special processing.

I store help text in a table so I can maintain it without changing source code. If you restructure tables and add fields or change the way one works, you can edit the help table to correspond. The table has two keys, table name and field name. Figure 9-7 shows its structure. The sample data is for the Price 1 field in the Invent table.

Field Name	Type	Sample Data
Tblname	A8*	INVENT
Fldname	A32*	PRICE 1
Text	M10	

Figure 9-7. *Help text table structure.*

You must define a form for Helptbl that includes all fields. Place it unlinked on each master form where you want to access field-level help. Specify that it is display-only so users cannot change help text. An application should not help those who help themselves.

Once a WAIT command with a form begins, Paradox cannot move to tables unless they are on it. You can make the embedded form invisible by selecting the same foreground and background color so it does not distract the user. This is the only way to make the help table available during maintenance.

Paradox uses F1 to invoke lookup table help so I use Ctrl-F1 as my help key. When a user presses it, the main program checks whether the table is in form view; if so, it then calls FldHelp (Program 9-5) with the table name and field name. Help is available only in form view because the help table is embedded on the form. If the program tries to move to it in table view, Paradox creates a script error.

FldHelp moves to the help table, locates the matching record, and displays help text until the user closes the window. Figure 9-8 shows a help screen for the price break field in the Gulag inventory table. If the company changes price breaks or other rules, revising text in the help table makes the new information available instantly without changing source code.

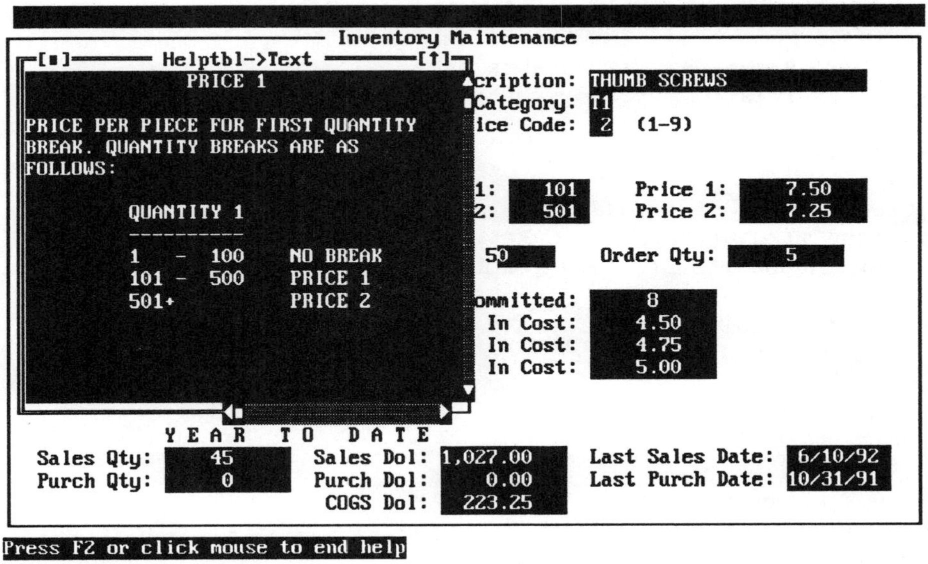

Figure 9-8. Help text for inventory price break.

Control returns to the main program and the original table when the user closes the editor window by pressing F2 or clicking the left mouse button.

```
;FldHelp.sc
;Display context-sensitive help when user presses
;Ctrl-F1 in a WAIT interaction. Move to Helptbl which
;should be embedded on the form and locate the table
;and field name. Display help until user presses any
;key, then return to main table.
PROC Fldhelp(Tbl,Fld)
PRIVATE
         Ans,        ;User keypress for message
         Embedtbls,  ;Array of tables embedded in form
         Found,      ;Switch indicating whether Helptbl
                     ; is on the current form
         Numtbls,    ;Number of tables on form
         Procname,   ;Procedure name
         Tbls        ;Loop controller to check for Helptbl

Procname = "Fldhelp"

;Create array of embedded table names
IF ISMULTIFORM(TABLE(), FORM()) THEN
  FORMTABLES TABLE() FORM() Embedtbls
ELSE
  MESSAGE "Help table is unavailable"
  SLEEP 2000
  MESSAGE ""
  RETURN
ENDIF

;Check array for Helptbl
Numtbls = ARRAYSIZE(Embedtbls)
Found = False
FOR Tbls FROM 1 TO Numtbls
  IF UPPER(Embedtbls[Tbls]) = "HELPTBL" THEN
    Found = True
    QUITLOOP
  ENDIF
ENDFOR

IF NOT Found THEN
  MESSAGE "Help table is unavailable"
  SLEEP 2000
  MESSAGE ""
  RETURN
ENDIF
```

```
;Locate table and field name in help table
MOVETO "Helptbl"
MOVETO [Tblname]
LOCATE UPPER(Tbl),UPPER(Fld)
IF NOT Retval THEN
  MESSAGE "No help available - take two aspirin and"+
          " call me in the morning"
  SLEEP 2000
  MESSAGE ""
  MOVETO Tbl
  RETURN
ENDIF

;Open editor on text field
MOVETO [Text]
FIELDVIEW
ECHO NORMAL
PROMPT "Press F2 or click mouse to end help"
WAIT TABLE
  PROC "Helpproc"
  MOUSE "ALL"
  KEY "F2"
ENDWAIT
ECHO OFF

IF ISFIELDVIEW() THEN
  DO_IT!
ENDIF

;Move to original table
MOVETO Tbl
ENDPROC
```

Program 9-5*. Display Field-Level Help*

You must include Ctrl-F1 (ASCII -94) or another key in the UNTIL clause to call FldHelp. Program 9-6 is a sample script that coedits the Gulag inventory table with a form. The form includes Helptbl as an unlinked embedded form that is invisible to the user.

```
;Editinv.sc
;Coedit an inventory table with context sensitive help.
;Ctrl-F1 (-94) is the help key.
COEDIT "Invent"
PICKFORM 1
WINMAX
WHILE True
  WAIT RECORD
    PROMPT "F2-Quit, Ctrl/F1 - Field Help"
  UNTIL "F2",-94
  SWITCH
    CASE Retval = "F2":
      QUITLOOP

    ;Call help when user presses Ctrl-F1
    CASE Retval = -94:
      IF ISFORMVIEW() THEN
        Fldhelp(TABLE(),FIELD())
      ELSE
        MESSAGE "Field help available only in form view"
        SLEEP 2000
        MESSAGE ""
      ENDIF
  ENDSWITCH
ENDWHILE
DO_IT!
```

Program 9-6. *Edit Inventory Table with Field Help*

Summary

A developer never has time to do everything users want. My daughter says, "The hurrieder I go, the behinder I get." Table driven applications reduce development time by allowing you to store system parameters in tables and reuse general purpose routines without reprogramming.

We discussed the three types of tables used in Paradox applications. Data tables contain information about entities such as inventory items. An application table can hold a report specification for a table constructed using Query-by-Example. System tables are the key to table driven applications. They hold general information such as passwords, menu choices, and printer setup strings.

By writing utility routines to process data in system tables, you can pass different table names to a procedure and change how it works without changing source code. By borrowing from previous systems, you need write new code only as a last resort!

> **Warning**
>
> Even if you employ table driven design and reuse as much PAL code as possible, you still cannot produce systems as fast as users want them. They always have the magic phrase 'Yes, but...' on the tips of their tongues! Too bad their checkbooks are not nearly so ready for action.

10

Improving Performance

McGinn's Law: Just about everything takes longer than they say it does, except sex.

—Jim McGinn

Introduction

If your applications already run fast enough to make users happy, you can skip this chapter and take a well earned rest. Just send me a list of your stock tips, favorite race horses, and preferred lottery numbers! You're a lucky person! If not, you are like most developers, always trying to squeeze more performance out of PAL applications. One method is to write small procedures (under 10K) and put them in libraries. If you include library names on an Autolib path, Paradox manages memory for applications automatically.

Using queries instead of coding solutions helps, as does creating secondary indexes on non-key fields used with LOCATE and ZOOM. Paradox optimizes queries and index searches. Tuning its memory allocations for table buffers, codepool operations, and cache may also help. And you can divide your application files into multiple directories to reduce DOS search times.

As with rich men and poor men, it is just as easy to love a high-powered system as a low-powered one. So why not spend some money on new equipment? Buying the best hardware you can afford will always improve performance. And the nice part is that better hardware is sure to be available and fun to buy besides! Who wouldn't rather have a shiny new disk drive, memory card, or CPU accelerator board than waste money on such humdrum things as food, clothes, rent, utility bills, and tax payments?

Networks introduce new performance problems. Less memory is available on workstations because network drivers use some of it. Most database applications are CPU intensive, so less memory means lower speed. Furthermore, data must often travel across the network between servers and local PCs. The more traffic, the slower the system. We discuss several ways of speeding up networked applications, including using read-only files and directories, and putting private directories and copies of system files on local drives.

After optimizing software and hardware, you can switch to a client server architecture if you still must give your application a boost. The final solution is to abandon your current users and find ones (perhaps in the South Seas) who value a more leisurely way of life!

Optimizing PAL Code

You can improve performance by taking advantage of Paradox's automatic memory management and query and search optimization.

One approach is to use procedure libraries and assign an Autolib path so Paradox can manage memory and swap procedures for you. Keep procedures small (under 10K) for efficiency.

Writing Efficient Procedures

The golden rule for writing an efficient procedure is that it should do just one job such as accept a customer number or display a message. If it does, it is almost certainly under the 10K limit and will be easy to maintain. I use a simple rule-of-thumb to decide if a procedure is efficient. If I can write a short sentence describing what it does, it is good. For example, Setport (Program 10-1) asks the user to select a local or network print destination. It returns the port name or a null string ("") if a user presses Esc.

You can reuse efficient procedures to reduce the amount of coding you must do. For example, an application can call Setport before printing and thus let the user switch between local and network printers.

```
;Setport.sc
;Ask user to select local or network printer destination
;Set port and return port name
;or null if user presses Esc.
PROC Setport()
PRIVATE
        Port,     ;Choice for printer output
        Portname, ;Port name, LPT1 or LPT2
        Procname  ;Procedure name

PROCNAME = "Setport"
;Ask where to direct output
STYLE ATTRIBUTE 79
@ 24,0  ?? SPACES(80) @ 24,27 ?? "Press 1-Local, 2-Network "
ACCEPT "S" MIN 1 MAX 2 TO Port
STYLE
IF NOT Retval THEN
  RETURN ""
ENDIF

;LPT1 local, LPT2 network
Portname = "LPT" + STRVAL(Port)
SETPRINTER Portname
RETURN Portname
ENDPROC
```

***Program 10-1.** Select Print Destination*

If a description includes words such as 'but', 'until', or 'except', the procedure is probably doing too much. You should break the task down into simple steps and write a separate procedure for each one.

A side benefit of the one job per procedure rule is easier maintenance. For example, you can add a third printer port to Setport easily.

CheckPoint 10-1. Efficient Procedures

Objective: Change procedure Setport to select among three available printers. LPT1 is local, LPT2 and LPT3 are network printers. Accept the user's choice and set the port.

Using Paradox Queries

Another way to speed up applications is to replace code with queries, as Paradox optimizes them automatically. For example, the following Changeto query is faster than a SCAN loop for changing (raising!) the sales tax rate for Connecticut customers.

```
Query
Customer   | State  | Sales Tax Rate   |
           | CT     | Changeto 6.00    |
Endquery
```

Another advantage is that Paradox creates a temporary table (Changed) containing the original records. You can add it back to Customer to reverse the change if you make a mistake such as entering the wrong percentage. Use the following menu path to restore the table:

```
Tools/More/Add/Changed/Customer/Update
```

If Customer is keyed, Paradox replaces the new records with the old ones by matching key values.

Use CheckPlus in queries rather than Check if the two create the same Answer table. CheckPlus ignores duplicate records, so it runs faster. You need one CheckPlus in a query form to get the advantage.

The following example selects all customers that have ordered more than a thousand units and includes each one's identification number and sales amount. The Answer table will have no duplicate records because Id numbers are unique. The query selects a customer record based on the amount in the Sales field. Using CheckPlus tells Paradox to skip duplicates.

```
Query
Customer | Customer Id    | Sales Total |
         | √_+            | √_ > 1000   |
Endquery
```

Using Secondary Indexes

A secondary index is another way to speed queries, ZOOMs, and LOCATEs. You can create up to 255 indexes for a table, each based on any number of fields. Indexes can be case sensitive. They can include duplicates, so you can use fields such as names.

You create a secondary index by specifying the table and field names. For example, the following command creates a case-sensitive one called Compind for the Customer table based on company name.

```
INDEX "Customer" LABEL "Compind" CASESENSITIVE
  ON "Company Name"
```

PAL overwrites an old index, if one exists, without any warning. Once you create an index, Paradox uses it automatically whenever it will speed an operation such as ZOOM.

By default, the secondary index is not maintained. In practice, Paradox marks it obsolete after a user changes records in the table. It rebuilds it completely the next time you search on its fields. The rebuilding can be slow if the table is large (say, over 5,000 records).

To keep the index current, include the MAINTAINED clause when creating it. This tells Paradox to update it when a user changes the table. The following example recreates the same index as maintained.

```
INDEX MAINTAINED "Customer" LABEL "Compind" CASESENSITIVE
  ON "Company Name"
```

Multi-field indexes must be maintained. You can create them by combining up to 16 fields. The following example creates an index for a mail order address table sorted on Zip Code and last name.

```
INDEX MAINTAINED "Mailordr" LABEL "Zipsort" ON
  "Zipcode","Lastname"
```

Queries will execute faster using maintained indexes, but maintenance will be slower. (There is no free lunch!) If an application works with historical data that seldom changes but involves many queries, such as a sales history table, maintain the index to speed the queries. If, on the other hand, users regularly coedit a table such as inventory, do not maintain indexes or maintenance will be slower.

Paradox ignores secondary indexes if you use wildcard patterns in a query. It uses them in a ZOOM or LOCATE with wildcards, but searches only for the first letter. For example, it will not be any faster to LOCATE "Water.." than "W.." in the Company Name field. Paradox uses the secondary index to locate the first "W" and searches sequentially afterward.

> **Tip**
>
> Avoid wildcards to speed searching in queries, ZOOMs, and LOCATEs. Paradox will not use secondary indexes in a query and will search only for the first character in a ZOOM or LOCATE.

Tuning Paradox Memory Management

> **Warning**
>
> Paradox must run in protected mode. Your PC must have at least 2MB of memory.

Paradox checks the PC configuration at startup and uses all available extended memory. You will usually get the best performance by letting it decide how much memory to allocate to its internal table buffers, codepool area, and cache.

It uses table buffers to perform queries, sorts, and indexing. It uses the codepool area for non-table operations such as changing variables, doing calculations, and controlling the user interface. The cache holds swapped copies of scripts, procedures, forms, and reports.

You can see how Paradox allocates memory by starting it with the -space option on the command line. Table 10-1 describes the allocations. All amounts are in kilobytes.

Table 10-1. Paradox Memory Allocations

Allocation	Purpose
Kgetm	Left after assigning table buffer space
Kpool	Codepool
Kswap	Table buffers
Ktot	Total before table buffers
Maxkswap	Maximum for queries and sorts

Table Buffers

If you query, sort, or index large tables (say, over 5,000 records), you should increase table buffer space. Think of the disk as your bank account and the buffer as your wallet. You withdraw money from the bank, put it in your wallet, and spend it from there. You need not revisit the bank until you have spent everything in your wallet (maybe you had an exciting weekend or went to the grocery store). Since the slowest part of most systems is disk access, the fewer trips to the disk for data, the better the performance.

The maximum number of table buffers depends on the table's block size. For example, if it is 4K and the buffer allocation is 24K, Paradox can use 6 buffers at once. (It is like having six wallets, each with four dollars—although what good four dollars would do you these days, I can't say!)

You can change the amount of memory allocated for table buffers by using the -tablek option when loading Paradox. The following example specifies 2,000K for buffer space.

```
Paradox -tablek 2000
```

Remember, you start Paradox with a fixed amount of memory. Increasing table buffer space automatically reduces the amount available for controlling the interface, doing calculations, and swapping scripts and procedures. You should change *tablek* only if the application regularly queries very large tables (5,000 records or more). It may slow performance rather than improve it otherwise.

> **Tip**
>
> Test the effect of changing *tablek* by designing a query for a large table. Run it with the default Paradox allocations and time it. Raise *tablek* 200K to 300K repeatedly and rerun the query as long as the speed keeps increasing. Use the best setting to test other parts of the system such as table maintenance. If adding keyed records seems slower than usual, reduce *tablek* until speed is acceptable.

Codepool and Cache

After allocating table buffers, Paradox divides most of the remaining space between the codepool and the cache. If an application has little table activity but uses many variables and a fancy interface with menus and windows, you may increase performance by giving more memory to the codepool. For example, you can allocate it 1,000K from the DOS prompt with

```
Paradox -codepool 1000
```

Paradox uses the cache to hold copies of PAL scripts, procedures, forms, and tables that it swapped for lack of space. If your application has many procedures over 10K each, you may improve performance by increasing the cache up to the maximum of 200K. To allocate that amount, use

```
Paradox -cachek 200
```

You can combine options on the command line by separating them with spaces.

Directory Management

Whenever you refer to an object such as a table or form, Paradox uses DOS to locate it in the current working directory or the user's private directory. If the directory contains more than 100 to 150 files, searching is slow. You can improve performance by subdividing it.

You must keep table families together, but you can put lookup tables in another directory. Dummy tables holding form and report specifications are not members of a family, so you can separate them also.

> **Tip**
>
> Keep scripts in the same directory with their libraries so they will be available for the debugger if a runtime error occurs.

Lastly, you can place tables with menu choices, printer options, and other system information in their own directory.

Table 10-2 shows a naming scheme for a sample directory layout.

Table 10-2. Sample Directory Layout

Directory	Contents
Applib	Application with starting script (home directory)
Dummy	Dummy tables with forms and reports
Library	Paradox libraries and source scripts
Lookup	Paradox lookup tables
System	System tables
Tables	Paradox tables and their families

Besides improving performance, this arrangement keeps the application together logically, and makes backup programs easier to use. Figure 10-1 is a directory tree for the example.

```
C:\ — Applib\
            |
            |
            |— Dummy
            |
            |— Library
            |
            |— Lookup
            |
            |— System
            |
            |— Tables
```

Figure 10-1. Example directory layout.

Applib is the working directory. You must reference all objects in PAL programs relative to it. For example, the following commands load a Customer table onto the desktop and select a form.

```
VIEW "\\Tables\\Customer"
PICKFORM 1
```

> **Tip**
>
> Design all application objects such as forms and reports in the working directory so Paradox records the correct path to them. Otherwise, it will not find them when you run the application.

Improving Network Performance

You can improve network performance by using a workstation's hard disk rather than the file server's whenever possible. If you put a user's private directory on the local PC rather then on the server, Paradox need not send private data such as Answer tables across the network. Queries thus run faster. Paradox also uses the private directory as a scratchpad for sorts and restructures, so they will run faster too.

You can install a standalone copy of Paradox on a local PC and configure it to read shared tables on the network. The installation program asks if you want this option. Paradox operates faster when installed locally because it need not access system files stored on the network, only data.

Paradox can cache table data if the file is locked exclusively (full lock) or the table is read-only or in a read-only directory. It does not cache for other configurations. Paradox checks the cache for data first, only going to the disk if it cannot find what it needs. Fewer trips to the disk mean faster performance.

You can also change the screen refresh rate. Paradox freezes actions while it refreshes the screen, thus slowing applications.

Using a Local Hard Disk

The file server processes disk requests one at a time. As more users make them, the backlog increases and performance slows.

You can reduce delays by using the standalone copy of Paradox mentioned earlier. You must change the PATH statement in a user's AUTOEXEC.BAT file to search the local directory first. Paradox will read system files from the local disk rather than from the server, thus reducing the request backlog and improving performance.

Placing a user's private directory on the local disk also improves performance. If it is on the server, Paradox moves private tables such as Answer, Changed, and Crosstab there. If it is on a local drive, no movement is necessary. This reduces network traffic.

Caching Data

Paradox does not usually cache network data. In practice, this means it makes extra trips to the disk. The result is lower performance, as disks are much slower than memory.

Paradox caches network data if the file has a full lock on it, it is a read-only file, or it is in a read-only directory. You use the LOCK command to place a full lock. The following example puts a full lock on the Customer table. Paradox sets Retval to True if it obtains the lock and False otherwise.

```
LOCK "Customer" FL
```

Remember to unlock the table when the application no longer needs it. Otherwise, other users will be locked out until the application issues a RESET command (unlocking all tables) or the current Paradox session ends. You unlock a table by including its name and the lock type in an UNLOCK statement as follows.

```
UNLOCK "Customer" FL
```

You can also make a file read-only by using the DOS ATTRIB command with the +R switch. You can set it for a group of files at the DOS prompt before starting Paradox, or use the RUN command in an application. The following command sets it for the Customer table family at the DOS prompt.

```
ATTRIB +R Customer.*
```

> **Warning**
>
> Set the read-only attribute for an entire table family, not just the data file. If you set the attribute for the data only, Paradox may corrupt family members such as forms and reports.

RUN suspends Paradox temporarily and transfers control to DOS. The user must type EXIT or put it at the end of a DOS batch file to return to Paradox. Paradox restores the environment afterward.

The following example transfers control to DOS and runs the batch file SETATTRB.BAT. It puts the read-only attribute on the Customer table and its family, then returns control to Paradox.

```
RUN "SETATTRB"
```

The SETATTRB.BAT file contains the following commands.

```
ATTRIB +R Customer.*
EXIT
```

You remove the read-only attribute from files using the -R switch. The following example restores read/write access to the Customer table and its family.

```
ATTRIB -R Customer.*
```

You can specify a shared directory as read-only, thus making all files in it read-only, regardless of their individual attributes, using the following Paradox menu path.

```
Tools/Net/Lock/DirLock/DirectoryPath/Set
```

DirectoryPath is the full path to the directory you want to make read-only. You can remove the setting with the same path and Clear instead of Set.

Setting the Refresh Interval

If users must have write access to shared data, you can change the screen refresh rate to improve performance. Paradox automatically refreshes table data displayed in table or form view based on a rate in seconds. This assures that all users are viewing the most current information. During refresh, Paradox freezes the screen until it redraws everything and then returns control to the application.

If operators are doing heavy data entry such as taking telephone orders, the default refresh rate of three seconds may be inconvenient. You can change it permanently using the Custom Configuration Program or temporarily in an application.

To change it permanently, play the Custom script and select the Net menu choice. Change the rate in seconds and save the configuration file. You can turn refresh off by entering 0. You can change the rate in an application similarly by selecting the Paradox menu path Tools/Net/AutoRefresh.

If a user begins to coedit a record that has changed since the last refresh, Paradox updates it before allowing him or her to continue.

Upgrading Hardware

You can always improve performance by upgrading your hardware. And hardware can always be upgraded, often at amazingly low prices. Most database applications are CPU intensive, so buying the fastest processor you can afford will provide a dramatic improvement.

A memory upgrade will also help. Paradox automatically uses all available extended memory. The space for time rule states that the more space an operation has, the faster it runs. Paradox swaps code and data among main memory, cache, and disk. The fewer disk accesses it makes, the better your application performs. You can also buy faster network interface cards with wider buses and more local memory. If you are not using SQL server technology, a tremendous amount of data is moving across the network. A faster card speeds data transfers.

The continuing rapid advances in hardware mean that better things are surely available. If you haven't visited your supplier lately (say within the last few months), you will probably be amazed. Bigger and faster disks, faster processors, faster cards, and larger memories—and at lower prices besides! What a business!

Using a Database Server

One way to reduce network traffic, thus improving performance, is to use client server technology. It places the intelligence at the network server rather than the local PC. With a file server configuration, even if Paradox is installed on the network and all tables are stored there, decisions are still made locally.

For example, suppose a user creates the following query for a 10,000 record Customer table stored on the network:

```
Query
Customer  | Company Name   | Total Sales  |
          | √              | > 5000       |
Endquery
```

Even with multiuser Paradox, all 10,000 records must travel across the network to the user's PC. The decision on whether to keep them is made there. Assume that 4,000 records match the query and the user's private directory is on the network. Paradox creates the Answer table there, so it will send 4,000 records back across the network.

With a client server architecture, Paradox is installed on the network along with shared tables, and decisions such as whether a record belongs in the Answer table occur there too. In the query example, no records would travel across the network. The user creates the request on a local PC and submits it to Paradox by pressing F2 to DO_IT!. The query runs on the network server, not the local machine. If the private directory is on the network, Paradox stores matching records in the Answer table there. Only the request travels across the network. The time savings are obviously enormous.

You need two software packages to switch from file server to client server organization, a database server and SQL Link. The server, such as Microsoft's SQL Server, allows processing at the network level. (Easy to explain but often difficult to configure!) Borland's SQL Link, an add-on to PAL, provides commands for accessing shared tables.

You can use SQL Link to perform queries on shared and local tables using Paradox's Query-by-Example facility. SQL Link also adds PAL commands to operate on server tables. The following command selects all fields from the Customer table for Connecticut customers and creates an Answer table.

```
SQL
  SELECT * FROM Customer WHERE State = "CT"
ENDSQL
```

SQL Link's biggest drawback is that it can update only in batch mode, not on-line. You may change tables using DataEntry mode only. All other options on the Modify menu, including Sort, Edit, and Coedit, are disabled. This may make it inappropriate for applications such as order entry where the user needs to see current inventory levels immediately.

Summary

Users often think sluggish systems are not working and complain about them bitterly. You can improve performance by packaging procedures in libraries. Assigning a series of library names to the Autolib variable also allows Paradox to manage memory automatically and frees you from the chore of explicitly reading procedures from libraries and releasing them when done.

Paradox optimizes queries, so using them rather than code will also help performance. You can speed up searches by creating secondary indexes on non-key fields, but Paradox will not use them for queries with wildcard operators.

Upgrading hardware helps performance, as does tuning Paradox memory allocation to match application needs.

DOS locates Paradox objects faster if you limit directories to 150 files. You can divide application files into multiple directories (as long as you keep families together). Paradox encourages strong family ties!

Paradox can cache read-only files or ones located in read-only directories. Making fewer trips to the disk for data improves performance. Paradox will also cache data from tables locked with a full lock.

If users must have write access to tables, you can change the screen refresh rate. Raising it means that Paradox waits longer between refreshes and thus does not slow data entry.

You may also consider changing your architecture from file server to client server to improve performance. This moves processing from the local PC to the server, thus reducing network traffic.

Appendix A
Paradox Keycodes

Table A-1. Paradox Extended Keycodes

Extended Code	Name	Keys
-2	AltSpace	Alt-Space
-3		Null
-4	ClipCopy	Ctrl-Ins
-5	ClipPaste	Shift-Ins
-6		Ctrl-Del
-7	ClipCut	Shift-Del
-15	Reverse Tab	Shift-Tab
-16		Alt-Q
-17		Alt-W
-18	MiniEdit	Alt-E
-19	Refresh	Alt-R
-20		Alt-T
-21		Alt-Y
-22		Alt-U
-23		Alt-I
-24	DosBig	Alt-O
-25		Alt-P
-30	ReplaceNext	Alt-A
-31	OrderTable	Alt-S
-32	DeleteWord	Alt-D
-33		Alt-F
-34		Alt-G
-35		Alt-H
-36		Alt-J

Extended Code	Name	Keys
-37	KeyLookup	Alt-K
-38	LockKey	Alt-L
-44	ZoomNext	Alt-Z
-45	Crosstab	Alt-X
-46	TogglePalette	Alt-C
-47		Alt-V
-48		Alt-B
-49		Alt-N
-50		Alt-M
-59	Help,F1	F1
-60	Do_It!,F2	F2
-61	UpImage,F3	F3
-62	DownImage,F4	F4
-63	Example,F5	F5
-64	Check,F6	F6
-65	FormKey,F7	F7
-66	ClearImage,F8	F8
-67	EditKey,F9	F9
-68	Menu,F10	F10
-71	Home	Home
-72	Up	Up Arrow
-73	PgUp	PgUp
-75	Left	Left Arrow
-77	Right	Right Arrow
-79	End	End
-80	Down	Down
-81	PgDn	PgDn
-82	Ins	Ins
-83	Del	Del
-84	F11	Shift-F1
-85	F12	Shift-F2
-86	F13	Shift-F3
-87	F14	Shift-F4

Extended Code	Name	Keys
-88	WinMax,F15	Shift-F5
-89	GroupBy,F16	Shift-F6
-90	F17	Shift-F7
-91	F18	Shift-F8
-92	F19	Shift-F9
-93	F20	Shift-F10
-94	F21	Ctrl-F1
-95	F22	Ctrl-F2
-96	F23	Ctrl-F3
-97	WinNext,F24	Ctrl-F4
-98	WinResize,F25	Ctrl-F5
-99	CheckDecending,F26	Ctrl-F6
-100	GraphKey,F27	Ctrl-F7
-101	WinClose,F28	Ctrl-F8
-102	F29	Ctrl-F9
-103	ToQpro,F30	Ctrl-F10
-104	F31	Alt-F1
-105	F32	Alt-F2
-106	InstantRecord,F33	Alt-F3
-107	InstantPlay,F34	Alt-F4
-108	FieldView,F35	Alt-F5
-109	CheckPlus,F36	Alt-F6
-110	InstantReport,F37	Alt-F7
-111	Clearall,F8	Alt-F8
-112	CoeditKey,F39	Alt-F9
-113	PalMenu,F40	Alt-F10
-114		Ctrl-PrtSc
-115	CtrlLeft	Ctrl-<
-116	CtrlRight	Ctrl->
-117	CtrlEnd	Ctrl-End
-118	CtrlPgDn	Ctrl-PgDn
-119	CtrlHome	Ctrl-Home
-120		Alt-1

Extended Code	Name	Keys
-121		Alt-2
-122		Alt-3
-123		Alt-4
-124		Alt-5
-125		Alt-6
-126		Alt-7
-127		Alt-8
-128		Alt-9
-129		Alt-0
-130		Alt--
-131		Alt-=
-132	CtrlPgUp	Ctrl-PgUp

Table A-2. Paradox ASCII Keycodes

ASCII Character	Name	Keys
0		Ctrl-@
1	Replace	Ctrl-A
2		Ctrl-B
3		Ctrl-C
4	Ditto	Ctrl-D
5		Ctrl-E
6	FieldView	Ctrl-F
7	Go	Ctrl-G
8	Backspace	Backspace, Ctrl-H
9	Tab	Tab, Ctrl-I
10		Ctrl-J
11		Ctrl-K
12	ResyncKey	Ctrl-L
13	Enter	Enter, Ctrl-M
14		Ctrl-N
15		Ctrl-O
16		Ctrl-P
17		Ctrl-Q
18	Rotate	Ctrl-R
19		Ctrl-S
20		Ctrl-T
21	Undo	Ctrl-U
22	VertRuler	Ctrl-V
23		Ctrl-W
24		Ctrl-X
25	DeleteLine	Ctrl-Y
26	Zoom	Ctrl-Z
27	Esc	Esc, Ctrl-], Ctrl-Esc
28		Ctrl-\
29		Ctrl-[

ASCII Character	Name	Keys
30		Ctrl-^
31		Ctrl-_
32	Space	Space bar Alt-Space Ctrl-Space Shift-Space
33	!	!
34	"	"
35	#	#
36	$	$
37	%	%
38	&	&
39	'	'
40	(	(
41	)	)
42	*	*
43	+	+
44	,	,
45	-	-
46	.	.
47	/	/
48	0	0
49	1	1
50	2	2
51	3	3
52	4	4
53	5	5
54	6	6
55	7	7
56	8	8
57	9	9
58	:	:
59	;	;

ASCII Character	Name	Keys
60	<	<
61	=	=
62	>	>
63	?	?
64	@	@
65	A	Shift-A
66	B	Shift-B
67	C	Shift-C
68	D	Shift-D
69	E	Shift-E
70	F	Shift-F
71	G	Shift-G
72	H	Shift-H
73	I	Shift-I
74	J	Shift-J
75	K	Shift-K
76	L	Shift-L
77	M	Shift-M
78	N	Shift-N
79	O	Shift-O
80	P	Shift-P
81	Q	Shift-Q
82	R	Shift-R
83	S	Shift-S
84	T	Shift-T
85	U	Shift-U
86	V	Shift-V
87	W	Shift-W
88	X	Shift-X
89	Y	Shift-Y
90	Z	Shift-Z
91	[	[
92	\	\

ASCII Character	Name	Keys
93	]	]
94	^	^
95	_	_
96	`	`
97	a	A
98	b	B
99	c	C
100	d	D
101	e	E
102	f	F
103	g	G
104	h	H
105	i	I
106	j	J
107	k	K
108	l	L
109	m	M
110	n	N
111	o	O
112	p	P
113	q	Q
114	r	R
115	s	S
116	t	T
117	u	U
118	v	V
119	w	W
120	x	X
121	y	Y
122	z	Z
123	{	{
124	|	|
125	}	}

ASCII Character	Name	Keys
126	~	~
127	CtrlBackSpace	CtrlBackSpace
128 - 255		Alt-Keypad # (Table B-1)

Appendix B
ASCII Character Set

Table B-1. ASCII Character Set

ASCII Character	Screen Symbol	Keys	ASCII Character	Screen Symbol	Keys
0	Blank		127	/	Alt-127
	Null	Ctrl-@	128	Ç	Alt-128
1	☺	Ctrl-A	129	ü	Alt-129
2	☻	Ctrl-B	130	é	Alt-130
3	♥	Ctrl-C	131	â	Alt-131
4	♦	Ctrl-D	132	ä	Alt-132
5	♣	Ctrl-E	133	à	Alt-133
6	♠	Ctrl-F	134	å	Alt-134
7	•	Ctrl-G	135	ç	Alt-135
8	◘	Ctrl-H	136	ê	Alt-136
9	○	Ctrl-I	137	ë	Alt-137
10	◙	Ctrl-J	138	è	Alt-138
11	♂	Ctrl-K	139	ï	Alt-139
12	♀	Ctrl-L	140	î	Alt-140
13	♪	Ctrl-M	141	ì	Alt-141
14	♫	Ctrl-N	142	Ä	Alt-142
15	☼	Ctrl-O	143	Å	Alt-143
16	►	Ctrl-P	144	É	Alt-144
17	◄	Ctrl-Q	145	æ	Alt-145
18	↕	Ctrl-R	146	Æ	Alt-146
19	‼	Ctrl-S	147	ô	Alt-147
20	¶	Ctrl-T	148	ö	Alt-148
21	§	Ctrl-U	149	ò	Alt-149
22	▬	Ctrl-V	150	û	Alt-150
23	↨	Ctrl-W	151	ù	Alt-151

ASCII Character	Screen Symbol	Keys	ASCII Character	Screen Symbol	Keys
24	↑	Ctrl-X	152	ÿ	Alt-152
25	↓	Ctrl-Y	153	Ö	Alt-153
26	→	Ctrl-Z	154	Ü	Alt-154
27	←	Ctrl-[	155	¢	Alt-155
28	∟	Ctrl-\	156	£	Alt-156
29	↔	Ctrl-]	157	¥	Alt-157
30	▲	Ctrl-6	158	₧	Alt-158
31	▼	Ctrl-_	159	ƒ	Alt-159
32	Blank	Space bar	160	á	Alt-160
33	!	!	161	í	Alt-161
34	"	"	162	ó	Alt-162
35	#	#	163	ú	Alt-163
36	$	$	164	ñ	Alt-164
37	%	%	165	Ñ	Alt-165
38	&	&	166	ª	Alt-166
39	'	'	167	º	Alt-167
40	(	(	168	¿	Alt-168
41	)	)	169	⌐	Alt-169
42	*	*	170	¬	Alt-170
43	+	+	171	½	Alt-171
44	,	,	172	¼	Alt-172
45	-	-	173	¡	Alt-173
46	.	.	174	«	Alt-174
47	/	/	175	»	Alt-175
48	0	0	176	░	Alt-176
49	1	1	177	▒	Alt-177
50	2	2	178	▓	Alt-178
51	3	3	179	│	Alt-179
52	4	4	180	┤	Alt-180
53	5	5	181	╡	Alt-181
54	6	6	182	╢	Alt-182
55	7	7	183	╖	Alt-183
56	8	8	184	╕	Alt-184
57	9	9	185	╣	Alt-185
58	:	:	186	║	Alt-186

ASCII Character	Screen Symbol	Keys	ASCII Character	Screen Symbol	Keys
59	;	;	187	╗	Alt-187
60	<	<	188	╝	Alt-188
61	=	=	189	╜	Alt-189
62	>	>	190	╛	Alt-190
63	?	?	191	┐	Alt-191
64	@	@	192	└	Alt-192
65	A	A	193	┴	Alt-193
66	B	B	194	┬	Alt-194
67	C	C	195	├	Alt-195
68	D	D	196	─	Alt-196
69	E	E	197	┼	Alt-197
70	F	F	198	╞	Alt-198
71	G	G	199	╟	Alt-199
72	H	H	200	╚	Alt-200
73	I	I	201	╔	Alt-201
74	J	J	202	╩	Alt-202
75	K	K	203	╦	Alt-203
76	L	L	204	╠	Alt-204
77	M	M	205	═	Alt-205
78	N	N	206	╬	Alt-206
79	O	O	207	╧	Alt-207
80	P	P	208	╨	Alt-208
81	Q	Q	209	╤	Alt-209
82	R	R	210	╥	Alt-210
83	S	S	211	╙	Alt-211
84	T	T	212	╘	Alt-212
85	U	U	213	╒	Alt-213
86	V	V	214	╓	Alt-214
87	W	W	215	╫	Alt-215
88	X	X	216	╪	Alt-216
89	Y	Y	217	┘	Alt-217
90	Z	Z	218	┌	Alt-218
91	[	[	219	█	Alt-219
92	\	\	220	▄	Alt-220
93	]	]	221	▌	Alt-221

ASCII Character	Screen Symbol	Keys	ASCII Character	Screen Symbol	Keys
94	^	^	222	▐	Alt-222
95	_	_	223	▀	Alt-223
96	`	`	224	α	Alt-224
97	a	a	225	ß	Alt-225
98	b	b	226	Γ	Alt-226
99	c	c	227	π	Alt-227
100	d	d	228	Σ	Alt-228
101	e	e	229	σ	Alt-229
102	f	f	230	μ	Alt-230
103	g	g	231	τ	Alt-231
104	h	h	232	Φ	Alt-232
105	i	i	233	■	Alt-223
106	j	j	234	Ω	Alt-234
107	k	k	235	δ	Alt-235
108	l	l	236	∞	Alt-236
109	m	m	237	φ	Alt-237
110	n	n	238	ε	Alt-238
111	o	o	239	∩	Alt-239
112	p	p	240		Alt-240
113	q	q	241	±	Alt-241
114	r	r	242	≥	Alt-242
115	s	s	243	≤	Alt-243
116	t	t	244	⌠	Alt-244
117	u	u	245	⌡	Alt-245
118	v	v	246	÷	Alt-246
119	w	w	247	≈	Alt-247
120	x	x	248	°	Alt-248
121	y	y	249	•	Alt-249
122	z	z	250	·	Alt-250
123	{	{	251	√	Alt-251
124	|	|	252	^{n}	Alt-252
125	}	}	253	^{2}	Alt-253
126	~	~	254	■	Alt-254
			255		Alt-255

Appendix C
Paradox Commands

Name	Description
=	Assign a value
?	Display text on next line
??	Display text to right of cursor
@	Position cursor at row and column
ACCEPT	Accept value entered on canvas
ACCECTDIALOG	Accept current dialog box
ADD	Combine two tables
ALTSPACE	Pull down system menu
APPENDARRAY	Append list of arrays to a table
ARRAY	Declare a fixed array
BACKSPACE	Move cursor back one character
BEEP	Sound beep
CALCDEBUG	Turn calculated field error message on or off
CANCELEDIT	Cancel changes, return to Main mode
CANCELDIALOG	Cancel current dialog box
CANVAS	Turn canvas display on or off
CHECK	Place or remove check mark
CHECKDESCENDING	Place or remove check descending mark
CHECKPLUS	Place or remove check plus mark
CLEAR	Clear all or part of canvas
CLEARALL	Clear all images from desktop
CLEARIMAGE	Clear current image from desktop
CLEARPULLDOWN	Clear current pulldown menu
CLIPCOPY	Copy editor text to clipboard
CLIPCUT	Copy editor text to clipboard and delete it
CLIPPASTE	Paste clipboard text at cursor in editor
CLOSE PRINTER	Close printer opened with OPEN PRINTER
COEDIT	Coedit a table
COEDITKEY	Place all desktop images in Coedit mode

Name	Description
CONVERTLIB	Convert 3.0 or 3.5 library to 4.0 format
COPY	Copy table and family to new name
COPYFORM	Copy form between tables
COPYFROMARRAY	Copy array to current record
COPYREPORT	Copy report between tables
COPYTOARRAY	Copy current record to array
CREATE	Create new Paradox table
CREATELIB	Create a new library
CROSSTABKEY	Crosstabulate current table
CTRLBACKSPACE	Erase current field contents
CTRLBREAK	Stop current task
CTRLEND	Move cursor depending on mode
CTRLHOME	Move cursor depending on mode
CTRLLEFT	Move cursor depending on mode
CTRLPGDN	Move cursor depending on mode
CTRLPGUP	Move cursor depending on mode
CTRLRIGHT	Move cursor depending on mode
CURSOR	Change canvas cursor appearance
DEBUG	Transfer control to PAL Debugger
DEL	Delete current record
DELETE	Delete table and its family
DELETELINE	Delete current text line
DELETEWORD	Delete current word in editor
DITTO	Copy last value for field to current field
DO_IT!	Complete an operation
DOS	Suspend Paradox, run DOS shell with 200K
DOSBIG	Suspend Paradox, run DOS shell with 500K
DOWN	Move cursor down one line or record
	Move cursor down one image
DYNARRAY	Create dynamic array
ECHO	Change desktop display status during script play
EDIT	Edit Paradox table
EDITKEY	Place all desktop images in Edit mode
EDITLOG	Record transactions during Edit and DataEntry for possible rollback

Name	Description
EDITOR EXTRACT	Save file to a variable
EDITOR FIND	Search file for a string
EDITOR FINDNEXT	Repeat last EDITOR FIND
EDITOR GOTO	Move cursor to specified location
EDITOR INFO	Create dynamic array for editor session
EDITOR INSERT	Write expression to editor session
EDITOR NEW	Open editor for new file
EDITOR OPEN	Open editor with existing file
EDITOR READ	Insert file at cursor in editor session
EDITOR REPLACE	Replace string in editor session
EDITOR SELECT	Select text in editor session
EDITOR WRITE	Write text to a file
EMPTY	Delete all table records
END	Move to last table record
ENTER	Press Enter key, result based on current mode
ERRORINFO	Create dynamic array for latest script error
ESC	Return to previous menu or exit command with no choice
EXAMPLE	Start example element in query
EXECEVENT	Execute event from dynamic array
EXECPROC	Execute procedure, do not accept arguments
EXECUTE	Execute procedure with optional arguments
EXIT	End script play, return control to DOS
FIELDVIEW	Change to Fieldview mode
FILEREAD	Read file into variable
FILEWRITE	Write expression to a file
FIRSTSHOW	Make current image the first image
FOR	Counting loop control structure
FOREACH	Dynamic loop control structure
FORMKEY	Toggle between form and table view
FORMTABLES	Create array of tables embedded on multi-table form
FRAME	Draw frame around current canvas
GETCOLORS	Create dynamic array of current palette
GETEVENT	Create dynamic array of specified event
GETKEYBOARDSTATE	Create dynamic array of keyboard state

Name	Description
GETMENUSELECTION	Start pulldown menu and get user's choice
GRAPHKEY	Graph current table
GROUPBY	Place or remove Groupby symbol in current query image
HELP	Display Paradox help system
HOME	Move to first table record
IF	Two-way programming decision
IMAGERIGHTS	Restrict access to current image
INDEX	Create secondary field index
INFOLIB	Create table of library procedures listing current size in bytes
INS	Insert a record or line
INSTANTPLAY	Play Instant script
INSTANTREPORT	Print report for current table
KEYLOOKUP	Move between records with duplicate keys in Coedit mode
KEYPRESS	Simulate pressing a key
LEFT	Move cursor left
LOCALIZEEVENT	Map mouse location from screen coordinates to window coordinates
LOCATE	Search for record with value in current field
LOCATE INDEXORDER	Locate record using secondary index
LOCK	Lock list of tables
LOCKKEY	Lock or unlock current record in Coedit
LOCKRECORD	Lock current record in Coedit
LOOP	Move to top of current loop
MENU	Display current menu
MENUDISABLE	Disable pulldown menu item
MENUENABLE	Enable pulldown menu item
MESSAGE	Display message in bottom right screen corner
MINIEDIT	Start editor session
MOUSE CLICK	Click mouse
MOUSE DOUBLECLICK	Double click mouse
MOUSE DRAG	Drag mouse
MOUSE HIDE	Hide mouse cursor (no skinning involved!)
MOUSE SHOW	Show mouse cursor

Name	Description
MOVETO	Move cursor to table, record, or field
NEWDIALOGSPEC	Change event list for dialog box
NEWWAITSPEC	Change event list for WAIT command
OPEN PRINTER	Open printer device
ORDERTABLE	Select or create secondary index
PAINTCANVAS	Color rectangular area of screen
PASSWORD	Present passwords to access encrypted tables
PGDN	Move down one page
PGUP	Move up one page
PICKFORM	Select form to display table
PLAY	Play a script
POSTRECORD	Post current record in Coedit mode
PRINT	Print expression list on printer or in file
PRINTER	Echo screen output to printer
PRIVTABLES	Create tables in private directory
PROC	Begin procedure definition
PROMPT	Assign prompt to display on line 24 of desktop
PROTECT	Assign master table password
QUERY	Define Paradox query
QUIT	Stop script play, return control to Paradox
QUITLOOP	Exit from current loop structure
READLIB	Load procedures from library to RAM
REFRESH	Update display images in Main or Coedit mode
REFRESHCONTROL	Refresh dialog box control element
REFRESHDIALOG	Refresh all dialog box control elements
RELEASE	Release variables or procedures from RAM
RENAME	Rename a table and its family
REPAINTDIAIOG	Repaint dialog box based on dynamic expressions
REPLACE	Replace highlighted value in editor
REPLACEFIELDS	Replace field values with expressions
REPLACENEXT	Find next occurrence of value in editor and replace it
REPORT	Send report to printer
REPORTTABLES	Create array of tables linked to current report
REQUIREDCHECK	Turn ValChecks for field on or off

Name	Description
RESET	Remove locks, close tables, and clear desktop
RESYNCCONTROL	Resynchronize control element in dialog box
RESYNCDIALOG	Resynchronize all control elements in dialog box
RESYNCKEY	Resynchronize detail record display for changed master record
RETURN	Exit current script or procedure
REVERSETAB	Move cursor to previous field
RIGHT	Move cursor right
ROTATE	Move current field to far right in current table image
RUN	Suspend Paradox, run external program
SAVETABLES	Write changed table buffers to disk
SAVEVARS	Write current variable values to disk
SCAN	Sequential loop structure
SCROLLPRESS	Press Scroll Lock plus direction key
SELECT	Select option from current menu
SELECTCONTROL	Move to control element in dialog box
SETAUTOSAVE	Set automatic save period
SETBATCH	Group operations in multiuser environment to improve speed
SETBW	Select black and white palette
SETCANVAS	Direct canvas commands to a window
SETCOLORS	Set palette from a dynamic array
SETDIR	Change working directory
SETKEY	Define keyboard macro
SETKEYBOARDSTATE	Set states of Num Lock, Caps Lock, and Scroll Lock keys
SETMARGIN	Set left margin for text display
SETMAXSIZE	Make disk block size larger than default, allowing larger tables
SETNEGCOLOR	Assign color used for negative number display
SETPRINTER	Set printer port
SETPRIVDIR	Assign private directory path
SETQUERYORDER	Set query order to table or image
SETRECORDPOSITION	Move cursor to specific record in multi-table form

Name	Description
SETRESTARTCOUNT	Limit number of times Paradox will try to restart query, report, or crosstab on shared tables
SETRETRYPERIOD	Set number of seconds for which Paradox will try a lock
SETSWAP	Set minimum amount of available RAM before swapping occurs
SETUIMODE	Select 3.5 or 4.0 user interface
SETUSERNAME	Set current user name
SHIFTPRESS	Press Shift plus direction key in editor
SHOWARRAY	Display Paradox style menu using two arrays
SHOWFILES	Display Paradox style menu of files in specified directory
SHOWDIALOG	Display dialog box
SHOWMENU	Display Paradox style menu
SHOWPOPUP	Display popup menu
SHOWPULLDOWN	Display pulldown menu
SHOWTABLES	Display Paradox style menu of tables in specified directory
SKIP	Skip number of records from current position
SLEEP	Pause script play up to 30 seconds
SORT	Sort records in a table
SOUND	Create sound with frequency and duration
STYLE	Change screen attribute for future text display
SUBTRACT	Delete records from a table that have matching ones in a second table
SWITCH	Multi-way branching structure
SYNCCURSOR	Position canvas cursor in same location as workspace cursor
SYSINFO	Create dynamic array of current hardware and software setup
TAB	Move cursor to next field
TEXT	Display text lines on screen
TOGGLEPALETTE	Turn color palette display on or off
TOQPRO	Suspend Paradox to run Quattro Pro
TYPEIN	Type string of characters into Paradox reports and forms

Name	Description
UNDO	Reverse latest table change
UNLOCK	Unlock list of locked tables
UNLOCKRECORD	Unlock currently locked record
UNPASSWORD	Remove access to tables opened with PASSWORD command
UP	Move cursor up one line or record
UPIMAGE	Move cursor up one image
VERTRULER	Display vertical ruler in report and script editor
VIEW	Display Paradox table
WAIT	Let user interact with table on desktop in table or form view
WHILE	Conditional loop structure
WINCLOSE	Close current window
WINDOW CLOSE	Close window
WINDOW CREATE	Create canvas window
WINDOW ECHO	Set echo state for specified window
WINDOW	Create dynamic array of window attributes GETATTRIBUTES
WINDOW GETCOLORS	Create dynamic array of window colors
WINDOW HANDLE	Get handle of current window
WINDOW LIST	Create fixed array of window handles
WINDOW MAXIMIZE	Maximize or restore original window size
WINDOW MOVE	Move window
WINDOW RESIZE	Change window size
WINDOW SCROLL	Scroll window to specified location
WINDOW SELECT	Make specified window current
WINDOW	Change window attributes from dynamic SETATTRIBUTES array
WINDOW SETCOLORS	Change window palette from dynamic array
WINMAX	Maximize or restore original window size
WINNEXT	Move to next window
WINRESIZE	Move or resize window using arrow keys
WRITELIB	Write procedures to specified library
ZOOM	Move cursor to first matching record with value in field
ZOOMNEXT	Move cursor to next matching record with value in field

Appendix D
Paradox Functions

Name	Returns
ABS	Absolute value
ACOS	Arc cosine of a number in radians
ARRAYSIZE	Number of array elements
ASC	ASCII version of a character
ASIN	Arc sine of a number in radians
ATAN	Arc tangent of a number in radians
ATAN2	4-quadrant arc tangent of angle in radians
ATFIRST	True if current record is first in image, False otherwise
ATLAST	True if current record is last in image, False otherwise
BANDINFO	Current report band
BLANKDATE	Blank date value
BLANKNUM	Blank number
BOT	True if MOVETO or SKIP will move cursor to table top
CAVERAGE	Average for table field values
CCOUNT	Count of non-blank record values in a field
CHARWAITING	True if character waiting in buffer, False otherwise
CHECKMARKSTATUS	Null if field not checked, or type of check present
CHR	One character string corresponding to ASCII value
CMAX	Largest value in field
CMIN	Smallest value in field
CNPV	Net present value
COL	Cursor column on canvas
COLNO	Column number for current image
CONTROLVALUE	Specified dialog box control element

Name	Returns
COS	Cosine of a number in radians
CSTD	Standard deviation of field
CSUM	Sum of field
CURSORCHAR	Character at cursor
CURSORLINE	Current text line
CVAR	Variance of field
DATEVAL	Date equivalent of string
DAY	Day of month
DIRECTORY	Current working directory
DIREXISTS	1 if directory exists, 0 if it does not, -1 if path is invalid
DOW	Day of week as a string
DRIVESPACE	Number of unused bytes on drive
DRIVESTATUS	True if drive is ready, False otherwise
DYNARRAYSIZE	Size of a dynamic array
EOT	True if MOVETO, SKIP, or LOCATE will move cursor to end of table, False otherwise
ERRORCODE	Current error code number
ERRORMESSAGE	Current error message
ERRORUSER	Name of user trying to lock currently locked object
EXP	Exponential
FAMILYRIGHTS	True if user has specified table rights, False otherwise
FIELD	Current field name
FIELDINFO	Current contents of mode indicator in form and report editor
FIELDNO	Physical field number in table structure
FIELDRIGHTS	True if user can modify field, False otherwise
FIELDSTR	Contents of field as a string
FIELDTYPE	Field type
FILESIZE	Size of file in bytes
FILEVERSION	Paradox version used to create a library or table
FILL	String filled with a single character
FORM	Current form number
FORMAT	Formatted string for display or printing

Name	Returns
FORMTYPE	True if form is type specified, False otherwise
FV	Future value for series of equal payments
GETCANVAS	Window handle for current canvas
GETCHAR	ASCII value of character collected from the keyboard
GETWINDOW	Handle for current window
GRAPHTYPE	Current graph type
HELPMODE	String of current help type
IFF	One of two values based on a condition
IMAGECAVERAGE	Average value of field in current view
IMAGECCOUNT	Number of nonblank values in field in current view
IMAGECMAX	Largest value in field in current view
IMAGECMIN	Smallest value in field in current view
IMAGECSUM	Sum of values in field in current view
IMAGENO	Current image number
IMAGETYPE	Current image type
INT	Greatest integer value of a number
ISASSIGNED	True if variable assigned, False otherwise
ISBLANK	True if expression is blank, False otherwise
ISBLANKZERO	True if Blank=Zero option true in configuration, False otherwise
ISEMPTY	True if table empty, False otherwise
ISENCRYPTED	True if table encrypted, False otherwise
ISFIELDVIEW	True if in field view, False otherwise
ISFILE	True if file exists, False otherwise
ISFORMVIEW	True if current image displayed with form, False otherwise
ISINSERTMODE	True if in insert mode, False otherwise
ISLINKLOCKED	True if current table link locked, False otherwise
ISMASTER	True if table is encrypted and master password specified, False otherwise
ISMULTIFORM	True if current form has embedded table, False otherwise
ISMULTIREPORT	True if current report has linked tables, False otherwise

Name	Returns
ISRUNTIME	True if script playing under Runtime, False otherwise
ISSHARED	True if table in shared directory, False otherwise
ISTABLE	True if table exists, False otherwise
ISVALID	True if current field conforms to ValChecks, False otherwise
ISWINDOW	True if argument is an active window handle, False otherwise
LEN	Length of string
LINKTYPE	Link between current master and detail tables
LN	Natural logarithm
LOCKSTATUS	Number of occurrences of lock type on current table
LOG	Base 10 logarithm
LOWER	String converted to lowercase
MATCH	True if pattern in string, False otherwise
MAX	Larger of two numbers
MEMLEFT	Number of bytes of RAM currently available
MENUCHOICE	Current menu choice
MENUPROMPT	Text of current menu choice
MIN	Smaller of two numbers
MOD	Modulus (remainder) from division
MONITOR	Monitor type as a string
MONTH	Month number from a date
MOY	Month abbreviation
NETTYPE	Type of network as a string
NFIELDS	Number of fields in table
NIMAGERECORDS	Number of records in current image
NIMAGES	Number of images on desktop
NKEYFIELDS	Number of key fields
NPAGES	Number of pages in current form
NRECORDS	Number of records in table
NROWS	Number of rows in current image
NUMVAL	Number equivalent of string
PAGENO	Page number of current form or report

Name	Returns
PAGEWIDTH	Number of characters per line for current report
PI	Value of Pi (π)
PMT	Loan payment per period
POW	Number raised to a power
PRINTERSTATUS	True if printer available, False otherwise
PRIVDIR	DOS path to private directory
PV	Present value of payments
QUERYORDER	Query order selected in custom configuration
RAND	Random number between 0 and 1
RECNO	Current record number
RECORDSTATUS	True if record in listed status, False otherwise
RETRYPERIOD	Number of seconds for which Paradox will retry a lock
RMEMLEFT	Number of bytes an application can borrow when memory gets low
ROUND	Rounded number
ROW	Current canvas cursor row
ROWNO	Row number in current image
SDIR	DOS path of currently executing script
SEARCH	Character position within string where match found or 0 if not found
SEARCHFROM	Position of substring within string, or 0 if no match found
SIN	Sine of number in radians
SORTORDER	Sort order selected in custom configuration
SPACES	String of spaces
SQRT	Square root
STRVAL	String equivalent for all data types
SUBSTR	Substring of specified length
SYSCOLOR	Color attribute of specified Paradox screen element
SYSMODE	Current Paradox mode
TABLE	Current table name
TABLERIGHTS	True if user may access current object based on password, False otherwise
TAN	Tangent of number in radians

Name	Returns
TICKS	Time of day as an integer
TIME	Current system time
TODAY	Current date
TYPE	Paradox data type of expression
UPPER	String converted to uppercase
USDATE	Data in U.S. format
USERNAME	Current user name
VERSION	Paradox version number
WINDOW	String with current workspace message
WINDOWAT	Topmost window handle with specified coordinates
YEAR	Number for year in specified date

Appendix E
Checkpoint Answers

CheckPoint 2-1. Recording Scripts

A Customer table has the following structure:

Field Name	Type
Cust Id	N*
Name	A15
Address	A15
City	A10
State	A2
Zip	A5

Press Alt-F3 to begin recording an Instant script to sort the Customer table by Name to a new table Sorttbl. Press the following keys to perform the sort.

```
{Modify} {Sort} {Customer} {Sorttbl} Down "1" Do_It!
```

Press Alt-F3 to stop recording when the sorted table appears on the desktop. Remember, if you play the Instant script again, Sorttbl already exists and Paradox displays the Cancel/Replace menu. Delete it with Tools/More/Delete/Table first.

CheckPoint 2-2. PAL Commands

The WHILE loop lets the user try to correct printer problems three times before it quits. Ctr equals 4 after the ENDWHILE statement if the printer is still not ready. Add the following statements to test the counter and display a message if the user could not correct the problem.

```
;If Ctr = 4, printer still not ready
;Display message for 2 seconds
IF Ctr = 4 THEN
  MESSAGE "Printer still not ready! - request abandoned"
  SLEEP 2000
  MESSAGE ""
ENDIF
```

CheckPoint 3-1. Add a Menu Option

All you must do is add a record to the Maint table to display the new option to delete customers. Procedure Domenu reads the table including the new choice the next time the user selects the maintenance menu. Add the following record to table Maint.

Item	Desc	Proc	Args
Delete	Delete Customers	Delit	

CheckPoint 3-2. Add a Submenu

Domenu calls the procedure in the Proc field of a menu table entry when a user selects an option. You can change the Edit choice to call a submenu by changing its Proc field to Domenu and the argument list to "Editcust".

Editcust is the table containing the menu choices. Use the Paradox COPY command to copy the Maint table to Editcust with the following path.

```
Tools/Copy/Table/Maint/Editcust
```

Modify Editcust so it contains the following choices for changing customer names and searching by city.

Item	Des	Proc	Args
Change	Change Cust Names	Chgname	
Search	Search by City	Srchcust	
Return	Return to menu		

Remember to include a Return option on the menu. A user can return to the maintenance menu by selecting it or by pressing Esc.

CheckPoint 4-1. Find Largest Array Element

Procedure Maxelement accepts an array and determines how many elements it has using the ARRAYSIZE function. It assumes the first one is the largest and compares the next one to it. If the successor is larger, the procedure saves it instead. The loop continues, comparing each element to the largest found thus far. When the loop ends, variable Biggest holds the largest number.

```
;Cp4-1.sc
;Find largest array element
PROC Maxelement(Numbar)
PRIVATE
        Biggest,  ;Largest array element
        Ctr,      ;Loop control variable
        Howmany   ;Number of array elements

;Find number of array elements
Howmany = ARRAYSIZE(Numbar)

;Initialize biggest value to first array element.
;Compare all others to it.
Biggest = Numbar[1]

;If array has only one element, return it
IF ARRAYSIZE(Numbar) = 1 THEN
  RETURN Biggest
ENDIF

;Compare rest of elements to largest found so far
FOR Ctr FROM 2 TO Howmany
  IF Numbar[Ctr] > Biggest THEN
    Biggest = Numbar[Ctr]
  ENDIF
ENDFOR
RETURN Biggest
ENDPROC
```

The following statements create a test array for Maxelement. The message displays 99, element number 4, and waits for two seconds before clearing the screen.

```
ARRAY Numb[4]
Numb[1] = 10
Numb[2] = 25
Numb[3] = 6
Numb[4] = 99
Largest = Maxelement(Numb)
MESSAGE "The largest element is " + STRVAL(Largest)
SLEEP 2000
MESSAGE ""
```

CheckPoint 4-2. Inserting an Array Element

Procedure Arinsert accepts an array of numbers, the position to insert at, and the value to place. It is easier to move the elements down starting with the last one and working up to the insertion position. This eliminates the need for temporary variables to avoid overwriting values. The routine drops the last array element if it exists (there is nowhere to move it!)

```
;Cp4-2.sc
;Inserts element at Spos from array. Shifts all
;elements past it down one position.
;Checks whether indicated position is within
;array bounds. Drops last element if it contains
;a value.
;Spos <= ARRAYSIZE(Sarray)
;Svalue is value to insert.
PROC ArInsert(Sarray,Spos,Svalue)
PRIVATE
        Arsize,  ;Size of array
        Sloop    ;Loop variable

Arsize = ARRAYSIZE(Sarray)
IF Spos <= Arsize THEN
  IF Spos = Arsize THEN
    ;Just insert value if last one specified
    ;It will overwrite an element if one exists
    Sarray[Arsize] = Svalue
  ELSE
    ;Work backward in array. Move each element
    ; down one position starting with the last one.
    ; Overwrites the last element if it exists.
    FOR Sloop FROM Arsize TO Spos STEP -1
      Sarray[Sloop] = Sarray[Sloop - 1]
    ENDFOR
    ;Insert new value
    Sarray[Spos] = Svalue
  ENDIF
ELSE
  MESSAGE "Position ",STRVAL(Spos), " is not in the array"
  SLEEP 1500
ENDIF
ENDPROC
```

The following statements create an array of five numbers. The script calls Arinsert to insert the value 15 in position 3. Because the array is filled, the Arinsert drops the value in Numbar[5] (8) when it moves elements down to make room for the new one. It displays the array to show that the procedure worked.

```
ARRAY Numbar[5]
Numbar[1] = 4
Numbar[2] = 6
Numbar[3] = 0
Numbar[4] = 1
Numbar[5] = 8
;Insert 15 in element 3 and move all elements down.
;Procedure drops element 5. No room!
ArInsert(Numbar,3,15)
;Display array to confirm
FOR Ctr FROM 1 TO 5
  ? Numbar[Ctr]
ENDFOR
;Wait for user to press a key
Ans = GETCHAR()
```

CheckPoint 5-1. Introductory Screen in a Window

A *splash screen* is a text window displayed before the first application menu. Before changing the title, create a dynamic array of default attributes. Create the window afterward. Use ECHO NORMAL or the window will not be visible. The following script displays a splash screen.

```
;Cp5-1.sc
;Display a text window for two seconds
;Turn echo on or window is hidden
ECHO NORMAL
DYNARRAY Atts[]
;Change title in default attributes
Atts["Title"] = "A LONG DAY'S JOURNEY INTO PAL"
WINDOW CREATE ATTRIBUTES Atts @ 7,15
  HEIGHT 10 WIDTH 50 TO Textwindow
@ 3,6 ?? "Life is a journey, not a destination"
;Display window for 2 seconds
SLEEP 2000
;Close window and turn echo off
WINDOW CLOSE
ECHO OFF
```

CheckPoint 5-2. Using the Paradox Sort Facility

You can use the Paradox sort facility in your applications. Select the source and target tables and use the ECHO command to let the user specify sort fields. The following example deletes the target table Sortcust if it exists. It passes user keystrokes such as arrow keys to

Paradox until the mode changes. This happens when the user presses F2 to begin sorting.

```
;Cp5-2.sc
;Sort customer table into new table.
;Let user select fields to sort on using Paradox
; sort facility.
;If Sortcust table exists, delete it

;Delete Sortcust if it already exists
IF ISTABLE("Sortcust") THEN
  DELETE "Sortcust"
ENDIF

{Modify} {Sort} {Customer} {Sortcust}

;Reveal desktop with sort facility
ECHO NORMAL
;Accept keystrokes as long as in Sort mode
WHILE SYSMODE() = "Sort"
  ;Get a key and press it
  Key = GETCHAR()
  KEYPRESS Key
ENDWHILE

;Turn echo off when user leaves Sort mode
ECHO OFF
```

If Sortcust exists, you could ask for confirmation before deleting it. The test at the beginning would change to

```
IF ISTABLE("Sortcust") THEN
  MESSAGE "Sortcust exists - Continue? (Y/N)"
  Ans = GETCHAR()
  ;Check for Y (ASCII 89) or y (ASCII 121)
  IF Ans <> 89 AND Ans <> 121 THEN
    RETURN
  ELSE
    DELETE "Sortcust"
  ENDIF
ENDIF
```

CheckPoint 5-3. Keypress-Driven WAIT

You must change the program in three places to add F7 as the form toggle key. First, add text to the prompt statement so the user knows the key is available.

```
Prmpt = "F2-Quit, Ins, Alt/E-Edit, Del-Del, F7-Chg View,"+
        "Ctrl/Z-Zm, Alt/Z-ZmNxt"
```

You must also add F7 to the UNTIL list in the WAIT statement. This tells Paradox to trap it.

```
WAIT RECORD
  PROMPT Prmpt
UNTIL "F2","Ins",-18,"Del","F7","Zoom","ZoomNext",
      "Up","Down","PgUp","PgDn","Dos","DosBig",5
```

Paradox will drop out of the WAIT command when the user presses a key in the UNTIL list. You must add a CASE to handle the F7 key and tell Paradox to switch views.

```
CASE Retval = "F7":
  FORMKEY
```

CheckPoint 5-4. Event-Driven WAIT

You must add the DEPARTTABLE trigger to the WAIT command so Paradox will trap any key used to leave the TIME table as shown in the following example.

```
WAIT WORKSPACE
  PROC "EventHandler"
  TRIGGER "DEPARTFIELD","DEPARTROW","DEPARTTABLE"
  KEY "F2"
ENDWAIT
```

Paradox calls EventHandler when a user presses a key to leave either table. You must test explicitly for table name and display total hours only if departing the TIME table. The following example uses SCAN to sum total hours and MESSAGE to display them until the user presses a key.

```
;Cp5-4.sc
;Display total hours when user departs TIME table
;Remove message when user presses a key.
PROC EventHandler(TriggerType,EventRecord,CycleNumber)

;Check for F2 (-60) to end Coedit
IF EventRecord["TYPE"] = "KEY" AND
```

```
  EventRecord["KEYCODE"] = -60 THEN
     RETURN 2
ENDIF

;Check for departing Time table.
;Calculate total hours.
IF UPPER(TABLE()) = "TIME" AND
  TriggerType = "DEPARTTABLE" THEN
     TotalHours = 0
     HOME
     SCAN
       TotalHours = TotalHours + [St Hours] + [Ot Hours]
     ENDSCAN
     MESSAGE "Total Hours = "+STRVAL(TotalHours)+
       " - Press any key"
     Ans = GETCHAR()
     MESSAGE ""
     ;Event Ok
     RETURN 0
ENDIF

;Check for departing Date field in Time table
;Duplicate date not allowed
IF UPPER(TABLE()) = "TIME" AND
   UPPER(FIELD()) = "DATE" AND
   TriggerType = "DEPARTFIELD" THEN
     ;Lock record to post it
     POSTRECORD
     IF NOT Retval THEN
       MESSAGE "Duplicate date not allowed"
       SLEEP 2000
       MESSAGE ""
       ;Deny event
       RETURN 1
     ELSE
       ;Event Ok, let it happen
       RETURN 0
     ENDIF
ENDIF

;Check for departing record in Time table.
;Overtime not allowed unless standard
;time = 8 hours
IF UPPER(TABLE()) = "TIME" AND
   TriggerType = "DEPARTROW" THEN
     IF [St Hours] < 8.00 AND
         [Ot Hours] > 0.00 THEN
          MESSAGE "No overtime allowed unless "+
```

```
                  "standard hours = 8!"
        SLEEP 2000
        MESSAGE ""
        ;Deny event
        RETURN 1
    ELSE
        ;Event ok
        RETURN 0
    ENDIF
ENDIF

;Just a regular event, process it
RETURN 0
ENDPROC
```

CheckPoint 5-5. Adding Menu Help

All SHOW commands include a KEYTO option to trap keys besides handling menu selections. Paradox stores the key name in the specified variable if a user presses one in the list. In the following example, it traps F1 for SHOWPOPUP.

```
;Cp5-5.sc
;Controlling menu for a Customer system with table
;maintenance and query options.
;Display menu help when user presses F1

;Clear workspace and canvas
RESET
CLEAR

;Declare autolib path Paradox will
; search for called procedure
Autolib = "Utility"

WHILE True
  ;Use entire screen
  SETCANVAS DEFAULT
  ;Initialize Helpkey for testing
  Helpkey = ""
  CLEAR
  PAINTCANVAS ATTRIBUTE 31 0,0,24,79
  ;Display system menu
  SHOWPOPUP "Customer System" CENTERED
    "Maintenance"       : "Customer Maintenance" : "MaintTag",
    "Query-by-Example"  : "Query by Example"     : "QbeTag",
```

```
    "Query-by-Form"     : "Query by Form"          : "FormTag",
    "Return"            : "Return to DOS"          : "ReturnTag"

ENDMENU
UNTIL "F1" KEYTO Helpkey
TO Mchoice
```

The following code displays a text window when a user presses F1 for menu help. It redisplays the menu when he or she presses any key.

```
  ;Check if user pressed help key
  IF Helpkey = "F1" THEN
    DYNARRAY Atts[]
    Atts["Title"] = "Menu Help"
    ECHO NORMAL
    WINDOW CREATE ATTRIBUTES Atts
      @ 7,15 HEIGHT 10 WIDTH 50 TO Helpwindow
      @ 2,2 ?? "Maintenance allows Add/Chg/Del for customers"
      @ 3,2 ?? "Query-by-Example uses Paradox query facility"
      @ 4,2 ?? "Query-by-Form uses a custom form for queries"
      @ 6,2 ?? "              Press any key    "

    Ans = GETCHAR()
    WINDOW CLOSE
    ECHO OFF
    LOOP
  ENDIF
```

CheckPoint 6-1. Data Dictionary

The following example loads the data dictionary and customer tables onto the desktop. It uses an event-driven WAIT to trap the F2 and Del keys. If the user presses Del, the event procedure checks for logically linked records in the data dictionary.

```
;Remove pulldown menu
SHOWPULLDOWN
ENDMENU

;Data dictionary table must be on workspace
VIEW "Datadict"

;Set prompt before starting WAIT
PROMPT "F2 - Finish, Del - Delete"
```

```
COEDIT "Customer"
WINMAX
;Toggle ECHO NORMAL to improve performance
ECHO NORMAL
WAIT TABLE
  PROC "EventHandler"
  KEY "F2","Del"
ENDWAIT
ECHO OFF
DO_IT!
CLEARALL
```

EventHandler assumes that Paradox can process keys normally so it sets the default return code to 0. It returns 2 to end the WAIT if a user presses F2. It changes the code to 1 if there are logically linked records in other tables. This tells Paradox to ignore the Del key.

Because the program may load and remove many tables while looking for related records, the procedure turns ECHO OFF to avoid screen flicker. Note that the procedure does not issue the DEL command. If it returns zero, Paradox performs the action automatically.

```
PROC EventHandler(TriggerType,EventRecord,CycleNumber)
PRIVATE
        Keyfld,    ;Value of customer key field
        Key_Name,  ;Name of customer key field
        Ok,        ;True if no linked records
                   ;False otherwise
        Returncd,  ;Return code
        Save_fld,  ;Contents of key field
        Save_tbl   ;Original table name

;Assume everything will be all right
Returncd = 0

;Check for F2 (-60) and Del (-83)
IF EventRecord["TYPE"] = "KEY" THEN
  SWITCH
    ;Check for F2 to end WAIT
    CASE EventRecord["KEYCODE"] = -60:
      Returncd = 2
    ;Check for Del
    CASE EventRecord["KEYCODE"] = -83:
      ;Save current table name, field, and value
      Save_tbl = TABLE()
      Save_fld = FIELD()
```

```
        Keyfld = [Cust Id]
        Key_Name = "Cust Id"

        ;Close table and use dictionary to
        ; check if delete is allowed
        ;Turn Echo off so workspace does not flicker
        ECHO OFF
        DO_IT!
        Ok = Check_Del(Save_tbl,Keyfld)

        ;Restore cursor to original table and record.
        ;The record may no longer exist so check if
        ; still available
        MOVETO Save_tbl
        COEDITKEY
        MOVETO FIELD Key_Name
        LOCATE Keyfld
        IF NOT Retval THEN
          MESSAGE "Record no longer in table!"
          SLEEP 1500
          MESSAGE ""
          ;Deny this event
          Returncd = 1
        ELSE
          MOVETO FIELD Save_fld
          ;If delete allowed, lock record and delete
          IF Ok THEN
            LOCKRECORD
            IF Retval THEN
              ;Record locked, let Paradox delete it
              Returncd = 0
            ELSE
              MESSAGE "Record cannot be locked and deleted"
              SLEEP 1500
              MESSAGE ""
              ;Deny this event
              Returncd = 1
            ENDIF
          ELSE
            ;Linked records, deny event
            Returncd = 1
          ENDIF
        ENDIF
  ENDSWITCH
ENDIF

;Redisplay workspace
ECHO NORMAL
```

```
RETURN Returncd
ENDPROC
```

CheckPoint 7-1. File Locks

The following example assigns Lockstr a list of order entry tables. The backslashes tell Paradox to interpret quotation marks as characters, not end of string delimiters. Getflocks tries to lock the files for ten seconds. If it succeeds, it returns True; if not, it returns False.

```
Lockstr ="LOCK \"Orders\" PWL, \"Customer\" PWL, "+
         "\"Nextord\" PWL"
Locked = Getflocks(Lockstr,10)
IF NOT Locked THEN
  MESSAGE "Could not lock tables"
  SLEEP 2000
  MESSAGE ""
  RETURN
ENDIF
```

CheckPoint 7-2. Record Locks

Procedure Getlocks accepts two table names. It assumes Paradox has located the correct record in each one. The procedure calls Getrlock to lock each record. It returns True if the locks succeed and False if they fail.

```
PROC Getlocks(Tbl1,Tbl2)
PRIVATE
         AllLocked    ;True if both locks succeed, False
                      ; otherwise
         Locked,      ;True if record locked, False otherwise
         Savetbl      ;Original table position

;Save original location
Savetbl = TABLE()

;Assume locks will succeed
AllLocked = True

WHILE True
  ;Try to lock first record
  MOVETO Tbl1
  Locked = Getrlock(5)
  ;Test first lock
  IF NOT Locked THEN
    AllLocked = False
```

```
      QUITLOOP
   ENDIF
   ;Try to lock second record
   MOVETO Tbl2
   Locked = Getrlock(5)
   IF NOT Locked THEN
      AllLocked = False
      ;Unlock first record
      MOVETO Tbl1
      UNLOCKRECORD
      QUITLOOP
   ENDIF

   ;Locks succeed
   QUITLOOP
ENDWHILE
;Restore original table position
MOVETO Savetbl
RETURN AllLocked
ENDPROC
```

CheckPoint 8-1. Delete WordPerfect Documents

Add Alt/D (-32) to the PROMPT and UNTIL clauses for the WAIT command to delete a note. When the user presses Alt/D, check if the cursor is in the Notes tables. Display an error message if not. Use ISFILE to test whether the document exists. The user may have deleted it from WordPerfect or DOS and forgot to delete the Paradox record. I always ask the user to confirm deletions, as he or she may have pressed the key by mistake. If the user confirms, use RUN to transfer control to DOS temporarily and delete the document. Remember to delete the record also. The following example shows the new program to edit or delete WordPerfect documents for the Client table.

```
;Cp8-1.sc
;Edit client table. User presses Alt/N (-49) to
;edit client notes. Program transfers control
;to NoteMaint procedure with document name.
;Add Alt/D (-32) to delete a note.

;Remove pulldown menu
SHOWPULLDOWN
ENDMENU

COEDIT "Client"
PICKFORM 1
```

```
WINMAX
WHILE True
  WAIT TABLE
    PROMPT "F2-Done, F4-Notes, F3-Client, Alt/N-EditNotes, "+
           "Alt/D-DeleteNote"
  UNTIL "F2","F3","F4",-49,-32,"Del","Dos","DosBig"
  SWITCH
    CASE Retval = "F2":
      QUITLOOP

    CASE Retval = "F3":
      MOVETO "Client"

    CASE Retval = "F4":
      MOVETO "Notes"
    ;Alt/N for note maintenance
    CASE Retval = -49:
      IF UPPER(TABLE()) = "NOTES" THEN
        NoteMaint([Document])
      ELSE
        MESSAGE "You must select a note first..."
        SLEEP 1500
        MESSAGE ""
      ENDIF

    ;Alt/D (-32) Delete a note
    CASE Retval = -32:
      IF UPPER(TABLE()) <> "NOTES" THEN
      MESSAGE "You must select a note first..."
      SLEEP 1500
      MESSAGE ""
      LOOP
    ENDIF
    ;Check for file and delete it
    IF NOT ISFILE([Document]) THEN
      MESSAGE "File "+[Document]+" has already been deleted!"
      SLEEP 1500
      MESSAGE ""
      LOOP
    ENDIF

    ;Ask for confirmation
    MESSAGE "Delete this note? (Y/N)"
    Ans = GETCHAR()
    ;Check for Y or y
    IF Ans <> 89 AND Ans <> 121 THEN
      LOOP
    ENDIF
```

```
    ;Delete document
    RUN "Erase " + [Document]
    ;Delete Paradox note record
    DEL

  ENDSWITCH
ENDWHILE
DO_IT!
CLEARALL
```

CheckPoint 9-1. Menu Display

You can change the screen color by adding a parameter to the list for procedure Get_Choice. In the following example, Color contains a color attribute number.

```
PROC Get_Choice( Tbl,Title1,Title2,BoxTitle,
                 Tlr,Tlc,Hgt,Wid,Colm,Color,Logo)
```

The following shows a sample call to Get_Choice using black letters on a cyan background (48). You add the foreground number to the background number from Table 5-4 to get the color attribute. It uses the Mainmenu table for the Gulag Products inventory sysytem.

```
Get_Choice( "Mainmenu","Gulag Products",
            "Inventory System", "Main Menu",5,20,15,40,1,48,
            "Developed by V.S. Systems")
```

The procedure uses Color instead of an attribute number to color the screen as in

```
PAINTCANVAS ATTRIBUTE Color 0,0,24,79
```

CheckPoint 9-2. Add Printer Maintenance

You need only insert a record in the Mainmenu table to add printer maintenance to the inventory system as in the following example.

Item	Procnm	Parmlis
Add/Change Printers	Tblmaint	"Printers",-1,"Name"

The system will call procedure Tblmaint when the user selects this option. It is a utility program that maintains a single key table with or without a form. It accepts the table name (Printers), the form number or -1 for no form, and the key name (Name). The next time a user starts the inventory system, the new option appears on the menu.

CheckPoint 10-1. Efficient Procedures

You must change the message to allow three printers rather than two. You must also revise the ACCEPT statement to limit values. The printer port selection logic stays the same.

```
;Cp10-1.sc
;Ask user to select local or network print
;destination. Set port and return port name
;or null if user presses Esc.
;LPT1 is a local printer.
;LPT2 and LPT3 are network printers.

PROC Setport()
PRIVATE
         Port,      ;Redirect printer output
         Portname, ;Port name—LPT1, LPT2, or LPT3
         Procname  ;Procedure name

;Ask where to direct output
STYLE ATTRIBUTE 79
@ 24,0  ?? SPACES(80)
@ 24,12 ?? "Select 1-Local, 2-Network LaserJet,"+
           " 3-Network Dot Matrix "
ACCEPT "S" MIN 1 MAX 3 TO Port
STYLE
IF NOT Retval THEN
  RETURN ""
ENDIF

;LPT1 local
;LPT2 and LPT3 network
Port = UPPER(Port)
Portname = "LPT" + STRVAL(Port)
SETPRINTER Portname
RETURN Portname
ENDPROC
```

Acronyms

ASCII	American Standard Code for Information Interchange
BASIC	Beginners All purpose Symbolic Instruction Code
CCP	Custom Configuration Program
CPU	Central Processing Unit
DPMI	DOS Protected Mode Interface
DOS	Disk Operating System
EMM	Expanded Memory Manager
EMS	Expanded Memory Specification
FIFO	First In First Out
I/O	Input/Output
KB (K or **Kb)**	Kilobyte
LAN	Local Area Network
LIFO	Last In First Out
MB (M or **Mb)**	Megabyte
MS-DOS	Microsoft Disk Operating System
PAL	Paradox Application Language
PC	Personal Computer
QBE	Query By Example
RAM	Random Access Memory
SQL	Structured Query Language
TSR	Terminate and Stay Resident
VAR	Value Added Reseller

Glossary

Abbreviated menu command
PAL command used to replace a series of Paradox menu selections. For example, COEDIT "Cust" replaces {Modify} {CoEdit} {Cust}

Alphanumeric field
A field that can contain letters, numbers, or special characters in any combination.

Application
A collection of scripts, procedures, libraries, and Paradox objects that form a unit to accomplish a single task such as accounts receivable.

Argument
A value or variable passed to a Paradox function or user-defined procedure.

Array
A data structure consisting of multiple elements with a single name. Individual elements are referenced by their offset from the first element or by field name if the array contains record data.

Array element
A single member of an array, designated by its offset from the first element.

ASCII
American Standard Code for Information Interchange, a 7-bit code used to identify 128 characters, including letters, numbers, and special symbols.

Assignment
The action of giving a Paradox variable, array element, or field a specific value.

Backslash
A special character that tells Paradox to interpret the next character literally.

Band
A horizontal section on a report specification.

Breakpoint
A location in a script or procedure at which the debugging facility is invoked.

Calculated field
A user-created field defined by an arithmetic formula or other expression that can appear on a form or report.

Call by value
Paradox method of replacing arguments with their values before calling a procedure.

Canvas window
Rectangular area of the screen used to display dialog boxes, menus, and messages, and get single values from the user.

Canvas cursor
Flashing bar that indicates the current position on the PAL canvas. It differs from the workspace cursor.

Case sensitive
Distinguishing between capital and lowercase letters.

Character
A single letter, digit (0-9), or symbol.

Click
A rapid press and release of a mouse button.

Clipboard
Editor object that contains text copied or removed from the current document.

Close box
Solid square displayed in the upper left frame of a window. A user clicks on it to close the window.

Closed procedure
A self-contained procedure that does not recognize variables unless they are passed through its parameter list, included in its USEVARS statement, or defined as private to it.

Closed script
A script called from the DOS prompt. Paradox returns control to DOS when it stops playing.

Command
A Paradox programming instruction, such as BEEP, that does not return a value.

Computed macro
A string expression that Paradox evaluates and executes as a sequence of PAL commands with the EXECUTE command.

Concatenation
Placing strings one after the other to form a single string.

Concurrent access
The ability of more than one person to use the same Paradox object such as a table simultaneously.

Context sensitive help
Information presented to the user about the current state of the application.

Control structure
A branching command that affects the order in which Paradox executes subsequent instructions.

CPU (central processing unit)
The part of a computer that executes instructions, accesses memory and input/output devices, and performs arithmetic and logic.

Current cursor position
The object field, record, image, window, or table the cursor is on.

Current window
The window containing the current image or involved in the current action such as displaying a menu.

Cursor
A bar character that indicates current screen position.

Cut and paste
A technique used to mark a block of text and move or copy it elsewhere in the same or another file.

Data
A piece of information such as client id or sales amount.

Database server
A combination of hardware and software that allows information processing to occur on the network CPU as well as on the workstation.

Data integrity
The state that exists when data has the correct values.

Data type
The kind of information that a field, variable, or array element contains. The Paradox field types are:

A#	Alphanumeric of length #
D	Date
L	Logical
M	Memo
N	Number
S	Short number
$	Currency

Debugger
A PAL facility used to test and trace the execution of commands interactively in a script or procedure.

Desktop
Area of the Paradox screen between the menu bar on line 0 (zero) and the status bar on line 24, used to display windows.

Detail table
A subordinate table linked to a master table by common data in fields.

Dialog box
Rectangular screen object with buttons such as Ok and Cancel. A user interacts with information in the box by pressing keys, typing text, or selecting choices from a list.

Directory
A file containing information about other files such as their names, locations, and sizes.

Display image
A picture of data in a Paradox table displayed in either table or form view.

Domain
The set of legal values a field may contain.

Double click
Rapidly depressing and releasing a mouse button twice in succession.

Drag
Moving an object on the screen by positioning the mouse in it, pressing a button, and holding it down while moving the mouse. Releasing the button anchors the object in a new location.

Duplicate key
Two or more records that contain the same values in their key fields.

Dynamic scoping
A method Paradox uses to determine the current value of a variable, depending upon its placement in a script or procedure.

Element
A single array member.

Embedded form
A form placed within another form. It may be linked.

Encrypt
Change a table or script into a form that is unreadable unless a password is provided.

Example element
An arbitrary series of characters used to identify a column in a query statement. It is used like a variable during table linking and calculations.

Expression
A collection of values, variables, array elements, field specifiers, operators, commands, and functions combined to form a single PAL instruction. It can evaluate to a data type. For example, Thirty = TODAY() + 30 calculates the date thirty days from today.

Expanded memory
Optional hardware that adds up to 16MB of memory to a computer system accessible via special software. Paradox cannot access this memory directly.

Export
The process of transferring Paradox table data into an external format such as a spreadsheet.

Extended memory
Optional hardware that adds up to 16MB of memory to a computer system. Paradox can access it directly when run in protected mode.

Family
A Paradox table and its associated objects, including forms, reports, indexes, and ValChecks.

Field
A single column in a Paradox table that contains a particular data type.

Field specifier
The PAL method used to indicate a field by enclosing its name in brackets. For example, [Name].

File
A collection of data stored under one name on an external storage device such as disk or tape.

File lock
Paradox object that limits operations a user may perform on a table.

File server
A network computer that contains programs and data for access by multiple users.

Format specification
A collection of symbols used to define the appearance of Paradox variables, fields, and array elements on forms and reports.

Form view
Used to display Paradox table data via a form defined with the form editor.

Function
A code sequence that returns a value to its caller.

Function keys
The 10 or 12 keys located at the top or left of the keyboard, labeled F1 through F10 or F12.

Global variable
A variable assigned in a PAL script whose value is available throughout an entire application.

Group lock
Group of Paradox record locks applied to a master record and its linked details on a multi-table form.

IBM extended codes
Keys or key combinations not defined in the standard ASCII character set. They are available to PAL using the extended code numbers -1 through -132 to represent them.

Image
A picture of a Paradox table or query form shown in a workspace window.

Image type
The type of an image, display for tables or query for query forms.

Import
The action of bringing data in a foreign format such as a spreadsheet into Paradox.

Index
A table family member based on a single field value that allows Paradox to locate records directly.

Key
A field in a Paradox table used to order records.

Keyboard macro
A sequence of recorded keystrokes that can be replayed.

Keycode
A code representing a character in PAL scripts or procedures. It may be an ASCII value, an IBM extended code number, or a string representing a valid Paradox keyname such as "F2".

Keyword
A reserved word used in a command. It cannot also be used to name a variable, array, or procedure.

Kilobyte
1,024 characters (bytes) of data. Abbreviated K or KB.

LAN
Local area network. A group of computers and peripherals wired together over a short distance for the purpose of sharing programs and data.

Landscape
Horizontal positioning of text on a page.

Link key
In a multi-table form, the detail table's key field that Paradox links to the master key field.

List box
Dialog box element with items a user may select.

Lock
A method Paradox uses to assure a user's right to view or change an object such as a table or form.

Logical operator
AND, OR, or NOT, used in PAL expressions.

Logical value
A value of True or False that Paradox assigns to an expression after evaluation.

Lookup table
A table with one key field linked logically to fields in master tables. A user must enter one of its values in the master table field.

Loop
A control structure that repeats a sequence of commands until specified conditions are met.

Many-to-many relationship
A condition in which one or more records in one table are related to one or more in another. Abbreviated M-M.

Many-to-one relationship
A condition in which one or more records in one table are related to one in another. Abbreviated M-1.

Master table
A table that contains a single record for each major entity in an application. Examples are Customers, Vendors, and Products.

Megabyte
1,048,576 characters (bytes) of data. Abbreviated M or MB.

Memo field
A variable length text field that can contain up to 64 MB of data.

Menu
A display of the options currently available in an interactive Paradox session or during script play.

Miniscript
A choice available on the Paradox extended menu that allows the user to construct a script from a series of PAL commands consisting of up to 175 characters. Paradox executes it when the user presses Enter.

Mode
The current Paradox state that determines what actions are valid. There are 15 major modes such as Coedit and several minor ones such as FieldView.

Mode indicator
The text displayed at the bottom of the screen indicating the current mode.

Mouse
A handheld device that moves a pointer on the screen.

Multiuser
Allows several users to access objects such as a table at the same time.

Normalized table structure
A table that does not contain repeating groups of information in a single record, and in which all non-key fields depend on all key ones. Also, no non-key fields depend on each other.

Object
A member of a Paradox table family, such as a form, report, or ValCheck.

One-to-many relationship
A condition in which one table record can be related to one or more in another table.

One-to-one relationship
A condition in which one table record can be related to one record in another table.

On-line data
Data available for immediate retrieval from an external storage device such as a disk.

Operating system
Program that performs the basic procedures required to run a computer.

Parameter
The variable in a procedure header that receives the value of an argument passed to it.

Parsing
Analyzing a piece of data and separating it into its components.

Pathname
The full description of a file's location on disk. It specifies the drive or volume, directory, and file name.

Pick list
A menu of items in a dialog box.

Picture
A pattern of characters used to restrict the type of data a user may enter during PAL commands such as ACCEPT.

Popup
Information that appears on the screen as the result of a user action.

Portrait
Vertical positioning of text on a page.

Post
Save or change a record in Coedit mode.

Primary Index
The index Paradox creates using a table's key fields. Paradox uses it to order records in the table.

Private directory
A directory reserved for a single user where Paradox performs tasks such as sorting and restructuring. It also stores private tables such as Answer and Crosstab there.

Private variable
A variable declared in the PRIVATE statement of a procedure. Its value is available to that procedure and all others it calls unless the original procedure is closed.

Procedure
A named series of PAL commands that does not execute unless it is present in memory and explicitly called by another procedure or script.

Procedure library
A collection of procedures stored in a single file. Individual procedures must be loaded into memory via the READLIB command before executing, or the library must be listed on an Autolib path.

Prompt
An instruction displayed on the canvas.

Protected mode
A microprocessor feature that allows Paradox to access all available extended memory automatically without requiring an additional program.

Prototyping
A process used to simulate the final application for demonstration purposes. Prototype software often lacks important features such as data validation and error handling.

Pulldown menu
An extended menu that appears below a menu choice as the result of a user action.

Query
A request formulated by the user about data in Paradox tables.

Query by Example
Paradox's nonprocedural language that allows a user to form queries based on examples of the data he or she is seeking.

Query by Form
A programming technique that hides Paradox's query form behind a custom form. An application uses the custom form to collect information and transfers it to the query form before execution.

Query form
The table image where a user enters examples, checkmarks, and selection criteria to extract data from the table.

Query image
The table image used on a query form.

QuerySave
A choice on the Scripts menu that allows a user to save the current workspace query in a script.

QuerySpeedup
A choice on the Tools menu that allows a user to create a secondary index on a non-key table field.

RAM
Memory used by the computer to save temporary data and results. Common types require power to retain their contents (that is, they are volatile).

Real mode
A microprocessor feature that limits programs such as Paradox to operating in 640K. Paradox will automatically run in protected mode if the computer has extended memory. A user can force it to run in real mode by using the -real switch.

Record
A row in a Paradox table containing related information about a single entity, such as a customer's name and address.

Record lock
An object applied by Paradox or an application to a single record to stop users from accessing its data.

Record number
The unique sequential number that identifies each record in a Paradox table.

Recursion
A language feature that allows a procedure to call itself.

Redirection
A language feature that allows source code to be used as data.

Referential integrity
The ability to assure that all links between records are maintained properly.

Refresh
Process Paradox uses to update screen images to reflect changes made by other simultaneous users.

Relational database system
Related information such as customers and orders stored in different tables and related by a key such as a customer id.

Reserved word
A keyword, function or command name, or system variable name that cannot be used as a PAL variable or array name.

Restricted view
The records shown in a linked detail table on a multi-table form which contain data matching the controlling master record data.

Runtime error
An error that occurs during script play due to a logic mistake or an attempt to access unavailable Paradox objects or physical devices such as printers and disk drives.

Script
A sequence of PAL commands stored in a file. A user can execute it by selecting the menu choice Scripts/Play or by using the PAL command PLAY with the script name.

Script editor
The word processor-like facility built into Paradox for creating and editing scripts.

Scroll bar
A highlighted bar that the application moves vertically over a screen area where multiple records are displayed, usually one per line.

Secondary index
An index based on non-key fields and created via the QuerySpeedup menu choice or the PAL INDEX command.

Source code
Computer program written in a language the programmer can read and understand. It must be translated before the computer can execute it.

String
A sequence of alphanumeric characters enclosed in quotation marks.

Structure
The physical arrangement of fields in a Paradox table.

Syntax
The set of rules governing the structure of expressions.

Syntax error
A script error caused by an incorrect expression.

Table
A structure consisting of rows and columns. The rows represent individual occurrences of an entity such as a customer. The columns represent entity attributes such as customer name and address.

Table lookup
Locating a value in a table based on another piece of data rather than via an explicit calculation. For example, locating the country "UNITED STATES OF AMERICA," given the abbreviation "USA".

Table view
Used to display Paradox table data using a format of rows and columns.

Text box
An area in a dialog box where a user types information.

Tilde variable
A PAL variable preceded by the tilde sign (~) used in a Paradox query. Paradox substitutes its value before executing the query.

Transaction
A group of instructions that must be completed to perform a particular task.

Unlock
To remove a table or record lock.

User
An individual who runs an application.

User interface
The visual part of an application that tells the user what to enter and how to respond.

Validity check
A constraint on the type of acceptable data for a field, variable, or array element.

Variable
A name used to represent a place in memory where Paradox stores the current associated value.

Wildcard
A special character used to represent one or more characters in a field.

Working directory
The disk directory Paradox searches to find objects unless given a specific pathname to them.

Workspace window
Rectangular area of the screen where Paradox performs table operations such as Coedit.

Workspace cursor
Flashing bar that indicates the current position on the Paradox workspace. It differs from the canvas cursor.

Trademarks

Clipper	Computer Associates
dBASE	Borland
EMM-386	QuarterDeck Office Systems
FoxPro	Microsoft
InterBase	Borland
LaserJet	Hewlett-Packard
1-2-3	Lotus Development
PAL	Borland
Paradox	Borland
PC-Kwik	Multisoft
QEdit	Semware
Quattro Pro	Borland
SQL Link	Borland
SQL Server	Microsoft
386Max	Qualitas
WordPerfect	WordPerfect

Other brand and product names may be trademarks or registered trademarks of the respective holders.

Index

D

E

F

G

H

I

M

N

O

P

T

U

V

W

X

Y

Z

Reader Comments
Paradox 4 Programming Guide

This book has been edited, the material reviewed, and the programs tested and checked for accuracy, but bugs find their way into books as well as software. Please take a few minutes to tell us if you found any errors, and give us your general comments regarding the quality of this book. Your time and attention will help us improve this and future products.

Did you find any mistakes? ______________________________

____

____

Is this book complete? (If not, what should be added?) ______________________________

____

____

What do you like about this book? ______________________________

____

____

What do you not like about this book? ______________________________

____

____

What other books would you like to see developed? ______________________________

____

____

Other comments: ______________________________

____

____

To be notified about new editions of this and other books of interest, please include your name and address, and mail to:

Name ______________________________

Address ______________________________

City/State/Zip ______________________________

Microtrend® Books
Slawson Communications
2075 Corte Del Nogal, Suite E
Carlsbad, CA 92009-1414

The Lance A. Leventhal Microtrend® Series
Lance A. Leventhal, Ph.D., Series Editor

Upgrading, Maintaining, & Servicing IBM PCs & Compatibles

by Julian Moss

Upgrading, Maintaining, & Servicing IBM PCs & Compatibles is the ideal book for those who depend on their PCs and want to keep them up-to-date and working as efficiently and trouble-free as possible. The author provides extensive guidance for those who want to do their own upgrading, maintenance, and repair. He covers hardware basics, problem solving, power supplies, motherboards, expansion buses, keyboards, video displays, diskettes, hard disks, serial ports, modems, mice, and printers. He describes how to remove and replace components, test them, diagnose problems, upgrade memory, enhance performance, recover files, and check connections. Includes complete chapters on tools and techniques, installation and use, preventive maintenance, configuration and tuning, computer viruses, and networking. Also has a glossary, acronym list, and appendixes covering power on self test error codes, hard disk data, and common PC viruses. A highly readable guide for typical PC owners.

Special features:

- Basic introduction to processors, memory, I/O ports, system buses, clocks, and timers for those unfamiliar with hardware.
- Detailed procedures for removing and replacing power supplies, motherboards, diskette drives, and hard drives.
- Extensive lists of common symptoms and how to diagnose and correct them.
- Includes a 1.2MB disk with original and shareware utilities.

7 x 9, 448 pages, trade paperback, ISBN 0-915391-70-8 $29.95 U.S.
Order #MT70

Available from your favorite book or computer store, use the order form at the end of the book, or call 1 (800) SLAWSON.

**Slawson Communications, Inc. • 2075 Corte Del Nogal, Suite E
Carlsbad, CA 92009-1414**

The Lance A. Leventhal Microtrend® Series
Lance A. Leventhal, Ph.D., Series Editor

IBM PC and PS/2 Graphics Handbook

by Ed Teja and Laura Johnson

This single source will answer all your questions about what the standards are, what works with what, what features languages and operating systems offer, how to upgrade systems, what to buy for specific applications and requirements, and how to make programs run on a variety of computers. The book contains many easily referenced tables and charts for quick access and rapid comparisons of systems, hardware, programs, and standards.

Special features:

- Covers adapters, monitors, printers, standards, file formats, languages, and applications packages.
- Includes summaries, a resource list, a glossary, an acronym list, and an annotated bibliography.
- Focuses on widely used hardware and software for word processing, business graphics, presentation graphics, CAD/CAM/CAE, and desktop publishing.
- Emphasizes current and emerging standards, such as VGA, 8514/A, Multisync monitors, GKS, IGES, TIFF, Borland Graphics Interface, Microsoft Windows, and Presentation Manager.
- Describes how to identify the graphics adapter on a system and how to convert between different screen and printer aspect ratios.

Ed Teja and Laura Johnson have been writing professionally about computers and electronics since 1976. A former computer and peripherals editor for *EDN* magazine, Teja has written articles for more than 35 magazines and has published three books.

7 x 9, 480 pages, trade paperback, index, ISBN 0-915391-35-X $24.95 U.S.
Order #MT35

Available from your favorite book or computer store, or use the order form at end of book, or call 1 (800) SLAWSON.

Slawson Communications, Inc. • 2075 Corte Del Nogal, Suite E
Carlsbad, CA 92009-1414

The Data Based Advisor® Series
Lance A. Leventhal, Ph.D., Series Director

Designing User Interfaces

by James E. Powell

User interfaces are often the key to the success or failure of software. Today's users demand software that is easy to learn, intuitive, and efficient. Experienced program designer James E. Powell provides a thorough, common-sense approach to creating effective user interfaces. Drawing from real-world applications, he asks readers to apply design techniques and compare their results with recommended solutions. The book covers analysis of user needs, visual design, data entry, error handling, menus, help, graphics, output, installation, tutorials, user manuals and documentation, creativity, legal issues, and future directions.

Special features:

- Many practical examples and sample problems drawn from actual applications.
- Extensive discussions of seldom-described topics, such as error handling, data entry design, help design, installation design, tutorial design, and considerations for handicapped users.
- Emphasis on a friendly interface with gentle tone and non-antagonistic approach.
- Descriptions of methods for creating interfaces for both beginners and experienced users.
- Thorough coverage of visual design, windowing, menus, graphical interfaces, and output design.
- Example programs using the popular FoxPro database manager.

James E. Powell is a program designer with over 20 years of practical experience. He is also a frequent contributor to major computer magazines.

7 x 9, 448 pages, trade paperback, ISBN 0-915391-40-6, $27.95 U.S.
Order # MT40

Available from your favorite book or computer store, use the order form at the end of the book, or call 1 (800) SLAWSON.

Slawson Communications, Inc. • 2075 Corte Del Nogal, Suite E
Carlsbad, CA 92009-1414

The Data Based Advisor® Series
Lance A. Leventhal, Ph.D., Series Editor

SQL and Relational Databases

by Soren Vang

An excellent book for those with no SQL experience. Soren Vang provides a clear, practical introduction to SQL for database programmers and users. Structured Query Language (SQL) is an IBM-developed standard for obtaining information from databases. It works on a wide range of computers and databases, allowing for data sharing among mainframes, minicomputers, workstations, PCs, and terminals. It is also the standard way to handle information requests on networks and other distributed systems via the popular servers available from many sources. The book includes many examples taken from IBM's SQL/DS, Oracle, and the OS/2 database manager.

Special features:

- Coverage of all aspects of the ANSI SQL standard.
- Discussions of Oracle utilities such as SQL *Forms.
- Entire chapters on normalization and data integrity issues in multiuser environments.
- Entire chapter on embedded SQL.
- Many examples of practical SQL queries.

Soren Vang has been a professor at the Engineering Academy of Copenhagen since 1985. He specializes in SQL/DS, PC databases, and other PC programs.

7 x 9, 350 pages, trade paperback, ISBN 0-915391-42-2 $24.95 U.S.
Order #MT42

Available from your favorite book or computer store, use the order form at the end of the book, or call 1 (800) SLAWSON.

Slawson Communications, Inc. • 2075 Corte Del Nogal, Suite E
Carlsbad, CA 92009-1414

The Lance A. Leventhal Microtrend® Series
Lance A. Leventhal, Ph.D., Series Editor

Turbo C Quickstart

by Lance A. Leventhal

Bestselling author Lance Leventhal provides an easy-to-understand, straightforward self-teaching guide to Borland's Turbo C. *Turbo C Quickstart* is ideal for those who want to learn the basics of C quickly on their own. Based on practical examples and exercises, it shows the key features needed to write real applications. It's like having an expert at your side. *Turbo C Quickstart* will help you master Turbo C quickly and confidently, regardless of your previous programming background. It has been extensively class-tested with a wide variety of students.

Special features:

- Provides hands-on experience with actual programs drawn from a variety of applications. All examples are clear, consistent, well-structured, fully documented, and tested. They are also available on the accompanying disk.
- Has question-and-answer sections that cover common problems and describe typical errors and how to correct them.
- Highly readable style that makes concepts easy to grasp.
- Step-by-step coverage insures thorough understanding of major language features such as conditionals, loops, arrays, strings, pointers, structures, and disk files.

Lance A. Leventhal is the author of 25 books that have sold over 1,000,000 copies and have been translated into many foreign languages. He conducts seminars and classes on C and other computer topics. Dr. Leventhal has a Ph.D. from the University of California, San Diego.

7 x 9, 700 pages, trade paperback, ISBN 0-915391-67-8 $29.95 U.S.
Order #MT67

Available from your favorite book or computer store, use the order form at the end of the book, or call 1 (800) SLAWSON.

Slawson Communications, Inc. • 2075 Corte Del Nogal, Suite E
Carlsbad, CA 92009-1414

Order Form

Thank you for purchasing this Microtrend® book. To order additional copies of this book or any of our other titles, please complete the form below, or call **1-800-SLAWSON**.

Name ____________________

Address ____________________

City/State/Zip ____________________

Country ____________________

Qty	Code #	Title	Price Each		Total	
	MT70	Upgrading, Maintaining, & Servicing IBM PCs & Compatibles	$29	95		
	MT35	IBM PC and PS/ 2 Graphics Handbook	$24	95		
	MT40	Designing User Interfaces	$27	95		
	MT42	SQL and Relational Databases	$24	95		
	MT67	Turbo C Quickstart	$29	95		

Subtotal		
Sales Tax: CA residents add 7.75%		
Shipping Charge: $3.50 per item		
TOTAL		

U.S. Shipping

Books are shipped UPS except when a post office box is given as delivery address.

Form of Payment

☐ Visa ☐ MasterCard ☐ Check

Card#: ____________________

Expiration date: __________

Signature: ____________________ Date __________

Mail your order to:

Microtrend® Books
Slawson Communications, Inc.
2075 Corte Del Nogal, Suite E
Carlsbad, CA 92009-1414